THE MAKING OF MODERN LIBYA

SUNY SERIES IN
THE SOCIAL AND ECONOMIC HISTORY
OF THE MIDDLE EAST

DONALD QUATAERT, EDITOR

Issa Khalaf, *Politics in Palestine: Arab Factionalism and Social Disintegration, 1839–1948*

Rifaʿat ʿAli Abou-El-Haj, *Formation of the Modern State: The Ottoman Empire, Sixteenth to Eighteenth Centuries*

M. Fuad Köprülü, *The Origins of the Ottoman Empire*, translated and edited by Gary Leiser

Guilian Denoeux, *Urban Unrest in the Middle East: A Comparative Study of Informal Networks in Egypt, Iran and Lebanon*

Zachary Lockman, ed., *Workers and Working Classes in the Middle East: Struggles, Histories, Historiographies*

Palmira Brummett, *Ottoman Seapower and Levantine Diplomacy in the Age of Discovery*

Ali Abdullatif Ahmida, *The Making of Modern Libya: State Formation, Colonization, and Resistance, 1830–1932*

THE MAKING OF

MODERN LIBYA

State Formation, Colonization, and Resistance, 1830–1932

Ali Abdullatif Ahmida

State University of New York Press

Published by
State University of New York Press, Albany

Printed in the United States of America

For information, address State University of New York Press,
State University Plaza, Albany, N.Y., 12246

Production by Diane Ganeles
Marketing by Theresa Swierzowski

Library of Congress Cataloging-in-Publication Data

Ahmida, Ali Abdullatif, 1953–
The making of modern Libya : state formation, colonization, and resistance, 1830–1932 / Ali Abdullatif Ahmida.
p. cm. — (SUNY series in the social and economic history of the Middle East)
Includes bibliographical references and index.
ISBN 0–7914–1761–1 (hc acid-free). — ISBN 0–7914–1762–X (pb acid-free)
1. Libya—History—1551–1912. 2. Libya—History—1912–1951.
I. Title. II. Series.
DT233.A38 1994
961.2'02—dc20 93–18526
CIP

10 9 8 7 6 5 4 3 2 1

To the memory of my grandfather, Ali, who fought against Italian colonialism and told me his life story when I was a child; to the memory of my grandmother, Aysha, who died in exile in northern Chad before I was born; to that generation of Libyans who fought for freedom and human dignity, I dedicate this book.

CONTENTS

ILLUSTRATIONS

Figures

Maps

ACKNOWLEDGMENTS

This book, based on my doctoral dissertation, would not have been possible without the guidance, encouragement, and criticism of a group of special individuals, and the services of a number of institutions in Libya, Italy, and the United States.

I am grateful to Ellis Goldberg, Resat Kasaba and Daniel Lev who provided me with direction, support and valuable critiques. Special thanks goes to my supervisor, Daniel Lev, for his open-mindedness and tolerance which allowed me to formulate my arguments. Peter Gran and Don Quataert, and especially to Rifaat Abou El-Haj whose critical remarks helped me to tighten my arguments while I was revising the dissertation into a book manuscript.

I thank Mr. Yusuf Jalala and Mr. Ali al-Dukali of the University of Sebha in Libya, Dr. Muhammad al-Jarrari, and Mr. Hamid Wuhayda of the Center for Libyan Studies, as well as Mr. Ramadan Gidida of the Libyan National Archives. In Rome, the staff of the Italian African Institute and Mr. Abd al-Rahman Shalgam, the head of the Libyan bureau, helped me collect my data.

In the United States, I am deeply grateful to the staff of the Inter-Library Loan Section of Suzzallo Library of the University of Washington for their wonderful service in getting me a vast array of material from all around the U.S. Also, I thank Karen Zollman of Whitman College for typing this manuscript.

Finally, I am grateful to my wife, Beth Ahmida, for her moral support and encouragement during the frustrating period of writing and revising this study. Above all, the credit for finishing my education and this book must go to my parents, whose love, encouragement, and parental sacrifice allowed me to pursue higher education.

Though many individuals helped me to gather and articulate my arguments, responsibility for the final draft remains mine alone.

ABBREVIATIONS

DMT	Dar al-Mahfuzat al-Tarikhiyya, Libyan archives (Tripoli).
MDJL	Markaz Dirasat al-Jihad al-Libi, Center for Libyan Studies (Tripoli).
PRO	Public Record Office (London).
GB	Great Britain.
CO	Colonial Office.
FO	Foreign Office.
ASMAI	Archivo Storico de Ministero Africa Italiana, Ministro degli Affair Esteri (Rome).
USNA	United States National Archives (Washington, D.C.).

A NOTE ON THE TRANSLITERATION

The proper names of persons and places are spelled according to the Arabic transliteration system followed by the *International Journal of Middle East Studies*. Turkish names of persons and administrative terms are spelled according to Arabic translation, as most of the sources of this study were written in Arabic. Exceptions to this system of transliteration are commonplace names or proper names that are widely used, such as "Fezzan" instead of "Fazzan" and "'Abdulnabi Bilkhayre" instead of "Abu al-Khayr."

INTRODUCTION

My childhood in central and southern Libya in the 1950s and 1960s was influenced by a specific social and cultural environment. It was shaped by memories of upheavals, wars, defeats, and resistance during the colonial period of 1911–1943. The generations who lived through that period, as my grandparents did, or witnessed its last phase, as did my parents, passed along to their children a vivid oral history of their displacements, anguish, and the struggle for survival. It was estimated that at least half a million Libyans died in battle, or from disease, starvation, or thirst. In addition 250,000 more Libyans were forced into exile in Chad, Turkey, Egypt, Palestine, Syria, Algeria, and Tunisia. It is telling that the population of Libya, which was one and a half million in 1911, remained at the same figure in 1950.

The educated elite of the Tripolitanian Republic, the Conference of Gharyan, and the Sanusi state were either killed or exiled. The leaders who were killed included R. al-Suwayhli, A. Belkhayre, A. Tantush, K. B. ʻAskar, H. Kaʻbar, F. al-Zawi, and S. al-Suwayhli; others lived in exile, such as S. al-Baruni, who went to Turkey and finally settled in Oman, and who served, until his death in 1940, as an advisor to its sultan. Shaykh S. al-Mahmudi, T. al-Zawi, A. al-Mariyyad, ʻAbd al-Jalil Saif al-Nasir, and Idris al-Sanusi lived in Egypt; Amad Saif al-Nasir and his brothers in Chad; Bashir al-Saʻdawi and Khalid Al-Gargani lived in Syria, becoming advisors to King Abd al-ʻAziz of Arabia.

The long and brutal colonial war pushed many peasants and tribesmen into the hinterland as refugees, including newly settled peasants who had begun to settle in the late nineteenth century. Thus, the hinterland's population increased, contributing to "retribal-ization," especially in the populated region of Tripolitania. Many peasants and transhumants were pressured to herd and cultivate cereal away from their coastal settlements. The Italian colonial policy showed no interest at that time in settling the tribes, nor in using them as cheap labor as the French did in neighboring Tunisia. Thus, the military defeat destroyed tribal and peasant autonomy, but did not yet incorporate tribes and peasants into the newly founded capitalist agricultural system. Instead, landless peasants and workers were brought from Italy and settled on the most fertile coastal land of the country.

The political and cultural legacy of the resistance has been powerful. The resistance strengthened an all-Libyan nationalism and gave the Libyan people prodigious examples of legendary heroes and martyrs. Further, those active in the resistance emphasized an anticolonial culture, which led to a conservative reaction in the revival of strong attachments to Islam and the clan. In other words, Islam and nationalism became synonymous. Anticolonial Islam had its roots in popular culture and this brand of Islam became a defining element of the postcolonial Libyan state.

The memory of this tragic and vivid period has not yet faded, and the postcolonial state has attempted to link its legitimacy to anticolonial resistance. Between 1951 and 1969 the Sanusi monarchy celebrated the role of King Idris and family (minus Ahmad-al Sharif) at the expense of the radical memory of 'Umar al Mukhtar and the Tripolitanian Republic, both of which were suppressed. After 1969 the young officers led by Colonel Gadhdhafi based part of their legitimacy on being the heirs of Ahmad al-Sharif, 'Umar al Mukhtar, and the Tripolitanian Republic. A center was inaugurated in 1977 for the study of the Libyan *jihad;* every important battle was celebrated, and most of the surviving ex-guerrillas were given medals and other awards. The fiery anticolonial sentiments of Colonel Gadhdhafi must be understood against the bitter colonial experience of the Libyan people between 1911 and 1943. Regardless of how nationalist elites use or manipulate the social history of the colonial period, the essential point is that Islam and anticolonial nationalism were products of a specific history and a reflection of ordinary people's collective memory.[1] This history clearly refutes essentialist and orientalist views of Muslims as "natural fanatics."

For the generations of the colonial period, the first half of the twentieth century was indeed a long tragedy. Hard times shaped the personal and collective memory of generations. This collective memory was conveyed to children of my generation through stories, songs, proverbs, and oral poetry. These forms of oral history tell not only tales of suffering and anguish; they also provide examples of resistance and human sacrifice, culled from the lengthy resistance to colonialism by hinterland peoples, which lasted for 21 years, from 1911 to 1932. Arriving in the United States to study in graduate school, I brought with me this social history.

Inevitably, as I chose to write about Libyan social history between 1830 and 1932, I found myself relying more and more heavily on certain elements of this lived history. That I was born in central Libya and was raised in the south; that my parents and grandparents experienced the colonial period firsthand; that my grandfather spent 10 years as a militant opponent of Italian colonialism; that my grandmother gave birth to my mother in exile (northern Chad) and later died without being able to return to her native land; and that my other grandmother lost two of her children to famine—these facts form the deepest part of my sensibility about this social history. The rich human history of resistance and the struggle for survival that was so important in my upbringing conflicted in fundamental ways with ethnocentric theories and analyses of third-world peoples. In these analyses, third-world peoples are inevitably portrayed as passive and manipulated traditional peoples without history.[2]

The study of modern North Africa or the Maghrib has been dominated by scholars concerned with French and Italian colonial studies and British social anthropology, and, to a lesser degree, by the modernization school, especially in the United States. French and Italian colonial studies focused on the needs of the colonial states to administer the natives, and many researchers were colonial officers. Their image of precolonial society is that it was "traditional," inhabited by unruly tribesmen on the one hand, and governed in the towns by corrupt patrimonial states on the other. According to this view, tribes and towns rarely cooperated.[3]

The most popular approach to modern North Africa has been, without a doubt, the segmentary model as articulated by British social anthropologists, particularly E. E. Evans-Pritchard and Ernest Gellner. The segmentary model assumes the existence of a tribal society comprised of homogeneous tribal segments. In the absence of state control, order was kept through mutually deterring tribal segments in any clan that threatened to disrupt the balance of power. This model was derived from colonial literature and official tribal ideologies. The segmentary model, like colonial literature, perceives the precolonial Maghrib society as an agglomeration of tribes or tribal states basically isolated from the larger social and economic structures of the region.[4]

Modernization theorists like Daniel Lerner viewed the modern Maghrib and the rest of the third world as composed of traditional societies that began to modernize under European colonialism. Traditional tribal and religious values were said to be passing away, replaced by modern, western, "rational" values.[5] Even some French Marxists such as Lacoste have viewed the precolonial Maghrib as an instance exhibiting the classic "Asiatic mode of production." Put briefly, the notion of the Asiatic mode assumes the existence of a strong state and self-sufficient village communities. Marx, because of his sketchy knowledge of India, saw this structure as being different from the European feudal mode of production. Yet Marx not only relied on orientalist European images of India, but abandoned his dialectical method when he assumed that change came mainly from the outside, in the form of European colonialism. The notion of the Asiatic mode of production is inadequate, since it was based on only vague knowledge of India and Asia. This sketchy knowledge came from orientalist European views of the Orient that denied the pre-existence of private property, described a strong state without the existence of classes, and finally omitted the dialectical method in predicting that change came from outside—for example, from British colonialism. The state in the precolonial Maghrib can hardly be viewed this way, since it was weak and quite different from the despotic image in Marx's Asiatic model.[6]

The literature suffers from two major deficiencies. First, Eurocentric views of Maghribi society as unruly, segmentary, traditional, or Asiatic assume change to have come from Europe—the "rational," revolutionary, and detribalized region that produced capitalist transformation. This line of reasoning also assumes that Europe has had a history that is dynamic, whereas North Africa has had a passive history, one composed of "closed Muslim tribes" doomed in the face of progressive, capitalist Europe. This point of view is Eurocentric in that it negates the existence of a fluid social history in North Africa prior to the colonial period, and it is also simplistic, ahistorical, and essentialist in the way it reduces North African social history to some changeless emanation from "the Muslim mind"—an allegedly static force informing tribal structure.[7]

The second inadequacy of existing analyses, especially modernization theories, is their inability to explain social transformation and the nature of politics in today's North Africa. Despite capitalist colonialization and postcolonial modernization, one is nevertheless struck by the persistence of noncapitalist relations such as sharecropping, tribal ownership of land, and self-sufficiency in household production even as late as the 1970s. This is especially true in Libya and Morocco.[8]

My first attempt to examine these issues was as a graduate student in the United States, using Weberian and structural-functionalist theories in which kinship and ideology are assumed to have autonomy from social and economic conditions. Utilizing this methodology in a long essay on the impact of religion and kinship on politics in Libya during the 1950s, I was unable to provide very convincing answers to the question of why noncapitalist relations persisted in Libya after the colonial period.[9] Also, a number of apparently historical discrepancies between the three regions of Libya became increasingly puzzling. Why, for example, did the coastal towns (with the possible exception of Tripoli) play an economic and political role subordinate to that of the hinterland tribes? Why and how were the hinterland tribes able to resist both the Ottoman and colonial states up through the mid-1930s? Why did Cyrenaica (the eastern region) have no major urban centers in the precolonial period, and why did Fezzan, in the south, decline economically at the end of the nineteenth century?

This book challenges Eurocentric theories of social change, such as state building, class formation, and cultural resistance, that ignore the internal dynamics of native social history. It also suggests that states and tribal confederations reacted to colonialism in the roles of major historical protagonists through resistance, collaboration or other survival strategies. Contrary to the dependency theory, the process of incorporating Libya into the colonial capitalist world system was not a linear progression from precapitalist to capitalist relations. Rather, the process was resisted and in fact modified during the colonial period. Sufi Islam, tribal military organization, and oral traditions were crucial cultural and social weapons in the fight against colonialism.

This book analyzes the social and political history of Libya from the early nineteenth through the early twentieth centuries, a period of intense change initiated in part by the expansion of the Ottoman and European colonial powers into the countryside. Local response was both determined and circumscribed by the imperatives of social organization in the agrarian regions that resisted colonial expansion. This tended to limit the impact of colonial economic and social influences, primarily in the cities. This study will show that powerful tribal and peasant alliances ruled Libya before the Ottomans and that the construction of a modern urban-centered state began in alliance with the Ottomans. The displacement of the Ottoman Empire by Italian colonialism renewed the need for tribal-peasant confederations as governing centers and thus explains their dominance over social life even after independence in 1951. The persistence of noncapitalist relations and ideologies in the postcolonial period, then, is the product of a long history of struggle carried on by various tribal-peasant alliances and can be appreciated fully only by an examination of the historical perspectives of member tribes and the peasants of the hinterland.

In its attempt to reconstruct Libyan history, this book adopts an approach emphasizing the mode of production in a flexible way; this approach has the advantage of linking economics to politics by analyzing the relationship between ecology, production, and the land tenure system, as well as legal, political, and social structures. E. P. Thompson's approach to class as a social and cultural formation is a fruitful way to understand the links between the labor process, culture, and ideology.[10] Thompson provides a convincing analysis of how English workers in the nineteenth century used traditional institutions and culture to resist the pressures of the capitalist market. Peter Gran, in his pioneering study, *Islamic Roots of Capitalism*, attempts to study social classes in an Islamic cultural context in eighteenth- and nineteenth-century Egypt. He argues that the rise of capitalism in Egypt was related to the production and new interpretations of Islamic law, especially in the writings of Shaykh Hasan al-'Atar.[11] Like Thompson and Gran, I take "traditions" seriously as the ideologies of social classes and strategies for resistance. Culture is approached as a process and not as a static concept.

This book begins with the year 1830, a year generally considered to mark the beginning of the capitalist penetration of coastal Tripolitania which led to the fall of the Qaramanli State when its pasha failed to broaden Tripolitania's social base. The book concludes with the year 1932, the end of the armed anticolonial resistance.

The designation "Libya" was used during Greek and Roman times and was revived by the Italian colonialists in 1911. This revival was an integral part of the policy justifying colonialism by linking it with the Roman rule of the Mediterranean.[12] Since the sixteenth century, the Ottomans had designated the province Tarabulus al-Gharb (Tripoli of the west, in contrast to the Tripoli of Lebanon). Although the eastern province was called Barqa, the ancient Greek name Cyrenaica was also used, especially by Europeans. Prior to the nineteenth century, the province of Tarabulus al-Gharb formed an essential component of the larger Maghrib, a region which, until 1900, connected the Muslim inhabitants from

Morocco to Egypt economically, socially, and culturally.[13] Contrary to the essentialist nationalist historiography, the use of the terms "Libya" and "Libyans," when used in reference to the nineteenth century, must be understood as referring specifically to the regency of Tarabulus al-Gharb and not to suggest (as many nationalist historians have attempted) that a contemporary nation-state existed prior to the colonial period. Similarly, the Tunisian, Algerian, and even Moroccan states are relatively recent constructs. The current phenomenon of national fragmentation in the Maghrib contrasts markedly with the integration of the precolonial period, during which time larger regional economies and different state models existed.[14] The modern Libyan nation-state is a recent construction, a product of the colonial period and the reaction to its impact.

The focus of analysis varies in its historical movement from tributary regional modes of production to the world capitalist system. Before being incorporated into the European capitalist market, regional economies (understood as those of the larger Maghrib and the Sahara) existed and are here the unit of analysis. The focus shifts necessarily, when reference is made to the period after incorporation. In regard to the incorporated areas, the focus is then on the international capitalist economy and the way this system interacts with communal and social classes. Because they neglect these regional and international units of analysis, studies of the modern Maghrib that focus primarily on the nation state during the pre- and postcolonial periods are inadequate.[15]

Other important concepts, as applied in this book, are defined as follows. *Reproduction* refers to "renewal of one round of production."[16] *Transformation* concerns the process of "undermining production, and the recombination of some of the old elements of production into new relations."[17] *Social class* is a term that was applied by Marx to analyze a class in and of itself in terms of the objective relationship of a group of individuals to the means of production as well as the group's consciousness of its reality when it develops organization through struggle with other classes.[18] This third concept, although useful, takes into account neither the politics of class formation, the cultural context of class, nor factionalism. Again, E. P. Thompson, in his study of the formation of the English working class, stresses the need to view class always in relationship to other classes, since a class does not exist on its own. Further, a class is not only an economic category, but a cultural one as well. Thompson argued not only that class has its culture, but that the struggle for the creation of social classes is fought ideologically and culturally.[19]

The process of class formation varies in the Maghrib. In Libya, class formation differs from that of the western European classical models. This study analyzes the differences. At this point, it is important to reiterate the deficiencies of the studies of tribes and tribalism proposed by the social anthropologists of the segmentary school: by assuming that "tribal" social structure is unchanging and classless and often in conflict with coastal states in North Africa, they ignore economic and social ties along peasant trade routes, in markets, and in states, promoting the image of an anarchic balance of power within a monolithic tribal structure.[20]

As other works have demonstrated, class actions are not always uniform since, in some cases, the origins and processes of class formation lead to the emergence of factions within the same class. Competition among factions (or strata) of one class appears often in the absence of a serious threat from lower classes.[21] The emphasis of this book is on the old communally organized social strata and the political struggle during the creation of newer classes such as the peasant and working classes. The emergence of a peasantry generally occurs when nomadic tribes settle land, whereas the process of proletarianization refers to "the historical process by which direct producers were deprived of alternative means of livelihood and were compelled to sell their labor power as a commodity."[22]

State and social formation are also key concepts to this study. States are formed by conquests, revolutions, and demographic and economic differentiations. State formation concerns basically the process of enlarging the capacity of state control over its subjects either internally or externally.[23] Social formation refers to the most dominant mode of production over other modes in a given period of history. In concrete social reality no single mode of production exists by itself.[24] Concrete social reality, the ways people make their living, refers to land tenure systems, regional and ecological settings, water resources, communal and class relations, legal and cultural symbols, and ideologies.

Recovering social history requires an acute awareness of alternative sources because state archives, newspapers, and secondary literature provide mainly the views of the state and European consuls.[25] Consequently, this study recovers history from Arabic sources, since the history of the hinterland in the Maghrib has been mainly Arabic, either written or preserved in various oral traditions such as songs, proverbs, epics, and poetry.[26]

I have relied on these "new" original and secondary sources of the state and the hinterland in constructing this social history. Oral traditions have specific significance simply because not all historical evidence is in written form, nor is statistical evidence always credible. The very word "statistics" originates in and is linked to attempts to collect data by those who control the state. Victorious groups and conquerors tend to destroy and bury the views of the oppressed. One is then justified in reconstructing the past by exploring the potentialities of buried or suppressed historical processes.[27]

Following the introduction, this book is divided into five chapters. The first chapter traces the social origins of pastoralism and regionalism in the nineteenth century. The second chapter deals with the general characteristics of precolonial social formations, such as trade, production, and the state. The third and fourth chapters treat the regional political economies of Tripolitania, Fezzan, and Cyrenaica. The fifth chapter is an analysis of collaboration with and resistance to Italian colonialism.

The contentions of this study can be summarized as follows: First, because of different historical processes, the three regions of Libya faced Italian colonialism with different economic and social confederations and forces. Second, colonial Italian settlement in Libya (1911–1943) occurred relatively late compared to that in Algeria and Tunisia, and was geared toward settling Italian peasants and workers; hence, there was no need at that time to destroy noncapitalist relations outside of the fertile coastal land. Third, the ability of local populations to resist colonialism from 1911 to 1932 kept relations of production in the hinterland out of the direct reach of colonialism. These varying and dynamic responses to Italian colonialism must be retrieved so as more fully to explain and understand a history that people of my grandparents' generation and experience know was not merely a one-sided story of the adventures of European colonials and capitalists.

CHAPTER 1

ECOLOGICAL AND SOCIAL ORIGINS OF REGIONALISM AND PASTORALISM: THE MYTH OF THE HILALI CONQUEST

"If Abu Zayd the Hilalian did not cultivate his own land, then why would he care if another land became a desert?"

—Libyan proverb

The purpose of this chapter is to trace the ecological and social origins of regionalism and pastoralism in Ottoman Libya, known as the Regency of Tarabulus al-Gharb, in the nineteenth century. This requires looking back to the eleventh century in order to determine why regionalism and pastoralism persisted into the nineteenth century. Of course, one is not doing justice to earlier periods; nevertheless, such a discussion will help set the historical background for the nineteenth century. This chapter will focus on three specific issues: the nature of regionalism and pastoralism; the geography of the Regency, that is, climate, rainfall, soil, and underground water; and the origins of pastoralism.

In 1911, Italian colonialists encountered in Ottoman Libya a pluralistic society. Strong tribal alliances competed with each other and contested the central state in Tripoli. These grew from roots in nineteenth-century Ottoman Libya, the most salient characteristics of which were regionalism and pastoralism as modes of social organization. These characteristics emerged out of a long process of interaction between desert ecology—soil, rain, underground water—and nomadic migrations and conquests.

Regionalism refers to the political and economic autonomy of the regions of Cyrenaica and Fezzan from the weak state in Tripoli. The Qaramanli state (1711–1835) and the Ottoman state after it (1835–1911) was confined to the coastal towns. Nineteenth-century Ottoman state formation was characterized by a weak central state and the power of the tribes, as demonstrated by their ability to carry arms, in contradistinction to European feudalism, where the use of arms was monopolized by the professional warrior class. Further, the Ottoman state since 1551 had to compete not only with armed tribal confederations but also with regional states such as the Awlad Muhammad in Fezzan (1550–1812) and the Sanusi state in Cyrenaica (1870–1911).

The ability of regional states and tribes to contest the power of the central state in Tripoli derived not only from an ecological distance from the central state, but also from strong socioeconomic ties with other regional markets and tribes in neighboring countries. One has to keep in mind that prior to the colonial period and the colonial conquest in 1911, strict borders were nonexistent, as were local ties to just one state. The tribes of western Tripolitania and southern Tunisia had strong confederations and were tied to the larger Muslim community of the Maghrib and the Sahara. The state of Awlad Muhammad in Fezzan was linked to the Lake Chad region for trade and the recruitment of soldiers. It also formed a strategic refuge from the Ottoman state in time of war. Equally important to note are the strong socioeconomic ties between the tribes of Cyrenaica and western Egypt. Cyrenaican tribes viewed western Egyptian cities and the desert as both sanctuaries to escape wars and as markets for agropastoral products. The development of these markets was due to ecological and social processes prior to and during the nineteenth century.

A review of the Regency of Tripoli's geography may provide some answers to the question of the origins of regionalism and pastoralism. The country is predominantly arid desert, without major rivers. The climate of the northern coast is Mediterranean. The interior is part of the huge desert of North Africa, *al-Sahará al Kubra*. Along parts of the coast, like the Gulf of Syrte, the desert and the sea come face to face, making a natural barrier between Tripolitania and Cyrenaica. (See Map 1.)

Rainfall is scant and inconsistent: The coast of Tripolitania averages only 300 millimeters annually; the Green Mountain of northern Cyrenaica receives up to 500–600 millimeters; Fezzan and southern Cyrenaica receive less than 10 millimeters.[1] Thus, only 5 percent of the entire country is suitable for cultivation. During the last century, settled agriculture was limited to the coast of Tripolitania, parts of the Jafara plain, the western mountain (al-jabal al-Gharbi, or Nifusa), the Green Mountain (al-jabal al-Akhdar), the Marj plain in Cyrenaica, and oases in Fezzan and Cyrenaica.

The geography of western Libya (Tripolitania) includes three major divisions: the coast, the plain, and the mountains. The

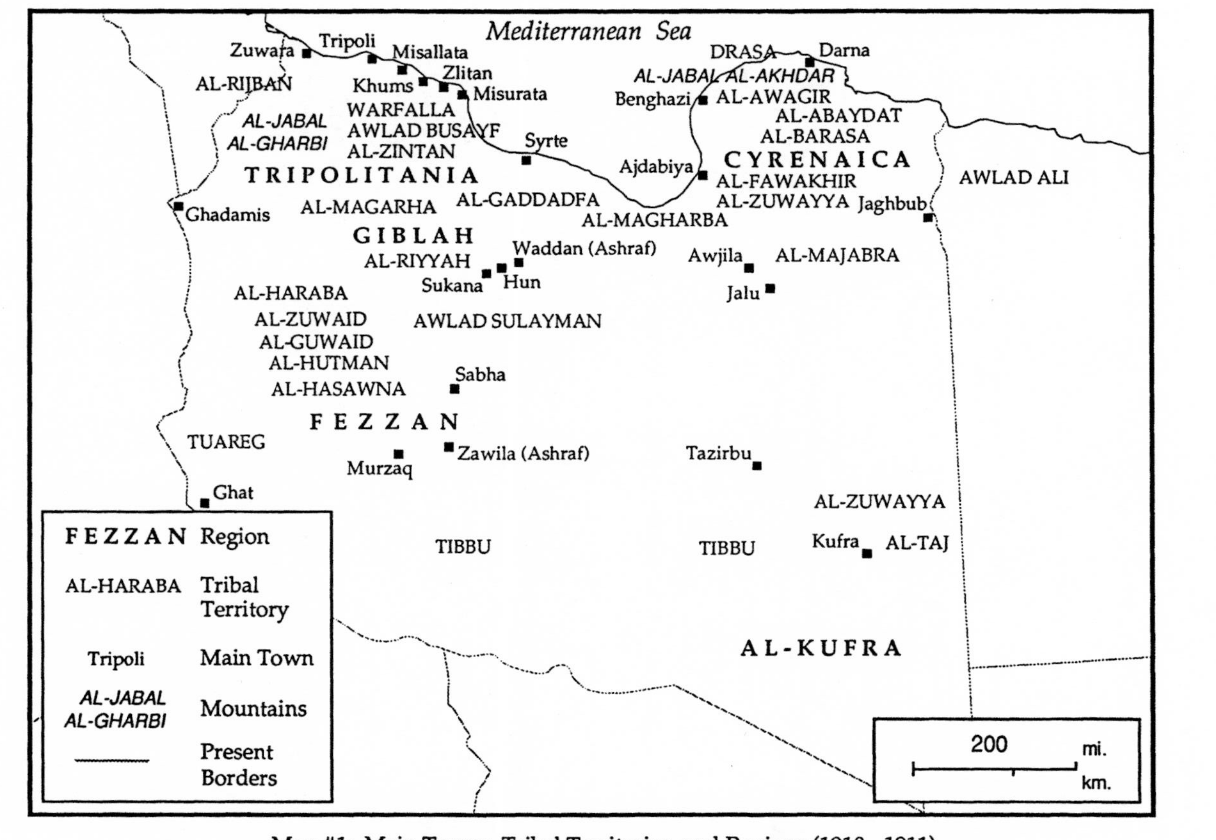

Map #1: Main Towns, Tribal Territories, and Regions (1910 - 1911).

Source: E. De Agostini, "Le populationi della Tripolitania," 39, and "Handbook of Libya," 97.

coastal area from Zawiya to Misurata was called the Sahil and the Manshia. Along this area settled agriculture was practiced in the form of sharecropping and small peasantry in the nineteenth century.[2] The plain of the Jafara expands to southern Tunisia and varies in width from 8 miles to 40 miles toward the coast. During the nineteenth century, the Jafara plain was partly covered by sand dunes and had only a few plots of cultivated land and green pastures. The plain is crossed by dry valleys (*widiyan*) which, during the rainy winter season, channel water runoff from the mountains to the Mediterranean Sea.[3]

Beyond the Jafara plain appears the western mountain range of Libya, *al-jabal al Gharbi*. The Jabal receives more rainfall than the plain; in addition, the Jabal has many springs which have allowed settled agriculture to take place. The Jabal nears the coast at Misurata, yet its southern sides are dry and rocky until it becomes part of the vast plateau of the *Hamada al-Hamara*. The Hamada plateau covers around 40,000 square miles; beyond that is the region of Fezzan. The eastern part of Tripolitania, the *Gibla*, stretches to the Syrte desert, and was inhabited up until the late nineteenth century by nomads and seminomads.

Fezzan, the southern region, is mainly desert crossed by *widiyan* where underground water is accessible and abundant. The population of Fezzan is either settled in major oases located along the *widiyan*, especially Wadi al-Shatti and al-Ajal, or is nomadic and seminomadic. The four major seminomadic tribal confederations were the Arab tribes of Wadi al-Shatti, those of the Gibla and Syrte, the Tuareg tribes of the southwest, and the Tebu tribes of the southeast. These groups interacted with each other and exchanged pastoral and agricultural products.[4]

Cyrenaica, the eastern region, extends to the north as a peninsula jutting into the Mediterranean Sea. It is separated from Tripolitania in the west by 403 miles of desert which reaches to the sea. That camels were the major means of travel in the desert in the nineteenth century indicates how much of a barrier the desert posed between the two regions. In the east and south, Cyrenaica is bordered by deserts—the western Egyptian desert in the east and the south Cyrenaican plateau, which eventually becomes part of the great Sahara, the largest desert in the world. Unlike the geography of Tripolitania, Cyrenaica has no large plains like the Jafara. Instead, the coast of Cyrenaica is narrow, with *al-jabal al-Akhdar*, the Green Mountain, rising almost immediately from the sea. Beyond the mountain there is the plain of *Marj*, followed by a plateau, but with limited underground water. The southern Cyrenaican desert, like Fezzan, restricts life to a few oases such as Jalu, Awjila, Jikhara, Tazirbu Jaghbub, and Kufra.

Pastoralism in this region, as in other parts of the world, developed as a human reaction to arid-zone and desert climates. Historically, water and land were owned collectively by tribes united by common descent. The tribe moves from one area to another, usually herding animals and in rainy seasons cultivating cereal. Such harsh climatic conditions demand mobility and militarism to ensure reproduction and defend the tribal homeland in the face of attacks from other tribes. In short, the tribe became a socioeconomic and political organization. Each tribe produced and exchanged with other tribes and peasants and had political and legal counsels; hence the tribes were able to survive in such arid-zone areas.[5]

Nineteenth-century Ottoman Libya was dominated by various nomadic and seminomadic types of social organization. In 1850 the urban population was very small. Tripoli City and Misurata in Tripolitania had only 12,000 inhabitants each; Murzaq in Fezzan had 5,000, as did the major towns of Cyrenaica, Benghazi, and Darna.[6]

The population in these areas had not changed much by 1911. In fact, the entire regency had only between 1 and 1.5 million inhabitants. Tripolitania had around 570,000 inhabitants of whom 126,000 were seminomads and 86,000 were nomads. The urban towns' population had increased somewhat by this time. For example, Tripoli City's population rose to 29,000. But the population of major Fezzani oases such as Murzaq, Ghat, and Sukana was limited to just a few thousand each.[7] Cyrenaica's population was estimated to be around 200,000, pastoralists comprising the majority. The urban population continued to be marginal—Benghazi had only 19,000 inhabitants and Darna 10,000 by the end of the nineteenth century.[8] In short, pastoralists dominated the Regency's social structure with the exception of the people who lived in Tripoli City. Why is this so? And when did it become the case for these populations? These questions are inviting, especially since many historians bring to bear on their studies the settled agriculture in northern Libya during the Roman period (A.D. 145–450).[9]

The standard interpretation of the origins of pastoralism in North Africa stresses ideological and religious factors in the migration of 200,000 to 300,000 "lawless" and "Mongol-like" tribesmen from Arabia to North Africa in the eleventh century. These tribesmen destroyed agricultural irrigation systems and urban life and consequently perpetuated nomadism as the dominant type of social organization up to the time of European colonialism.

According to this standard view, the eleventh-century Bani Hilal conquest was motivated not only by the politics of North Africa at that time, but by religious zeal. Their conquest of the region was enabled by a plan of the Fatimid Khalifa al-Mustansir who invited them from Arabia and sent them to Ifriqiyya to punish al-Muʿiz Ibn Badis al-Sanhaji, who rebelled against the Fatimid and declared his allegiance to the Abbasid Khalifa in Baghdad.[10] In short, the Hilali conquest was responsible, in this view, for destroying irrigation systems and settled agriculture, ushering in the process of desertification and nomadization in North Africa.

This interpretation was advanced by French colonial historians such as E. F. Gautier, a colonial officer in Madagascar and later in Algeria. He and other French and Arab historians popularized the so-called myth of the Hilali invasion of the Maghrib. The tribes of Bani Hilal and Salim came from Arabia, manipulated by the Fatimid Khalifa al-Mustansir's desire to punish his governor al-Muʿiz Ibn Badis in Ifriqiyya in the middle of the eleventh century. The Bani Hilal, motivated by religious zeal, advanced to the Maghrib, devastated settled agriculture and urban life, much as the Mongols did in Baghdad and West Asia in the thirteenth century. The Maghrib did not recover from the Hilali "catastrophe" for centuries; ostensibly, only the coming of European colonialism restablized the area and made settled life possible once again. Oddly, this interpretation of North African history was based on a selective reading of Ibn Khaldun, the famous fourteenth-century Muslim historian.[11]

Recently, other scholars have begun to challenge colonialist historiography. British archeologist Robert Goodchild points out that settled agriculture has been on the decline since the third century, long before the Hilali conquest. This, he argues, was due to Roman economic policy and the Vandal invasion. J. Poncet and C. Cahen agree with Goodchild and demonstrate that settled agriculture declined as a result of trade route changes and the weakening of the Ziri State before the Hilali. They call for revised analyses of the Hilali migration.[12]

Yves Lacoste has taken this critical approach further by showing that the Hilali myth is based on questionable evidence. It is motivated by an ideology that attempts to justify colonialism by disparaging the precolonial period as "barbaric and stagnant." It also ignores the complexity of Ibn Khaldun's history and politics, which do not promote themselves as being "value-free."[13] Ibn Khaldun came from a wealthy urban family and served as a judge and advisor in many states.[14] But the colonial view of the Hilali destruction ignores the fact that the Hilali migration was not Ibn Khaldun's major focus and that he praised nomads as state builders.[15]

Two recent historians go beyond methodological criticism of the myth of the Hilali invasion to reconstruct social history. Mahmud Abu-Swa and Radi Daghfus rely on original Arabic sources from the seventh and eleventh centuries. Abu-Swa shows the inadequacies of idealist and religious interpretations of the spread of Islam into North Africa. He points out that the rapid Islamization and Arabization of North Africa were due to the fact that both Berbers and Arabs practiced nomadism as a means of social organization. This mutual practice of nomadism facilitated their intermixing and eventually led to the Islamization and Arabization of the Berbers.[16]

Radi Daghfus's reading of al-Maqrizi and Ibn Thaghr-Bardi shows that the Hilali migration to the Maghrib was not motivated by Fatimid's political decisions to punish rebellious al-Mu'iz Ibn Badis alone, but was actually forced by severe droughts and famines in upper Egypt. In other words, the Hilali migration to the Maghrib was mainly motivated by economic needs.[17]

The decline of settled agriculture and the spread of different types of pastoralism were, then, the results of a long process of change in the climate, conquests, nomadic migrations, and the weakness of the central state. Interpretations of the Hilali migration must take into account these socioeconomic factors prior to, during, and after the eleventh century.

This eclectic interpretation of the Hilali migration does not deny the socioeconomic impact of the Hilali on North Africa; rather, it situates the migration as the result of the broader impact of climate, trade, other nomadic conquests, and state policies—whether Roman, Fatimid, or Ziris. Indeed, the Hilali conquest added new energy to pastoralism in North Africa. Its impact was a turning point in the eleventh century. The Hilali tribes took most of the land and water resources and turned many Berber and Arab tribes of the seventh century into clients and vassals. Further, Islam and the Arabic language replaced other religions and languages by the turn of the fourteenth century. Finally, the oral narrative of the Hilali Migration from Arabia to North Africa became the most popular epic in the precolonial modern history of the region. During the anticolonial resistance in Libya, leaders of the resistance, such as

Umar al Mukhtar, were compared to Abu Zaid and Dhiyab, legendary knights of the Hilali tribes.[18]

In 1908 a scientific expedition arrived in Cyrenaica, sent by the Jewish Territorial Organization in Europe. The aim of the expedition was to study the possibility of settling European Jews in Cyrenaica. A number of British and French university-affiliated scientists were financed by this organization and asked to evaluate the ecological and economic conditions of the region. Their findings shed new light on the previous debate over settled agriculture and pastoralism.

The scientists concluded their study of Cyrenaica by stressing that first, rainfall was scantier than had been believed. Second, the underground water in Cyrenaica was very limited even though most of the rainwater was concentrated in Cyrenaica rather than the rest of the region. Moreover, Tripolitania had more underground water than Cyrenaica. The solution to this puzzle was found in the nature of the soil in each region. Cyrenaican soil did not retain rainwater but allowed it to escape into the sea. Thus, the geology of Cyrenaica limited the quantity of reservoir water in the ground.[19] These findings suggest the possibility that there was a significant climatic change after the sixth century A.D., which may have reduced the amount of rainfall and consequently forestation. Further, it seems that both climatic change and pastoralist nomadic migrations contributed to the persistence of pastoralism in the period between the eleventh and mid-nineteenth centuries.

From this discussion of the geography of Ottoman Libya, two crucial conclusions must be drawn. First, regionalism and pastoralism persisted as a result of ecological and socioeconomic factors.[20] The nature of the soil, rain, and underground water limited the choices available to social groups, determining their mode of production. Also, the introduction of the camel by the Romans in the third century B.C. provided pastoralists with a remarkable resource, since camels endure desert harsh environment and go without water for 2 weeks. Camels became the major means of transportation as well as a source of milk, meat, and clothing. But equally important is the nature of the central state, the interaction with settled communities, trade routes, and regional economics outside of the Regency.

CHAPTER 2

OTTOMAN SOCIAL FORMATION: A TRADING AND COMMUNAL POLITICAL ECONOMY, 1830–1911

"You send your navy and demand that I must pay my debts to you, and the expenses of your expedition. But how could I pay my debts when you have reduced my revenues to just taxes on agriculture and especially when we did not have enough rain in the last four years?"

—Yusuf Pasha, the besieged Ruler of Tripoli's answer to the British Consul in Tripoli, 1831

The nineteenth-century Ottoman regency, Tarabulus al-Gharb (Libya), had a tributary social formation.[1] The state and ruling groups extracted tributes and taxes in both kind and money from foreign ships, tribesmen, peasants, and the caravans of the trans-Sahara trade between Bilad al-Sudan (today's Chad, Niger, Mali, and northern Nigeria) and the Mediterranean world and Middle East. Tripoli's agropastoral production was inconsistent given that rainfall was minimal and unpredictable. Drought and famine occurred frequently as in 1784 when it took hundreds of lives in the city of Tripoli alone.[2] The Regency suffered again in 1856, 1859, 1881–1882, 1888, and 1901–1903.[3] In short, Libyan agriculture promised little surplus.

Conversely, the transit trade across the Sahara, between the more stable agrarian political economies of Europe and Central and West Africa, provided a more reliable source of income than the unpredictable agropastoral production of the Regency. This was true as late as the 1880s, when the trans-Sahara trade through western Libya declined. Hence, in the nineteenth century, the tributary social formation of Tripoli was dominated by the extraction of tributes, collected by a standing army, and direct taxation. The tributary economy dominated and coexisted with other forms of tributary labor organizations: the small commodity production of artisans and peasants in Tripolitania; a semipastoral economy in rural Tripolitania, Cyrenaica, and Fezzan; semifeudal production in Fezzan; and capitalist enclaves in Tripolitania. As in other parts of the empire, then, the Ottoman tributary state-class in Tripoli faced diverse regional political economies: a peasant-pastoralist political economy in Fezzan, and a pastoralist political economy in Cyrenaica.

This chapter analyzes the trading economy as the major source of surplus; the nature of the state; and the agropastoral economy, which became, after the 1880s, the primary source of state income. Finally, it examines the impact of British and Italian commercial penetration.

The Transit Trade Across the Sahara

The trans-Sahara trade stretched as far back as Roman times, when the urban towns of Tripolitania, Subratha, Lipta, and Tripoli were major trading ports.[4] North Africa was a strategic zone linking Europe, the Middle East, and West Africa. Of the four major trade routes in the nineteenth century, then, three went through Libya:[5] Two routes, the Tripoli-Fezzan-Kawar-Bornu and the Tripoli-Ghadamis-Ghat-Air-Kano, went through western Libya. The third trade route crossed eastern Libya from Benghazi through Kufra to Wadai (see Map 2).[6]

Ottoman control over trade was aided by alliances with a number of tribes along the oases and tribal homelands in Tripolitania and Fezzan as well as the ruling dynasties of Bilad al-Sudan (Kanim, Bornu, and Wadai).[7] During the first Ottoman empire, from 1551 through 1711, trade was unstable because Ottoman control was limited to the coast and the state of Awlad Muhammad in Fezzan (1550–1812) contested Ottoman sovereignty and power.[8]

Historical Background

The Ottoman expansion into North Africa came during European-Muslim conflict after the expulsion of the Muslims from Spain and the Iberian Crusades to occupy North Africa. During the classical period, the Ottoman empire needed tributes, and so conquered new territories as an integral part of its tributary state formation. For their part, North African Muslims viewed Ottoman sultans as

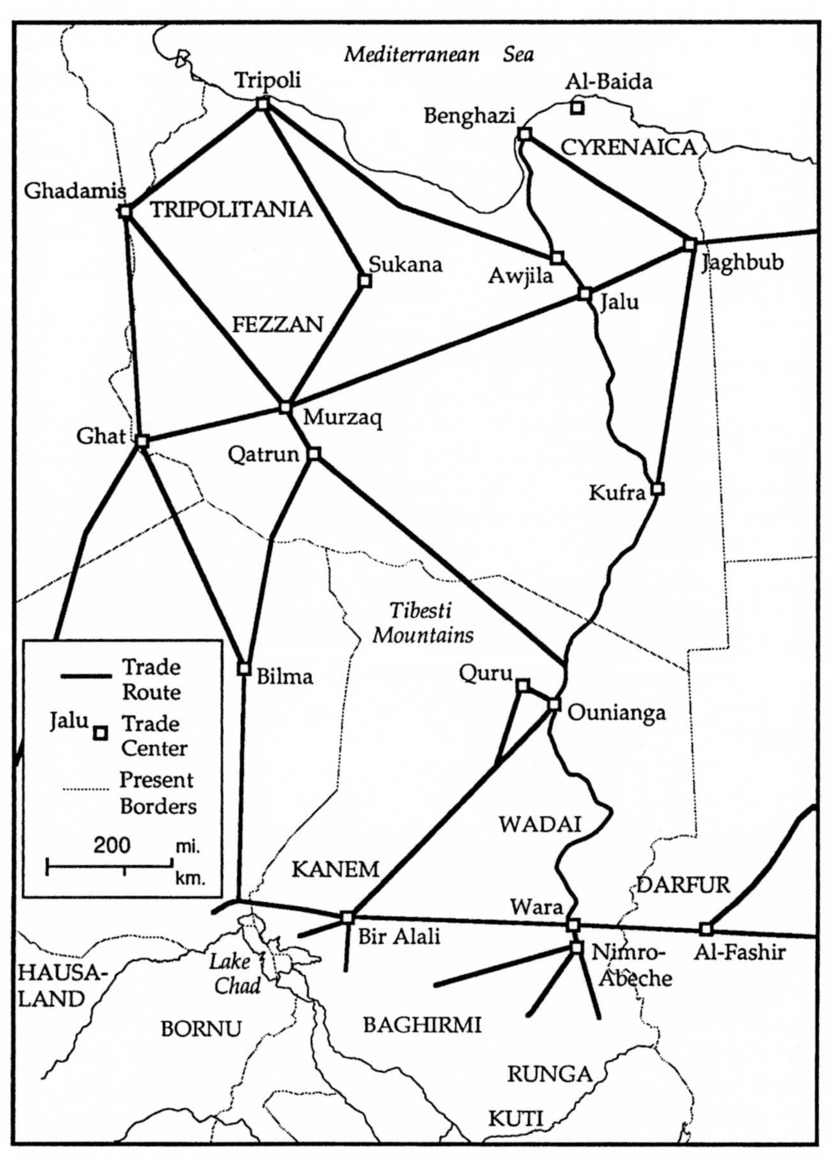

Map #2 : 19th Century Caravan Routes
Source: D. Cordell, "Eastern Libya, Wadai...," p. 25.

natural allies against the onslaught of Portuguese and Spanish naval attacks. Tripoli was occupied in 1510 by Spain, as were parts of Algeria and Morocco.[9] The Ottoman navy arrived on Tripoli's shore and took the city from the Knights of Saint John of Malta, who were allies of Spain in 1551. Tarabulus al-Gharb became an Ottoman province.[10] However, Ottoman sovereignty did not penetrate the hinterland because of the desert ecology, the lack of revenues for a major cross-desert campaign, and the existence of another state, that of Awlad Muhammad, in Fezzan.[11]

The state of Awlad Muhammad was founded around 1550 by a Sharifian (one who claimed descent from the Prophet's family) from Fes in Morocco. The descendants of Muhammad al-Fasi ruled the region of Fezzan and made alliances with other states in the region of Lake Chad.

The Awlad Muhammad state was a trading state. It emerged as a station for organizing and protecting trade caravans; in exchange, trade merchants paid the state tributes for each camel load. Fezzan provided the state of Awlad Muhammad with the largest market in the Sahara trade between Bilad al-Sudan, the Maghrib, and Egypt. The richness of the Fezzani markets naturally lured the Ottoman administration in Tripoli to take over the trade; Ottoman governors in Tripoli began to send armies to Fezzan for the purpose of collecting tributes. Awlad Muhammad sultans resisted the Ottomans; whenever defeated, they would withdraw into Lake Chad's region to recruit soldiers, especially their allies the rulers of Katsina, and return when the Ottoman army had left Fezzan.

A compromise with the Ottoman army was arranged by the Ulama of Fezzan in 1639. This compromise gave the Awlad Muhammad state Ottoman recognition in exchange for paying a yearly tribute in gold and slaves. The compromise ended when Sultan Najib M. Jhaym refused to pay the tribute in 1682. The Ottoman army attacked Murzaq, led by Murad al-Malti, who killed the Sultan. His son, Sultan Muhammad al-Nasir, agreed to pay tribute until 1689.[12] Once again, Governor Muhammad Sha'ib al-'Ain dispatched the Ottoman army. But al-Nasir defeated the army and did not pay tribute until 1715.[13] At that time, Ahmad al-Qaramanli took power and founded an autonomous state in Tripoli.

As mentioned earlier, the rise of the Qaramanli state was part of a larger phenomenon throughout the empire in which provisional governors and urban notable tax collectors, *'Ayan*, paved the way for the rise of autonomous states in the eighteenth century. The

Qaramanlis, for example, were members of the Cologhli class. As Turks themselves, they became a powerful group because of their ties to the Ottoman military aristocracy. They were landowners, military personnel, policemen, and members of a tax-exempt class.

In 1711 the Cologhlis became the ruling class. Even so, the Qaramanlis kept some formal ties with the Porte. Qaramanli pashas needed political protection from European states. They requested an Ottoman decree, or a Firaman, from the Porte prior to the appointment of any new pasha. Aside from these formal ties, the Qaramanlis acted independently and often opposed imperial Porte policy, as in 1815, when Yusuf Pasha allied with France against Ottoman policy.[14]

The Qaramanlis, however, did not have enough resources to crush all tribal confederations, nor to eliminate the state of Awlad Muhammad. Most of their revenue came from the sea: their success in building a small but effective navy enabled them to receive *Atawa* tributes from commercial ships, especially those from small European states.[15]

The tribes of the hinterland were armed and self-sufficient. A claim to land depended on the tribe's ability to defend the land against other tribes. As a defense strategy, regional tribal alliances developed to counter state armies, foreign conquest, and war over land with other tribes.

The Qaramanli pashas, like Yusuf, followed two policies: one was to incorporate strong chiefs by granting them the right to collect taxes in exchange for either a percentage or exemption, as in the cases of the Nuwair clan of the Mahamid in the western Tripoli family, the Haduth clan in Cyrenaica, and Saif al-Nasir of Awlad Sulayman in the 1820s. The second policy was to send the army and loyal tribes to punish rebellious tribes or states. This occurred against the Awlad Muhammad in 1715 and the Juwazi tribes in 1817.[16]

The Qaramanli state's strength reached its peak during the reign of Yusuf Pasha from 1795 to 1832 as a result of an increase in *Atawa* and *Kharaj* tributes from the sea. These tributes allowed the Pasha to expand state authority into the hinterland. After the decline of sea tributes following the war with the United States and the restrictions imposed by England and France, Yusuf Qaramanli shifted his trade policy to compensate for his losses.[17] The Fulanis' expansion in Lake Chad, under the leadership of 'Uthman B. Fudi, led to their domination of the Sahara trade. Yusuf Qaramanli directed his policy southward to compensate for his loss of sea tributes, attempting to control the Sahara trade directly. He occupied Ghadamis in 1810 and destroyed the state of Awlad Muhammad in 1812.[18] To further his effort he sent 'Abd al-Jalil, the chief of Awlad Sulayman, with 6,000 troops to aid his ally, Muhamad al-Amin al-Kanimi of Kanem (1775–1837), in 1817.[19] The army arrived with 6,000 camels and large tributes of slaves. In 1826, Mustafa al-Ahmar, the Qaramanli governor of Fezzan, aided the Kanimi against his enemies in Kanem, arriving with large tributes.[20]

Yet, in the late 1820s, Yusuf Pasha became unable to generate more revenues, and he was not willing to endanger his social base to do so. Rather, he continued to rely on his sons and servants to rule the state. Many other North African states began to borrow money from European merchants. In 1830 the pasha's French debt alone was around 500,000 American dollars.

In desperation, the pasha attempted to increase agropastoral taxes to pay European merchants; but this was not enough. He then imposed new taxes, not only on poor peasants and artisans, but even on members of his own ruling class, the Cologhli, who had previously been exempt. This led to their revolt against him. Finally, he resigned in favor of his son, Ali, but this was ineffective since the rebels rallied behind his grandson, Mihammad. The British consul, Warrington, supported the rebellion to counter the French consul, who supported Ali Qaramanli.[21]

This crisis could have led to the British occupation for which Consul Warrington was lobbying. Fear of this possibility and the occupation of Algeria by the French in 1830 persuaded the Porte to salvage one of its last territories in Muslim North Africa.[22]

The Nature of the State

The first third of the nineteenth century witnessed a period of intense conflict over the provinces of the Ottoman empire. European capitalist pressure and capitalist transformation within the empire—toward the goal of asserting authority over the periphery—culminated in the brutal colonial conquest of Ottoman Libya in 1835. In Tripoli, the Qaramanli state felt the pressure of the European powers in the Mediterranean and shifted its policy toward the frontiers of the Sahara to control the Sahara trade.

A tributary state generally extracts tributes directly from the producers and claims ownership of land; but there are variations, as in the case of capitalist states.

The state in nineteenth-century Ottoman Libya shared power with regional powers such as the tribal confederations of the Mahamid, the Awlad Sulayman, and the Sa'adi, or states such as the Awlad Muhammad in Fezzan (1550–1812) and the Sanusi brotherhood (1860–1932). These tributary states had different social bases. Some states were premodern because of both European capitalism and internal capitalist development in the second half of the nineteenth century. For example, a distinction must be made between the Qaramanli and the Awlad Muhammed states. Though both were tributary states, the Qaramanli state was stronger because of the tributes it exacted from sea trade and agropastoralism. The Awlad Muhammad state was basically a regional tributary state along the trans-Sahara trade route.

The second half of the nineteenth century witnessed the rise of a new type of state. The Ottoman empire became dominated by capitalist relations and began to enforce individual cash payment over the old collective tribute in kind. In short, the new state became "early modern" and less tributary—an early modern state being one at the transition stage when capitalist relations begin to dominate tributary ones. The Sanusi order, even though it was based on payment of tribute in kind, had other characteristics that justify treating it as an early modern state.

Many factors contributed to the rise of the early modern states. In the eighteenth century, the Ottoman empire underwent the process of decentralization; the Porte authority weakened because of wars against the Russian and Safavid empires; the flow of American silver in addition to an increase in the empire's population led to inflation between 1556 and 1625. This inflation affected the salaries of local commissioners in the provinces; hence, the Ottoman state began to rely more on provincial revenues. Because of the need for security in the provinces, many autonomous notables and governors became semi-independent. The Azms in Syria, the Jalilis Mosul, the Shihabis in the mountains of Lebanon, Shaykh Dhahir al-'umar and Ahmad al-Jazar in Palestine, and Ali Bik al-Kabir in Egypt all became virtually independent—that is, they did not pay taxes to the Porte. However, most local states kept some nominal allegiance to the Porte as a means of appeasing the sultan and protecting themselves from European expansion.[23]

In North Africa, decentralization existed even before the eighteenth century as a result of the distant location of the North African Ottoman regencies. Yet as in the earlier cases, and because of competition among the elite janissary, strong military officers from the Cologhli class claimed power, eliminated the janissary, and ensured security. Hussain B. Ali founded the Husaynid state in Tunis around 1705 and Ahmad Qaramanli built another local state in Tarabulus al-Gharb.[24]

The Qaramanli state reached its apogee during the reign of Yusuf Pasha Qaramanli (1793–1832). He organized a strong army and an active navy, allowing them to collect large tributes from commercial ships passing along Tripoli's coast, as well as from the Sahara trade. The army was composed of members of the Cologhli class, and was around 10,000 strong. Qaramanli's guards, slaves and irregular tribal allies numbered 40,000, especially in time of war or foreign conquest.[25] The Cologhli, numbering 30,000 in the 1830s, descendants of the old Ottoman janissary and local women, were exempted from taxes.[26] As for tribal troops, they were self-equipped and their chiefs were exempted from taxes. Their motive for allying with the state was basically that the state had promised them loot.[27] Managed by European mercenaries and local families, the navy surprised commercial ships, especially from small European states, and demanded tribute at the risk of confiscating ships and capturing nationals.[28]

Yusuf Pasha focused on building a navy and encouraged private ships to impose *Atawa*, or tribute, on European commercial ships passing by the Tripolitanian coast. This policy was branded by Europeans as piracy or corsairing. The image of the pirate implied that the tributes of North African states were nothing but plunder for its own sake, and ignored the fact that sea-tribute was a reaction of North Africans and southern Europeans to northern European piracy and monopoly of trade.[29]

The Qaramanli navy became strong enough to impose a tribute of passage on ships; otherwise, these ships were attacked. Many states agreed to pay tribute and give gifts to Yusuf Pasha, especially small states like Italy and Scandinavia. For example, between 1796 and 1807 the Qaramanli navy took in $84,000 from Austria and $12,000 from Sweden and Denmark. In 1798, Sweden and Denmark each paid Tripoli $100,000 each for returning their captive ships and nationals.[30]

In 1805, Yusuf Pasha demanded a higher tribute from European states. The United States refused to pay and a war began in which the Tripoli navy captured an American ship. The U.S. Navy occupied the eastern port of Darna with the help of the Pasha's brother, Ahmad. A peace treaty was signed in 1805, but Yusuf Qaramanli lost his first battle when the U.S. stopped paying him passage fees. In 1815, European states signed the Treaty of Vienna, which banned "piracy" and slave trade. This year marks the beginning of the Qaramanli party's decline. Yusuf Qaramanli did not modernize his state and army, nor did he broaden his elitist Cologhli-controlled state by appealing to the larger population; in the face of these misguided policies, he also continued his extravagant lifestyle. He began to borrow money from European merchants. As state revenues declined, however, he could not pay back his debts. To make things worse for him, England and France restricted their payment of tribute to Tripoli in 1820.[31]

This European pressure led to a change in the policy of Yusuf Pasha. As sea-tributes declined, he turned to agropastoral taxes and the Sahara trade tributes as alternative sources of surplus. After Tripoli's war with the United States, Qaramanli reoriented his policy toward the hinterland and the Sahara trade. He exempted strong tribal chiefs from taxes, as in the cases of the Nuir clan of the Mahamid, the Saif al-Nasir clan of Awlad Sulayman, and the Haduth of the Brasa. In exchange, these chiefs agreed to aid the state in collecting taxes and tributes.[32] As for the Sahara trade, the pasha aimed to control it directly, which meant a change from his predecessors' policy of coexistence with the Awlad Muhammad state. Instead of forming a partnership with Awlad Muhammad, the Pasha organized a large *Mahalla,* or expedition, which destroyed the Fezzani state in 1812.[33] Further, he sent two mahallas to Kanem in 1819 and 1827 to aid his ally, Shaykh Muhammad al-Amin al-Kanimi, the ruler of Kanem.[34] This drastic new policy highlights the importance of analyzing the state of Awlad Muhammad, essentially a trading state in Fezzan connecting Lake Chad's region with North Africa.

Fezzan's proximity to the Lake Chad region made it a strategic market for the many trade caravans. The market of Fezzan paved the way for the rise of local states. Many states had emerged along major trade routes in the Sahara and the rest of North Africa for centuries, so the rise of states in Fezzan was not an anomaly.[35] In Fezzan, two local states emerged: the Ibadi Banu al-Khatab state in Ziwaila in the tenth century, and the Awlad Muhammad state in Murzaq, which lasted from 1550 to 1812. A third attempt to build a state was made by the chief of Awlad Sulayman, Abd al-Jalil, who ruled the region from 1830 until 1842, when the Ottoman army killed him. This led to the flight of his tribal coalition into the Sahara frontiers in today's Chad. But the state of Awlad Muhammad lasted for centuries, and deserves further analysis.

The State of Awlad Muhammad, 1550–1812

According to old local traditions in Murzaq, which the Awlad Muhammad family built as the capital, this state was founded by a Sharifin Shaykh from Morocco named Muhammad al-Fasi in 1577. A station for the Sahara trade caravans, it was a tributary state like the sixteenth-century Ottoman state in Tripoli; it was dominated by the Awlad Muhammad family, tribal chiefs, and the merchants of Fezzan who needed secure routes, stations, and markets for their caravans.

Unfortunately, we still do not know many details about this Fezzani state except for those found in a few pages of the histories by the two local historians, Ibn Ghalbun and al-Ansari, those related by western travelers, and those found in a manuscript by an unknown writer called Tarikh Fezzan (*The History of Fezzan*). From these sources, we do know that the Fezzani state existed on tributes in the form of taxes extracted from the caravans of the Sahara trade that passed through Fezzan, for whom, in exchange, the state provided protection, a market, and housing for merchants.

The German traveler Friedrich Hornemann, who visited the region in 1789, wrote one of the earliest descriptions of the state. He observed that the state received tributes from trade caravans and raided oases and other states for spoils. Caravans from Cairo paid an equivalent of six to eight dollars for each camel load sold in the market of Murzaq, whereas caravans from Bornu and the Hausa lands had to pay two *mithqals* of gold for each slave they sold.[36]

Murzaq, the capital, was inhabited by merchants of different ethnic backgrounds—Arabs from Tripoli, Sukana, Jalo, and Egypt; blacks from Bornu and the Hausa lands; and Europeans.[37] The Awlad Muhammad state, in exchange for tributes from the merchants, provided the security of a large market where these merchants could buy food, rent houses and camels, hire guides, and meet other merchants. In addition, the capital Murzaq had a fine craft industry; dyed cloth from Murzaq was sought after by the merchants of the Sahara trade.[38]

When the Ottoman army conquered Tripoli in 1551, it targeted the rich Fezzan economy, which could provide tributes of dates, gold, and slaves. Further, the Ottoman state needed to ensure the flow of trade caravans to Tripoli City. Conflict was inevitable between a tributary empire and a regional state. Eventually, the Ottoman army was sent to Fezzan to demand a yearly tribute to the state in Tripoli. However, because the Ottoman state in Tripoli had only a small army between 1551 and 1711, a pattern persisted in its relations with the sultans of Awlad Muhammad: whenever the state in Tripoli weakened, the Awlad Muhammad refused to pay tributes. This in turn led to the retaliation of the Ottoman army, which tried to collect the tribute by force. The Awlad Muhammad, whenever defeated, would retreat to his allies in the Sahara frontiers in Bornu and the Hausa lands; he would return after he gained strength by gathering recruits and the Ottoman army departed.[39]

In 1639, Ibn Ghalbun described a truce that had been reached between the Ottoman army and the sultan of Awlad Muhammad. The sultan agreed to pay a yearly *jiziya*, or tribute, to the central government in Tripoli, made of

> four thousand mithqals of gold; two thousands in gold dior or dust and . . . the remaining two thousands in slaves. Each male slave would cost 25 mithqals, the price of a slave girl would be 30 mithqals. The Awlad Muhammad would bear the expenses of the slaves until they reached Sukana. Beyond Sukana the expenses would be the responsibility of the government in Tripoli.[40]

The Ottoman commander 'Uthaman Dey recognized the state of Awlad Muhammad and gave the title of Shaykh to Muhammad B. Jhaym.[41] However, the tribute to Tripoli was irregular whenever the state weakened; the Fezzani population supported Awlad Muhammad because of the brutality of the Ottoman army and its heavy taxation. Only after the rise of the Qaramanli state did the Awlad Muhammad pay tribute more regularly to the stronger Qaramanli state.

When Hornemann visited Fezzan in 1789, he observed that the tribute to Tripoli was $6,000, reduced in the following year to $4,000.[42] The state survived until 1812. Yusuf Qaramanli became heavily indebted to European merchants. To collect more revenues after the shrinking of the sea tributes, he shifted his policy southward toward the Sahara trade. Thus, the Awlad Muhammad became an obstacle to Qaramanli's new policy.[43]

Despite its military success in Fezzan, the Qaramanli state began to weaken as early as 1805. In that year the Pasha engaged in a war against the United States that ended in the restriction of his sea tributes. European pressure on North African states increased after the defeat of Napoleon in 1815.[44] The new conservative "concert of Europe" alliance restricted "piracy" and vowed to punish the Barbary states, which included the Qaramanli in Tripoli. The decline of sea tributes led to a shift in the Qaramanli policy toward the Sahara trade. Thus, the pasha wanted to claim all the tribute of Fezzan without the service of the Awlad Muhammad state. Further, he sent two expeditions to Lake Chad's region to help his ally Shaykh Muhammad al-Amin al-Kanimi in 1817 and 1826, which successfully brought in large tributes of slaves and animals. But even these revenues were not enough for the extravagant pasha and his family, who ruled most of the towns.[45]

As in the case of many states in the region, including the Ottoman state itself, Yusuf Qaramanli began to borrow money from French and British merchants. When he was not given an extension and these merchants demanded the repayment of their loans, the pasha sold them the right to collect agropastoral taxes from different districts such as Misurata and Benghazi. He became so desperate at one point that he gave more than one merchant the right to collect taxes from the same district. By 1830 the state began to collapse. The Qaramanli dynasty refused to reform its military and enlarge its social base, because the pasha, his sons, and the military elite did not want to give up their rule. The pasha, in desperation, raised new taxes and lifted the exemption that had been granted the Cologhli in order to pay his debts. He made these changes because the French navy in 1830 and the British in 1832 blockaded Tripoli and demanded that the pasha pay his $500,000 debt.[46]

This blockade led to a crisis within the ruling dynasty when the Cologhli class rebelled against the pasha and chose the pasha's grandson Mihammad as the only legitimate ruler. Not only did the Cologhli challenge his rule, but the major tribal confederation in Syrtica and the Jabal declared their autonomy from the state.[47] Yusuf Qaramanli, old and isolated, surrendered his throne to his elder son, Ali, in 1832. The crisis of the Qaramanli state set the stage for the coming of the Ottoman army and the formation of the second direct rule of the Ottoman state in Tarabulus al-Gharb.

The crisis of the Qaramanli state gave the sublime Porte in Istanbul a chance to build a firm administration in a time of expanding European imperialism. According to one document in the Tripoli archives, the Ottoman government studied the crisis and after a meeting decided to abolish the Qaramanli's rule and administer the Regency directly. This decision was motivated by a fear of losing Tripoli, the last Ottoman territory, to one of the European powers—especially after the French occupied Algeria in

1830—or to England, since British Consul Warrington sided with the rebels led by Mihammad Qaramanli. Tarabulus al-Gharb also functioned as a major gateway to Muslim Africa. Because of its importance the Porte decided to intervene and end the Qaramanlis' rule in 1835.[48]

The new Ottoman state in Tripoli (1835–1911) differed from the old states in part because of the changes that took place in the ruling class between the seventeenth and nineteenth centuries. By the end of the sixteenth century, the Ottoman state had changed gradually from the old tributary form to a capitalist form, which gained dominance over tributary relations by the middle of the nineteenth century. This transformation occurred internally and was only later, in the years after 1815, penetrated by European capital.[49]

In the late sixteenth century, the Ottoman population increased. The flow of American silver through Spain caused inflation and a fall in prices. The Porte needed cash to pay its bureaucracy. A farming-tax system was adopted in the late seventeenth century to meet these demands. Consequently, a new class of tax farmers, or *Malikin*, emerged in the provinces. In other words, the state sold state land to private owners to obtain quick cash for the treasury. Gradually, taxes were paid in cash instead of in kind. Thus, in the long run, capitalism developed internally and began to challenge the tributary structure, contrary to the argument of modernization theorists.[50] By the end of the eighteenth century, capitalist tendencies became dominant in the ruling class. Ottoman reforms during the period of Tanzimat (1839–1876) must be viewed mainly as the culmination of dynamics long at work in the Ottoman state.[51] Donald Quataert has shown that such capitalist processes were not a one-way street but were, rather, resisted and counterbalanced by many subaltern groups inside the Ottoman empire.[52]

Because the new centralized Ottoman state in Tripoli during the latter half of the nineteenth century was basically an early modern state dominated less by tributary production than by capitalism, its impact on the population was different from that of its predecessors. In the regency of Tripoli, the Ottoman state continued the efforts of the Qaramanli to strengthen the authority of the state over the autonomous tribal lords of the hinterland. By the 1850s trade started booming; in the 1870s it reached its apogee. However, by 1885 the Sahara trade had declined, until by 1911 it had become marginal, especially throughout western Libya.[53] A number of factors led to this decline. The French and British conquests of West

Africa shifted trade to the Atlantic coast, and the competition of new producers led to decline of the exports of commodities like ostrich feathers and esparto grass throughout the Sahara.

The region of Cyrenaica did not experience the same decline of the Sahara trade. On the contrary, a third major trade route was just starting to make its way through Cyrenaica. Thanks to the Sanusi order, missionaries and lodges in Cyrenaica, western Egypt, and Chad provided a cross-cultural and cross-ethnic network for the social organization of the Sahara trade. Thus, the tribes of Cyrenaica, living far from Tripoli, continued their exercise of autonomy, even when, after 1835, the state gained power over hinterland Tripolitania and Fezzan. The Sanusi brotherhood, unlike the regional Fezzani state of Awlad Muhammad, had a broader Islamic ideology which went beyond ethnicity and regionalism, offering a pan-Islamic appeal to the population of Cyrenaica, the western Egyptian desert, and northern Chad. The Sanusi success was due to education, missionaries, and trade management, all geared toward creating a society and state based on a North African Muslim model.

The Sahara trade in the eighteenth century was based on the exchange of luxurious commodities such as cloth, ivory, ostrich feathers, gold, goatskins, guns, and slaves. European merchants wanted to export their cloth, guns, and luxury goods, and West African kings and aristocrats needed and could afford these goods. The local economy profited as well from engaging in this transit trade. The state protected trade caravans and received taxes.[54] The local merchants made profits, and tribesmen from the Tuareq, Awlad Sulayman, Zuwayya, and Majabra tribes served as guides, guards, and camel renters while tribal chiefs received tributes from the merchants.[55] By the turn of the nineteenth century, Tarabulus al-Gharb and the Sahara became markets for cheap British textile cloth sold at that time to the population at large, and not just to the elite. It should be noted that there was no separation between the means and the forces of production; tribesmen worked for wages for a season, and after that returned to their tribal land. In other words, free labor was not separated from communal and collective tribal identity—at least not until 1850.

Prior to the discovery of the Americas, gold and slaves were the most valuable commodities of the trans-Sahara trade. Indeed, West Africa provided Europe with most of its gold. Slaves were an equally important commodity before slavery was effectively banned in 1860. Slave trade across the Sahara became politicized as European states, especially England, discovered the immorality of the slave trade and started a campaign to ban it at the turn of the last century. However, this moral goal was coupled with the British goal to explore the Niger River and control the Sahara trade. Indeed, many British consuls and travelers exaggerated the volume of the slave trade as an excuse to occupy the Sahara. It should be stressed that the slave trade was not as important in the nineteenth century as it has been made out to be in the twentieth, yet it caused much controversy. A summary of the history of the trade highlights the nature of this controversy.

Recently published documents of the Yushi' merchant family in Ghadamis shed new light on the Sahara trade. The transit trade was not, as European consuls reported, in gold and slaves, but was actually quite diverse. For example, the exports of Bilad al-Sudan were mainly wax, leather, ostrich feathers, and guns, while imports were British-manufactured cotton cloth, glass, mirrors, razors, papers, tea, sugar, and other commodities.[56]

But European travelers and consuls emphasized the slave trade. For example, the traveler Lyon estimated the number of slaves reaching Tripoli in 1819 at around 3,000 to 4,000, with 1,000 said to have reached Benghazi. The travelers Clapperton and Denham estimated the slave number at 2,000 in 1822–1824. In 1850, French Consul De Renaud appraised it at 2,708.[57] However, because the slave trade was an ideological tool in Europe to discredit Ottoman rule and justify colonial ambitions, the Yushi' family letters and Ibn Ghalbun's history are more reliable sources on the slave trade than the speculative evaluations of European consuls and travelers. After all, it was European traders and states who were engaged in the most massive slave trade in West and East Africa.[58]

Slaves were used as servants for wealthy merchants and as soldiers in Bilad al-Sudan, Fezzan, and the Qaramanli state. Other slaves formed the major part of the labor force in settled agriculture in Fezzan. Though the slave trade flourished in the eighteenth and early nineteenth centuries, it was not the most significant commodity of the trans-Sahara trade.

The trans-Sahara trade through western Libya reached its apex in the period between the 1860s and the 1870s. The trade's major commodities were ivory, ostrich feathers, and goatskins. The re-exports of ivory from West Africa to Europe reached a high of 4,000 pounds in 1871, but declined in the 1880s until they were just 2,000 pounds in 1904. (See Appendix.)

Ostrich feathers, which became fashionable in Europe during the Napoleonic wars, were used as pens, fans and decorations on women's hats.[59] The trade peaked in 1883, when the volume of exports reached 237,000 pounds; but this trade also declined by the end of the century. In 1904 the exports were only 23,000 pounds.

Goatskins were imported from West Africa and exported to cities in Europe and the United States. Following an increase in demand in the 1870s, the trade experienced a boom in the 1880s. However, as with other Sudanese commodities, trading in goatskins became marginal by the end of the nineteenth century. The decline of the Sahara trade through western Libya was caused by the impact of war around the region of Lake Chad, and as a consequence of French and British colonial expansion into West Africa after 1888. This expansion shifted the Sahara trade from the Sahara and North Africa to the Atlantic ports of West Africa.

The long-held view that the Sahara trade through Libya declined by the mid-nineteenth century can no longer be maintained. Studies assert that the route of Wadai-Kufra and Benghazi in western Libya actually boomed during most of the second half of the last century.[60] Actually, the decline of trade through western Libya was due to the instability of the Lake Chad region as a result of the dynastic war of Rabih al-Zubair, the French occupation of Kanem, Wadai, and Timbuctu in 1904, and the British opening of the Kano–Legos railway. The wars of al-Zubair made trading very difficult, and the British and French occupation of West and northwest Africa redirected the Sahara trade to the Atlantic Coast. But the French and British diversion of trade made it possible to make a profit without intermediaries, and the new route was cheaper than the long journey by camel caravans across the Sahara. Finally, Sudanese commodities such as ostrich feathers fell out of fashion in Europe and exports fell sharply. So it was a combination of internal factors like the wars in the Lake Chad region, and external factors like colonial expansion and the change in consumption trends, that led to the decline of the Tripolitania–Fezzan trade routes.

As Sahara trade declined the Ottoman administration began to focus on agriculture and the local economy. Its modernization program was part of a centralizing policy that coalesced around extending state administration to the hinterland, opening new schools and courts, settling tribes, registering tribal land privately, and experimenting with new agricultural crops such as rice, coffee, and cotton. To evaluate such programs, it is first necessary to delineate the nature of the agrarian structure and land tenure system.

Land Tenure and Property Relations

Different types of land tenure existed in Tripolitania, Cyrenaica, and Fezzan. The Ottoman Land Code of 1858 recognized the following types: privately owned land (*mulk*); state land (*miri* or *kharaj*); religious endowment land (*waqf*); "no man's land" (*matruka*); and "dead" land (*mawat*).

The Ottoman Land Code reflected a mixture of Turkish tribal practice and Islamic law. Islamic law recognized private property and state property. *Mulk* land granted the owner full ownership (*hiaza* and *ragaba* are terms for "full ownership") *tasaruf* (usufruct), whereas *kharaj* land granted only the right of possession while the state kept the right of usufruct. On the other hand, the Ottoman Land Code included the *timar,* in which the state owned the land and leased it to a territorial Ottoman cavalry called *sipahi.* The *sipahi* were appointed by the state to collect taxes from the peasantry, and the *sipahi* in turn had to provide supplies and men to the state in times of war. The *sipahi* kept part of the taxes for themselves. In short, the state recognized private property, state land (*miri*), *timar,* as well as public land. The Ottoman Land Code of 1858 was not applied equally around the empire, since ecological and local factors conditioned its enforcement.[61]

Mulk is land over which an individual or a family held full rights of ownership and usufruct as a result of succession, sale, donation, or development. Aside from paying taxes in kind to the state, the holders of the land were free to sell or donate their land. *Mulk* land existed in the settled agricultural gardens along the Tripolitanian coast of the Sahel and al Manshiyya, al-Jabal al Gharbi's villages, and in the gardens of the Sahara oases of Tripolitania and Fezzan. This type of land was worked either by the small peasantry, the family, or by sharecroppers. No large land-owning class existed in Libya, with the exception of landed merchants in the Fezzan, where semifeudal relations existed. The landed merchant class used sharecroppers and tenant-peasants to work the large palm groves of Fezzan, which provided Libya with most of its dates.[62]

The second type of land ownership was state land, or *miri.* The state had direct right of usufruct.[63] Individuals who had leases to cultivate *miri* land had no right of usufruct. Because of the tribal military autonomy no absentee landlords emerged in Libya as they did in Lebanon, Syria, and Palestine. Desert ecology and the lack of state revenues limited settled agriculture to coastal Tripolitania, the

Jabal, and the oases of the Sahara. But this situation held true only for the period prior to the 1860s. Ottoman state formation led to the creation of settlements by the end of the last century. The bulk of the population was organized into tribal and intertribal alliances.

The third type of land ownership, *waqf* or *habs* land, was *mulk* land donated to Islamic religious foundations such as mosques, shrines, or holy cities in Islam. This type of land could not be subject to any type of legal alienation. In urban North Africa, the urban-merchant classes acquired *waqf* to avoid state confiscation and to provide crucial services to major cities.[64] *Waqf* land was not predominant in western Libya and Fezzan.[65] Yet the bulk of agricultural land in Cyrenaica was *waqf* land because of strong tribal loyalty to the Sanusiyya. The Sanusi lodges' *zawaya* land was *waqf*, donated and cultivated by the tribes of Cyrenaica. The Sanusi order's land was estimated at 600,000 acres at the turn of this century.[66] Most of the land was used for cereal cultivation and the herding of animals.

The fourth type of land was called *matruka*, or waste land, that was owned by the state, but which a tribe or village possessed, or used collectively. Nevertheless, Libyan tribes regarded certain bed valleys as their tribal homeland. This type of land was not irrigated, but cultivated during rainy seasons with barley and wheat and used as animal pasture. It is essential to note that tribal land was held in common and could not be alienated for individual use without the consent of the tribe. Collective ownership of land was most common in the Regency, but in 1858 the Ottomans attempted to register land individually and settle tribes as a result of the capitalist change within the Ottoman ruling class in Istanbul. This policy enjoyed only partial success in rural Tripolitania, and none at all in Cyrenaica or Fezzan, for reasons which are later explained in detail in an analysis of the Tripolitanian regional economy.

The purpose of the Land Code of 1858 was to collect taxes efficiently, directly through individuals, and without village and tribal heads as intermediaries. Thus, the state administration took over the function of all tribal councils. By 1902 all tax exemptions were abolished in Libya. The Cologhli, the Ashraf, and some of the notables all lost their privileges. This change angered the powerful Cologhli class and some of them contacted the European, especially the Italian, consulates and collaborated with them. Hassuna Qaramanli, grandson of Ali Qaramanli, the last ruler of the Qaramanli Dynasty in 1835, exemplifies this collaboration. The application of the Land Code of 1858, however, did not succeed in every province of the empire. Instead, the application varied from one province to another as well as within each province. Consequently, in reality a combination of local tribal customs and Ottoman laws coexisted. The code was limited to urban Cyrenaica; but by the end of the last century tribal ownership in rural Tripolitania had changed and the state succeeded in encouraging land registration. Registration led to the rise in prominence of certain leading families who applied their names to land. Landless families migrated to Tripoli City and French Tunisia, attracted by urban jobs. The family consequently became more important than the tribe. The Gibla tribes, however, like their Cyrenaican counterparts, were not affected by the state land code and continued to reproduce their "corporate" character by owning tribal land collectively.[67]

Libyan agropastoral economy produced a limited and unsteady surplus as long as most of the production went for self-sufficiency and paying taxes and tributes. Traditional agriculture and pastoralism complemented each other. Pastoralists exchanged their surplus animals and products like barley and wheat for dates, oil, and other peasant products from the oases.

Yet in spite of the fragility of the Libyan agropastoral economy, during rainy seasons Libyan peasants and tribes reacted to market demand and exported to outside markets. In 1810, Libya became the major source of meat and grain for the British navy in Malta. During that year 500 cattle and 20,000 hectoliters of cereals were imported by the British in Malta from Libya.[68] Later, by the middle of the century, the French consul De Reynaud reported the total indigenous agropastoral exports from Tripoli as follows:

Commodity	*Value in Pounds Sterling*
Cereals	59,840
Olive Oil	29,680
Animals	16,320
Butter	16,240

The total sum of the Regency's re-exports from the Sahara trade added to the overall exports is 3,272,444 pounds sterling.[69] Obviously this was a good rainy year; in a bad year, when rain was either scant or nonexistent, there was danger of famine, and flour had to be imported.[70] Only Fezzan had a steady harvest of date palms, making that region a target for the starving nomadic tribes of the Gibla and Syrte.[71]

The period between 1885 and 1896 witnessed the commercial production and exporting of esparto or halfa, a wild grass that grows in rural Tripolitania. Indeed, this grass, since it was used in the British paper industry, brought rural Tripolitania into the European capitalist market. Two major British companies held a monopoly over the trade. Some small Tripolitanian coastal ports grew as a result—Khums, Zlitan, and Zawiya among them. Four major pressing centers were built in 'Aziziyya and Khums, and with these, the Regency witnessed the first formation of a working class.

After the decline of the Sahara trade, many tribesmen were attracted to jobs created by the halfa trade, such as collecting, processing, and shipping. In short, this trade contributed to the rise of wage labor and the separation of some tribesmen from the collective tribal melding of the forces and means of production.[72]

Libyan exports of esparto started in 1885 at 20,000 tons, and reached a peak of 210,000 tons in 1888. (See Appendix.) However, this trade began to decline when wood fiber, which proved to be cheaper, replaced esparto for making paper. In addition, the primitive hand method used to collect the grass adversely affected the growth of new grass and was harmful to the land. The demand for Libyan esparto grass declined as France and Sweden became major producers of wood fiber for the paper industry. In spite of this competition, esparto grass exports from Libya continued to be one of the main commodities well into the twentieth century. (See Appendix.)

The Impact of European Economic Penetration, 1830–1911

The incorporation of self-sufficient agrarian societies into the world capitalist market occurred either indirectly through trade or directly through imposition by a colonial state. Libya (or the Regency of Tripoli), as a province of the Ottoman empire, was influenced by the European economic penetration of the empire in general and by its own domestic conditions in the second half of the nineteenth century.

In 1887 strong European capitalist states began to divide the world into spheres of influence. European states pressured the Ottoman imperial authority to give European traders concessions to trade freely in the empire. These concessions were originally given as gifts, like one in 1535 to France. Libya obviously was not as rich a province as Egypt or Syria. Still, it was targeted by European traders as a strategic gateway to Africa and as a market for

European goods. By the late seventeenth century, major European countries such as England and France established commercial consulates in Tripoli.[73]

In the 1860s and 1870s, Tripoli's major trading partners were England, France, the Ottoman empire, Egypt, Tunisia, Austria, the United States, and Germany. During most of the second half of the nineteenth century, England was the Regency's leading trading partner. However, between 1899 and 1902, Italy moved up the ranks from being fifth to being Libya's second major trading partner. This change was not coincidental, but was engineered by specific plans on the part of Italy. (See Appendix B.)

Italian attempts to found colonies were focused on regions near the Red Sea and in East Africa during the era of Prime Minister Crispi (1870–1896). In 1882, Italy acquired the port of Asab through peaceful commercial means. But the army was used to take over Mussawa in 1885 and northern Somalia in 1889. However, colonial expansion collapsed after the defeat of the Italian army by the Ethiopian army in the Battle of Adawa in 1896.[74] Crispi resigned and colonial policy in general suffered from this defeat for quite a while.

When advocates such as industrialists, missionaries and extreme nationalists revised their colonial ambitions, Tripoli became a target, especially with the occupation of Tunisia in 1882. The Italian government secured the approval of the British, who wanted a buffer zone (Libya) to halt French expansion in North Africa toward Egypt. After initial diplomatic efforts, Italian policy makers shifted their policy to prepare economically and culturally to conquer the Regency of Tripoli. Italian policy makers and media waged a war of propaganda against the Ottoman administration in Libya, in which Ottoman Turks were accused of being backward and oppressive rulers who kept native Libyans in darkness for centuries. Italy, on the other hand, was going to bring progress and modernization to Libya.[75]

The Italian policy of cultural and economic penetration was organized through the Italian Consulate and the Banco di Roma. Between 1876 and 1911 the Italians built 12 schools in Libya, including a high school. An Italian-sponsored press was founded in 1909.[76] Italian schools and newspapers attracted mostly Tripolitanian Jews, who acted as middlemen because they had long been active in European trade and knew the Italian language and culture well. Some of them were even Italian citizens.[77]

The Role of the Banco Di Roma

The Bank of Rome was founded in 1880 by the Vatican with the encouragement of the Italian government, with whom the Bank was in partnership, with a budget of 5,000,000 Italian lire. The Vatican and the Italian government were the Bank's major investors. The president of the Bank, Romolo Tittoni, was the brother of the Italian Foreign Minister, Tomasso Tittoni, during the Bank's activities in Tripoli (1903–1909).[78] The Bank employed mainly urban Libyan Jewish and Muslim merchants and notables as middlemen. Merchants were mainly concerned with the protection and stability of political conditions so that they could pursue their business interests. They easily changed their loyalty from one ruler to another as long as security was guaranteed. Among these merchants were Jewish merchants such as the Hassan, Nahum, and Arbib families.[79] Tripolitanian Muslim merchants worked and collaborated with the Bank to buy land and invest in agriculture. Among these Muslim merchants and notables were the family of al-Muntasir of Misurata, headed by 'Umar al-Muntasir, Bik Darnas, Hassuna al-Qaramanli (grandson of Ali Qaramanli), Ahmad al-Ismirly of Tripoli City, and Mustafa Bin Gudara of the coastal town of Zlitan.[80]

The Bank began to penetrate the economy of the Regency first by opening branches in most major cities and towns. Second, it invested in real estate by buying 400,000 acres of land.[81] Third, the Bank loaned money at low interest rates—at 9 percent compared to the 20–60 percent charged by some local Jewish moneylenders. Fourth, it sponsored olive-oil and esparto processing factories, flour mills, an ice-cream factory, and a printing house. Also, it invested in trans-Sahara trade and controlled maritime transportation between Libya, Egypt, and Italy.[82]

The Bank's activities were opposed by some Ottoman governors, especially Rajab Pasha, and the local nationalist newspapers, especially *Abu-Qasha* and *al-Mirsad*.[83] Furthermore, ordinary tribesmen in their own way were aware of the Bank's activities. French journalist George Raymond described a case in Cyrenaica that reflected people's awareness of colonialism. The branch at Benghazi wanted to invest in animals, so the bank officials made an agreement with tribesmen that the tribesmen would herd sheep in exchange for a share of the profit. But in the following years, the shepherds came to the bank with large numbers of sheep ears and claimed that the plague had killed off most of the herds and that the ears were proof of what had happened. That year, the markets of Cyrenaica were full of earless sheep.[84]

The Bank found local allies in some Jewish and Muslim merchants. It offered them good pay in exchange for land and facilitating commercial activities in the Regency.[85] Eventually the Bank succeeded in buying 400,000 acres of cultivated and herding land.[86] Thus, despite an economic deficit, the Bank of Rome and the Italian Consulate finally succeeded in making Italy Tripoli's main trading partner. Culturally, the Italian language became widely spoken in the city because of the presence of Italian schools and newspapers. In addition, local merchants were won over to the Italian side. But the Bank's political achievement was marred by its failure to make a profit. This failure is not surprising—after all, the Bank's activities in Tripoli were not mere economic calculations but were intended to accomplish political goals.

CHAPTER 3

MARKETS, STATES, AND CLASS FORMATION IN TRIPOLITANIA AND FEZZAN, 1830–1911

"The policies of your predecessors [Ottoman governors] did not aim at reforming the conditions of our land, nor was it for the religion of Muhammad, but rather on collecting tributes from us."

—Ghuma, the leader of the Jabal Rebellion (1832–1858)

This chapter reassesses the nature of the state and the political economy of the western and southern regions of Ottoman Libya, Tripolitania, and Fezzan from 1830–1911. Fezzan was tied politically and economically to the central administration in Tripoli, whereas Cyrenaica, the eastern region, had weak political and economic ties with the Ottoman state in Tripoli until 1911. For this reason, the Cyrenaican regional economy is analyzed separately in the next chapter.

The objective is to show the impact on the regency of Ottoman state centralization, the decline of the Sahara trade through the region by the 1880s, and the penetration of European financial capital between 1880 and 1911. In other words, the questions addressed are: In what ways, where, and why did these three events change the tributary social formation of the Regency? How did the Ottoman state, local merchants, tribal confederations, and peasants react to these new developments in the nineteenth century?

Four topics relevant to the questions just raised are addressed: first, a brief summation of the historical background prior to 1835; second, an analysis of the nature of social groups—peasants, tribal confederations, and merchants in Tripolitania and Fezzan; third, a description of the process of Ottoman state formation and its impact on the extension of state bureaucracy and class formation and especially the consolidation of private property; and finally, the decline of the Sahara trade and the penetration of European finance capital, both of which led to the process of class formation.

Ottoman Libya was a regency removed from the central government, as well as a poor and marginal one when compared to those of other provinces such as Syria and Egypt. The Regency was composed of many communities competing with the central state in Tripoli. Tribal confederations, as independent socioeconomic and political organizations, were able to compete with the weak states in Tripoli from the sixteenth century onward. The central government often had to compete with regional states, as in the case of the Awlad Muhammad state in Fezzan from 1550 to 1812. Merchants and peasants sought protection and security either from states or tribal confederations. Hence, the burden of *kharaj, jiziya,* and *atawa,* various kinds of tributes, fell mainly on peasants, slaves, client tribes, and merchants. Further, there was no single national state with complete control, nor was there only one market; rather, communities competed in regions inside the Regency or with regions outside, like southern Tunisia, Bilad al-Sudan, and western Egypt. This was the general trend until the second half of the nineteenth century. Such mobile social formations require an examination of their historical origins.

Social Forces

Appraising the nature and impact of the new Ottoman administration requires first an analysis of major social groups, their economy, ideology, and social organization. Such an analysis allows the reader to trace the changes in and persistence of certain economic and social forms during the second half of the nineteenth century.

The population of Fezzan and Tripolitania in 1911 was approximately 570,000 and was composed of artisans, merchants, small peasants, ex-slaves, and tribesmen who were organized communally. The majority of the population came from Turkish, Arab, Berber, or black backgrounds, in addition to the religious minorities of Christians, Jews, and the Ibadi, among the Sunni Muslim majority. Some inhabitants, like the Cologhli, were descendants of the old Turkish ruling class, but the *Shwashna* were descended from ex-slave mothers and Muslim fathers, and were either peasants or servants. Jewish minorities had low social status but controlled trade with Europe, whereas *Ashraf* or *Shurufa,* who claimed religious knowledge and descent from the Prophet's family, had high social status, but not necessarily wealth. Furthermore, there were "noble," landowning tribes and vassal tribes who had to pay tribute to the "noble" landowning tribes in order to gain access to water resources and pasture. In short, the population was organized into competing tribal groups and social classes by members of the Cologhli class, the merchant class, the peasantry, or one of the major tribal confederations in different regions.

Nineteenth-century social groups were organized regionally. Merchants and artisans lived in urban coastal towns. The *Ayan* class refers to urban notables—merchants, bureaucrats, and *'ulama,* or religious scholars. The hinterland people were divided into a merchant class, small peasantry, slaves, and tribes. A peasant was a free cultivator who settled on land and paid taxes or tributes to the state or tribal protector. A slave, however, was either a domestic servant, a cultivator, or a shepherd; most slaves belonged to a household or tribe. Tribal social organizations varied from nomadic to seminomadic or transhumant. Tribes had varying relations to markets, peasants, and the central state.

Nomadic tribes were rare in nineteenth-century Ottoman Libya, but those that existed moved to places of pasture and water, as in the case of the Fawhkihr in Cyrenaica. Most Libyan tribes were seminomadic; that is, they practiced settled agriculture and pastoralism. Thus, seminomadic tribes would move between their homeland and oases, or, in rainy seasons, to valley beds or *widiyan.*

In the late nineteenth century, some seminomadic tribes became transhumants or completely settled peasants. Transhumants were peasants who moved to *widiyan* in rainy seasons or hired shepherds for their animals, but their movements were limited in comparison to seminomads. In other words, pastoral organizations varied in character from nomadic, seminomadic, and transhumant to a settled peasantry. Other differences among pastoralists are determined by the type of animals reared, laws of inheritance, relations to the state, and type of Sahara trade caravans. Writers who conflate tribes, bedouin, and kinship ties have not made the necessary historical differentiations. Nevertheless, because all of them engaged in tributary production and social formation, sharp distinctions between peasants and pastoralists must not be exaggerated. The interdependence of peasants and tribesmen justifies treating them together.

Tribesmen and Peasants

The origins of tribal differentiations and divisions can be found in the eleventh-century migration of the nomadic Arab tribes of Bani Hilal and Salim, which changed the socioeconomic and cultural structures of Tripolitania and the rest of North Africa.

The Hilali tribesmen, whose population was between 200,000 and 300,000, migrated with their families and herds. Whereas most of the Bani Salim settled in Cyrenaica and Syrte, the Bani Hilal conquered Tripolitania and Tunisia, where they intermarried with Berber tribesmen.[1] Intermarriage succeeded in Arabizing the whole Maghrib by the time of the Turkish conquest in 1550.[2] By the sixteenth century most of the fertile land was owned by mixed Arab-Berber tribes, like the Mahamid and Awlad Sulayman. Islam and tribal organization facilitated the Arabization and Islamization of the Berbers. Most of the Muslim population became followers of Malki-Sunni rites but some minorities in Tripolitania adhering to the Ibadi Khariji sect of Islam persisted in the coastal town of Zwara and part of the Tripolitanian Jabal of Nifusa.[3]

The Mahamid tribe conquered western Tripolitania in the fourteenth century. Consequently, the Mahamid not only acquired good pasture lands and water resources but also extracted tributes like wheat, olive oil, and barley from peasants, small tribes, and trade caravans. The Qaramanli dynasty during Yusuf's reign gave special tax exemptions to the leading aristocratic Suf clan of the Mahamid in 1795.

Another of Bani Salim's Arab tribes, the Awlad Sulayman, dominated eastern Tripolitania and Fezzan, collecting tributes from Fezzani peasants in the oases. Their leading clan, the Suf al-Nasir, ruled the region of Fezzan and Syrte from the late 1820s up to 1842.[4] To a lesser degree, other tribes such as the Zintan, Rijban, Magarha, Warfalla, Awlad Busaif, and Mashashiyya migrated between the Jabal, the Gibla, and the oases of Fezzan to collect dates from peasants; they also received tributes from the Sahara trade merchants.[5]

Most of the tribes were seminomadic, combining herding, cereal cultivation, and date harvesting in a traditional yearly migration. Though private property existed in urban towns and oases, collective ownership of land and water resources was the norm in the hinterland. Tribal land was used for pasture and cereal cultivation whenever rain came. Each clan had a plot to cultivate. Only movable property such as animals and equipment was owned individually.

These tribes in nineteenth-century Tripolitania became, in part as a consequence of collective ownership, not only social and economic units but also military and political organizations.[6] Tribal social structure was composed of the basic extended family, or *'ayla,* headed by a male patriarch followed by women and children. A group of families made a clan, or *lahma,* and clans made a tribe, a *qabila*. Finally, a number of tribes together made a confederation, or a *suff* (in the plural, *sufuf*). These *sufuf* provided tribes and peasants with a flexible political organization that could resist heavy taxes, foreign invasions, or threats from other tribes. Senior heads of tribal clans solved judicial and political problems after collective meetings.[7]

Intertribal wars were common in the nineteenth century. Drought led many tribes to attack other tribes' land and herds. Many wars occurred over land and water resources, as in the following cases: Awlad Sulayman and the Firjan in 1767; Awlad Busaif and the Mashashiyya against the Zintan and the Rijban in 1780; the Magarha and Awlad Busaif against Awlad Sulayman, Warfalla, and the Ghaddadfa in 1832–1842; and the Zintan against Awlad Busaif in 1910–1911.[8]

Most of the seminomadic tribes of Tripolitania followed a traditional cycle. During the winter they cultivated cereal and in the spring they harvested it; during the summer and fall they harvested or exchanged dates in the oases of the Jafara and Fezzan. This economic cycle reproduced tribal solidarity and ideology.

The semipastoralists of Tripolitania lived between the small peasants of the west and the Jabal on the Jafara plain, and also in the Syrte and the Gibla regions between northern Fezzan and eastern Tripolitania (see Map 1). The major difference between pastoralists and peasants was that peasants paid regular taxes to the state, but pastoralists paid only occasionally, when forced to do so by the army.

Small Peasantry

In Ottoman Libya small peasantry lived along the coast and in the Tripolitanian mountains, al-Jabal al-Gharbi, and the oases of Fezzan. These peasants cultivated their plots by using family labor or hiring sharecroppers. The coast and the Jabal received more rainfall than the rest of the region; in addition, the Jabal had many springs which were owned collectively by villages.[9]

Tripolitanian peasants were caught between the tributary state and the powerful nomadic tribes. Because they were settled, in contrast to the pastoralists, they had to pay tributes to the state or to strong tribal patrons. Their production was limited by the use of animals and hoes, and this contributed to their marginality and poverty. During the second half of the nineteenth century, the Tripolitanian peasantry continued to be marginalized and fragmented, consisting either of an extended family working a small plot of land, or sharecroppers and tenants working the land of wealthy peasants who did not have enough manpower. The size of the small farms, *swani* (in the singular, *saniya*), ranged from 0.25 to 1 hectare. In 1900, farms of this type numbered around 50,000.[10]

Tripolitanian peasants along the coast produced vegetables, fruits, dates, and cereals; the Jabal peasants produced figs, olives, and cereals. Peasants produced in order to be self-sufficient; the surplus was used to pay taxes and exchange products of wood, meat, and cereals with the seminomads. The cities of Tripoli, Gharyan, Misurata, and Zawiya were Tripolitania's major markets. These towns, especially Tripoli and Misurata, engaged in a vital craft industry of rugs, carpets, and traditional cloth financed by wealthy merchants.[11] The towns relied on the peasantry for foodstuffs and in turn the peasantry needed the towns as markets for their products and a place to buy their tools.

Due to scant and inconsistent rainfall, the peasants used underground water (springs and wells) for irrigating their small fields. They used a container made of goatskin called *dalu*, tied to a set of ropes and pulled by an animal, usually a donkey, guided by a peasant called a *jabbad.* A hoe was used for preparing the fields. Neither the *dalu* nor the hoe generated enough water or plowed land to cultivate more than a small plot. Inevitably, the agricultural surplus was scant.[12]

Because of the low population density, and thus the lack of abundant labor, three tributary methods of labor control were common: *khammasa, magharssa,* and *takhris.* In the *khammasa* system, rich peasants and merchants hired landless peasants to whom they leased land for a quarter, a third, or a half of the produce.[13] *magharssa,* another sharecropping system, entailed a written contract between a landowner and a tenant peasant. The peasant would agree to plant trees like palm or olive; when the trees were mature, he would receive a percentage according to the original agreement—a fifth, a third, or a half of the trees.[14] At harvest time—olives in Tripolitania and dates in Fezzan—rich peasants used the *takhris* method to overcome their need for labor. According to an agreement made between the owner of the trees and a peasant, the latter would harvest the trees in exchange for a percentage. Under these sharecropping systems the landlord provided seeds, food, and clothes to the peasant who sold his labor and received a share of the product. Rich peasants were either urban Cologhli or tribal chiefs, and small peasants were ex-slaves or tribesmen of low status.[15]

Seminomadic tribes lived in the Jafara plain, part of the Jabal, and the Syrte region prior to the second half of the nineteenth century. Most of them were seminomadic. The Siaan of the western Jafara plain are a case in point. Their homeland was near the powerful patron tribe of the Mahamid, who owned the best pastoral land and water resources. To survive, the Siaan moved between the Jafara and their own oases south of Tripolitania to collect dates. This cycle was typical of most Libyan tribes in Tripolitania, Cyrenaica, and Fezzan.[16]

Usually, powerful nomadic tribes like the Mahamid extracted tributes of barley, wheat, olives, and wood from client peasants and tribes. In exchange, the Mahamid provided protection from raiding tribes. Moreover, a form of nomadic sharecropping system existed among strong tribes, weak tribes, and peasants. Wealthy tribal clans employed clients and poor tribesmen to herd their animals. For example, in eastern Tripolitania, Jabal Tarhuna, Ja'afra and Hawara, tribesmen herded for strong tribal clans; in exchange, shepherds were given cloth, food, camels, and some goats and sheep according to the initial agreement. This type of share-herding shows that tribal structure was quite stratified and not egalitarian as claimed by Evans-Pritchard and other partisans of the segmentary tribal model.[17]

Pastoralists and peasants were not in conflict. On the contrary, they were economically tied to each other and, aside from drought years, were allied in a tribal confederation. A good example of such cooperation is the rebellion of the Mahamid tribe under Ghuma during the period 1832–1858. Many Ibadi peasants and rural tribes fought with Ghuma against the state administration and its harsh taxation.[18] This alliance brings us to the issue of the precapitalist ideologies extant in the first half of the last century.

Precapitalist Ideologies

Townsmen, peasants, and tribesmen identified their interests according to kinship, regional and religious ideologies. These ideologies persisted as a result of the self-sufficiency of seminomads and small peasantry, in addition to the distinct regional character of Tripolitania. Although distinct classes existed during the first half of the nineteenth century, as a consequence of the instability of the central state and private property the distinctions were not great. Private property existed in urban areas, while in the hinterland collective tribal ownership predominated.

Kinship ideology symbolized the collective ownership of land. A belief in a common ancestor unified households, clans, and tribes in order to help them survive in a harsh, arid environment where limited water and pasture land existed. Kinship ideology applied not only to full members of these groups but also to clients, slaves, and artisans who had lower status. The self-sufficiency of a tribe made it natural for its members to identify with their tribe and after that their allies.[19]

Tribal involvement in the Sahara trade, being mercantile and dealing in luxury goods, did not destroy tribal solidarity. Usually, income from the Sahara trade was used in intertribal wars over land and water resources, as in the case of the Tuareg of southwest Fezzan and the Awlad Sulayman of Eastern Tripolitania and Fezzan. As a general trend, seminomadism coexisted and allied with merchant capital.[20] Merchants allied with whoever gave them security. If the state was able to protect their trade, merchants would pay it tribute. But in the hinterland, merchants of the Sahara trade had to pay tribal chiefs tribute to ensure free passage.

Tripolitanian tribesmen and peasants identified themselves with Tripolitania as a region and Islam as a worldview. Tripolitanians, with the exception of the Jewish minority, believed in the Islamic *Umma*, a concept of universal brotherhood. Most Tripolitanian tribesmen and peasants practiced a form of folk Islam. They believed in saints or *'awliya'*, visiting their shrines and asking for blessings, cures and protection. From the fourteenth century onward, sufi orders spread in urban and rural Tripolitania. Some of these were the 'Arussiya, Tijaniyya, 'Issawiyya, Zaruqiyya, and Madaniyya. Sufi shaykhs democratized the abstract literature of Islam by simplifying it for Tripolitanian peasants and tribes. These Sufi shaykhs taught the Quran, mediated disputes, led religious festivals, and guarded saints' shrines. They were respected as teachers, judges, healers, and writers.[21]

Tribal Confederations—*Sufuf*

Libyan tribes were armed during the nineteenth and the first quarter of the twentieth centuries. They carried arms to protect their tribal herds and homeland from other tribes, since state authority was weak, especially in the hinterlands of Cyrenaica, Syrte, the Jabal of Nifusa, the Gibla, and Fezzan. The Ottoman state in Libya did not have enough resources to carry on a long, costly war against the tribes. Hence, by the turn of the century, Cyrenaica's tribes were armed with guns as follows: the Drasa, who numbered 28,000, had 6,000 guns; the ʿAwagir had 10,000 to 14,000 guns; and the Zawaya had 1,000 guns in Jaghbub and 10,000 more in Kufra.[22] In the 1920s, General Rodolf Graziani estimated the arms of western Libyan tribes as follows: the tribes of the Jabal and the Gibla (like the Zintan) owned 1,500 guns; the Rijban 1,000; the Siʿaan 5,000; the Haraba 5,000; and other small tribes 1,000.[23] By the end of the 1932 resistance, the colonial government had confiscated 70,000 guns: 40,000 from Tripolitania, 10,000 from Gibla and Fezzan, and 20,000 from Cyrenaica. In short, around 160,000 Libyans were active in the resistance against the Italians.[24] By contrast, the Ottoman state had only small garrisons in major cities and towns. Benghazi, for example, had only 1,100 troops in 1881 and 3,500 in 1890.[25] In 1889 the Ottoman army in Libya numbered their troops in terms of regions: Tripoli, 17,000-20,000; Fezzan, 300; Cyrenaica, 2,000; in addition to irregular troops who numbered 3,000.[26] However, in 1911 the Ottoman army was only 3,000 strong, as many soldiers were transferred to Yemen to face an anti-Ottoman rebellion.[27]

During foreign conquest or major tribal wars, Tripolitanian tribesmen and peasants revived the old intertribal confederations, *sufuf*. Among the most famous sufuf of the nineteenth century were the *suff* of Yusuf and Shdad in southern Tunisia and western Tripolitania; the interior *suff*, al-Fugi; and the coastal *suff*, al-Bahar, in western Tripolitania and the Syrte region.[28]

The *suff* of Yusuf included both the Tunisian tribal confederation of Warghumma and some Tripolitanian tribes like the western Mahamid. The rival *suff* Shaddad included most of the Mahamid, the Nuwail, and the Siʿaan. When a *suff* faced serious state pressure or foreign conquest, it unified with others against such threats. Two examples illustrate these tribal alliances. Between 1835 and 1858 the revolt of the Mahamid took place against the Ottoman army. The Mahamid chief Ghuma mobilized not only peasants, tribesmen, Arabs, and Berbers but also some of the tribes in southern Tunisia like the Warghumma. The rebels found aid and refuge in southern Tunisia during and after the revolt's defeat in 1858. Eighty thousand tribesmen and peasants emigrated to Tunisia.[29] In 1886 the French colonial army defeated the southern Tunisian tribes, whose revolt was led by Ben Ghadahum. Ben Ghadahum and his 100,000 tribesmen migrated to Tripolitania.[30]

Whereas the Mahamid dominated western Tripolitania, the Awlad Sulayman led the tribes of the Syrte and Fezzan regions. Their chief, ʿAbd al-Jalil, was appointed Governor of Fezzan by Yusuf Qaramanli in late 1820. ʿAbd al-Jalil ruled the region during the dynastic crisis (1832–1835) until 1842. Here, as in the case of the Mahamid's rebellion, chiefs led their tribesmen. ʿAbd al-Jalil led the tribal *suff* of the interior, al-Fugi. This tribal confederation included four clans of the Awlad Sulayman and the Gadaddfa, the Warfalla, and the population of the oases of Waddan and Hun.[31]

The Ottoman state countered this alliance by rallying its rival, the *suff* of the coast, al-Bahar. *Suff* al-Bahar included most of the population of the coastal "Makhzani" towns of the Khums, Zlitan, Misurata, Tajura, and the tribes of Awlad Salim, Hussun, Abadlla, Maʿadan, Firjan, Magarha of Fezzan tribesmen, and the populations of Sukana and Zalla (see Figure 1).[32]

The coastal *suff* paid taxes and was state-oriented, whereas the interior *suff* paid taxes regularly to the state but was independent. There were other differences between the two. Ghuma led the Mahamid to protect their tax exemption. ʿAbd al-Jalil wanted to build his own state, however, and did not compromise with the Ottoman state.[33]

The Political Economy of Fezzan

Fezzan was linked to the regional economy of the Sahara and Bilad al-Sudan because of its geographical location between Tripolitania and Bilad al-Sudan. The importance of this remote desert region was its strategic location between central and West Africa on the one hand, and Tripolitania and the Mediterranean on the other. Two international Sahara trade routes passed through Fezzan—one through Tripoli Ghadamis-Ghat and the other through Tripoli Sukana-Murzaq to Bilad al-Sudan. The Fezzani economy was based on one of the major markets of the Sahara trade, a market where merchants from Bilad al-Sudan, the Sahara, and even Europe met to exchange and barter European and Saharan luxury

Figure 1
Tribal *Sufuf* in Nineteenth-Century Tunisia, Tripolitania, and Fezzan

(A) Southern Tunisia and Western Tripolitania

Saff Shadad: Yazid, Nifzawa and Matmata (Tunisia) Nuwil, Hawamid, Mahamid (Awlad al-Marmuri), and Si'aan (Tripolitania).	*Saff Yusuf:* Warghumm Confederation, and the towns of the Sahil (Tunisia). Mahamid (Awlad Said B. Sulla), (Tripolitania)

(B) Tripolitanian Jabal and Gibla

Zintan, Ri-jban Mahamid (Ghaniama) Gdayrat, Sab'a	Awlad Bu-Saif, Mashashiyya Jadu, Fassatu

(C) Eastern Tripolitanian and Fezzan

Saff al-Bahar: (Coastal towns of Tripolitania) Khums, Zlitan and Misurta, the oasis of Sukana, and the Abadalla, Ma'adan, fir-jan, and Magarha tribes.	*al-Saff al-Fugi* Awlad Sulayman, Hasawna Huttman, Ghaddafa, Warfalla, Magharba and the oases of Hun and Waddan.

goods. Whenever the Sahara trade flourished, the region flourished, and vice versa.

In addition to the Sahara trade, Fezzan had a productive settled agriculture in its major oases along Wadi al-Shatti, Wadi al-Ajal, and Wadi 'Ataba. The self-sufficient Fezzani agriculture supplemented the Sahara trade and provided the local population, the caravan workers, and traders with dates, cereal, and vegetables. The region of Fezzan was the date basket of the whole regency for centuries. During the late nineteenth century there were two million palm trees.[34]

Fezzan's link was to both southern Tripolitania and the Sultanates of Bornu, Kanem, Wadai, and the Hausa states of northern Nigeria. The seminomadic tribes of the Gibla such as the Magarha, the Awlad Busaif, the Zintan, and the Mashashiyya were lured to the rich date groves of Wadi al-Shatti in northern Fezzan. These often starving Arab tribes either conquered the oases and extracted tributes from client Fezzan peasants or owned their own gardens worked by their own slaves.[35] The same was true for the nomads of the Syrte region where Awlad Sulayman, Warfalla, and Gaddadfa owned palm trees in the Jufra oases of Waddan, Hun, Sukana, and Zalla as well as central Fezzan's oases such as Samnu, Zighan and Sabha. Small nomadic tribes who had neither gardens nor clients exchanged with the peasants in the oases, as in the cases of the Jama'at and the Majir of the Jufra region.

In addition to the seminomads of Wadi al-Shatti and Syrte, there were the powerful Tuareg of the southwest and and the Tibbu of the southeast. The Tuareg had an elaborate class structure and extracted tributes from client tribes and slaves, whereas the Tibbu had less stratification but shared with other nomads an agropastoralist economy divided yearly between herding, cereal production, and date cultivation. In short, seminomadic tribes dominated the region. Still, chiefs of these nomadic tribes received tributes from the merchants of the Sahara trade, as in the case of the Tuareg, the Awlad Sulayman and the Mahamid, whereas other tribesmen (Hasawna, Riyyah, and Jama'at) worked as guides and guards for the caravans.[36] The Awlad Sulayman, under the leadership of their charismatic chief 'Abd al-Jalil, organized a strong tribal alliance when the Qaramanli state weakened in the 1830s. 'Abd al-Jalil even tried to build a state in Fezzan.

The Aborted State of 'Abd al-Jalil, 1830–1842

In 1830, during the dynastic crisis in Tripoli, the chief of Awlad Sulayman became virtually the ruler of Fezzan. He even had his own currency inscribed "'Abd al-Jalil, Sultan of Fezzan." He made alliances with the sultans of Bornu, contacted Muhammad Ali of Egypt, and sent politicians to France. But, to his disadvantage, the imperial Ottoman authority used the civil war to send the Ottoman army to Fezzan to build a strong state. 'Abd al-Jalil demanded political recognition of his autonomy, reduction of taxes, and the right to export trade from Syrte.[37]

'Abd al-Jalil led his tribal-peasant alliance, al-*Suff* al-Fugi. This *suff* included Awlad Sulayman, Warfalla, Gaddadfa, and the populations of the oases of Waddan and Hun. But in 1842 this remarkable chief was ambushed and killed by the Ottoman army. Consequently, his son and 1,000 warriors fled, making a historic trek to Kanem in today's Chad. Kanem is an arid desert region like the Awlad Sulayman's homeland in Syrte. Exile allowed the Awlad

Sulayman and allied tribesmen to live as seminomads.[38] As a result of their resilience, the Awlad Sulayman eventually returned to their homeland and fought the Italians in Fezzan under the grandsons of ʿAbd al-Jalil until they were defeated in 1927, when they again fled to Chad and Egypt.

The social base of the strong seminomadic tribes came from their mobility and military force. The Awlad Sulayman, the Arabs of Wadi al-Shatti, the Tuareg, and the Tibbu dominated the settled client peasantry of Fezzan. These seminomads herded animals in the winter, cultivated dates in the summer, and cultivated cereal during rainy seasons. They also leased their camels and worked as guides, as in the case of the Hasawna, the Magarha of Wadi al-Shatti, and the Tuareg of the Ghat region. In other words, the powerful seminomadic tribes and the merchant class were allies whose livelihood was based mainly on the Sahara trade.

The Merchant Class

The Tuareg and Awlad Sulyaman chiefs were the major military powers in Fezzan. But the Fezzan economy was dominated by the merchant class, who allied with the leading clans of the seminomads. And at the bottom of the social structure were slaves, client peasants, and tribes of low status. The merchant class continued to prosper after 1842 when the rebellion of the Awlad Sulayman and their allies was defeated. The Awlad Sulayman's rivals, the Arab tribes of Wadi al-Shatti—especially the tax-exempted Magarha and the Riyyah—replaced the Awlad Sulayman and supported Ottoman authority in Fezzan.[39]

The merchants of Fezzan came from Ghadamis, Tripoli, Sukana, Jalo, Misurata, and Bornu. Usually a whole corporate clan sent its sons to Fezzan, the Sahara, Tripoli, and Tunis. The wealthy merchants of Ghadamsi provide an example of this. In 1880 there were 73 Ghadamsi merchants: 19 in Kanu, 4 in Sokoto, 3 in Zaria, 3 in Nupe, 4 in Adomawa, 6 in Zinder, and 37 in Tunis and Tripoli City.[40] The recently published records of the Yushiʿa clan and the Faqih family in Tripoli City show the activities of these corporate merchants in the Sahara trade in Fezzan.[41]

The merchants of the Sahara trade paid tributes to tribes and the state to ensure the security of their caravans. These merchants, like the Ghadamsi of western Libya, hired guides and rented camels from the seminomads, as in the case of the Hasawna and the Magarha of Wadi al-Shatti. In addition, merchants had to pay tributes to powerful seminomads like the Awlad Sulayman and the Tuareg of the southwest. Failure to do so precipitated tribal raids. Raiding was a common phenomenon, but only during drought seasons or when caused by the nonpayment of tribute. When the Ghadamsi merchants could not secure contact with the Tuareg of Ghat, their caravan of 2,000 loaded camels was raided.[42]

Ottoman documents have left us records of raids between rival tribes over land, particularly during the rebellion of 'Abd al-Jalil. For example, the tax-exempt Magarha tribe attacked a caravan of the Gaddadfa, one of 'Abd al-Jalil's allies, in 1891. At the same time, the Timmama of the Awlad Sulayman attacked the herds of the rival al-Firjan in the *wadi*-s of Syrte.[43] 'Abd al-Jalil attacked the pro-Ottoman towns of Sukana and Ghuduwa in the 1830s.[44] Raiding increased during the period as a consequence of the rebellion. It should not be concluded that tribes were constantly engaged in raiding and feuding; economic cooperation and coexistence between tribes compose the other half of the story.

Raiding was common during drought seasons and times of conflict with the state over taxes. The merchants of Fezzan, in order to protect their tribe, had not only to pay off tribal chiefs but also to pay tributes to the state.[45] The Ottoman government lacked the resources to control these autonomous tribes in the Sahara. Its policy was to play on intertribal rivalries. For example, during the rebellion of 'Abd al-Jalil, some of the tribes of Wadi al-Shatti, his foes, were exempted from taxes, as in the case of the Magarha. The Magarha became an Ottoman police force like the Cologhli in Tripolitania. Even after the defeat of the rebellion in Fezzan, Ottoman authority was not assured outside of the oases of Sukana, Murzaq, Wadi al-Shatti, and Ghat. The seminomadic tribes were mobile and militarized, especially the Awlad Sulayman, the Tuareg and the Tibbu. The Tuareg tribe provides an example of the power and autonomy of the tribes in the nineteenth century.

The Ottoman authorities could not reach the town of Ghat, the capital of the Tuareg, until 1879. When the French armies began to expand in the Sahara, the Tuaregs' monopoly over the trade was threatened. The Tuareg of Ghat invited the Ottoman army to their town, fearing French expansion.[46] The Tuareg had a class structure more complex than that of any other Libyan tribe. At the top of the hierarchy was an aristocratic ruling class, followed by a class of vassals, a servant class; at the bottom were artisan client peasants and slaves. This class hierarchy forms a desert type of feudal structure.[47]

The Tuareg was the only Libyan tribe with a matrilineal system of kinship. Women among the Tuareg enjoyed high status and rights of inheritance, and men carried their mothers' names. The high status of women was in place until the Islamization of the Tuareg in the eighth century. Yet there is no agreement among the scholars who studied the Tuareg after Islamization on the nature of their social organization. The Danish anthropologist Johannes Nicolaison, who studied Libyan Tuareg, argued that their social organization changed to a patrilineal system after Islamization. Others, like John Gulick, insist that the Tuareg have kept their matrilineal system. The more persuasive argument is that the Tuareg of southern Libya have a mixed system of social organization. The spread of Islam in Africa has not been a one-way street—it has been shaped by ecological and pre-Islamic social organizations as in the case of the Tuareg. According to Lars Eldblom, a Swedish geographer who studied the Tuareg of southern Libya, women in the oasis of Ghat had their own *waqf* in 1960.[48] These details of Libyan tribal social organization are crucial for understanding their autonomy and alliances.

Ottoman State Formation, 1835–1911

In 1835, in order for the Ottomans to build a central state in Tripoli they had to face powerful tribal chiefs such as Ghuma and Abd al-Jalil in addition to less important ones like those of the al-Adgham in Misurata and the al-Maryyid of Tarhuna. These chiefs were exempted from taxes by the Qaramanli; during the civil war, they became autonomous lords of their districts.

By the end of the eighteenth century, the Ottoman empire became dominated by capitalist interests among the ruling classes. This change was echoed in provincial state policies. The Ottoman policy was to collect taxes directly and efficiently without major exemptions or mediation of the Shaykhs. The two powerful chiefs, Ghuma and 'Abd al-Jalil, refused to relinquish their status and autonomy, rebelling against the state from 1835 to 1858. In 1842, 'Abd al-Jalil was ambushed, and Ghuma was killed in 1858. Other chieftains such as 'Uthman al-Adgham and 'Abd al-Hadi al-Maryyid reconciled with the state.

Having eliminated the power of the autonomous chiefs, the Ottomans began to implement their state building program to generate revenues. This program necessitated such measures as abolishing tax exemptions, land reform to collect taxes directly without intermediaries, building schools and courts, and building up the administration, as well as a public force and an army to ensure the security and the authority of the state. As Figure 2 shows, the army received most of the funding, but new schools and a court system to administer the region and solve disputes received some of the monies.[49]

Figure 2
State Expenditures, 1881, in Piasters

Type of Expenditure	*Amount*
Interior department	998,600
Finance department	468,202
Religious courts	99,840
Justice department	946,188
Education	31,396
Other salaries	409,236
Quarantine office	1,200
Postal office	103,190
Military	6,785,140

Source: Abdallah Ali Ibrahim, "Evolution of Government and Society in Tripolitania and Cyrenaica (Libya) 1835–1911," Ph.D. dissertation (history), University of Utah, 1982, 347.

A postal and telegraph system was put into effect in 1867. All tax exemptions were abolished, including those for Cologhli military services, in 1892.[50] This policy outraged some leaders, who protested the decision by petition, first to Istanbul and later to the Italian authorities with whom they collaborated, as did the mayor of Tripoli, Hassuna al-Qaramanli. The Ottomans began to recruit from local populations for their police and the army: by 1881, there were 12,000 troops in Tripoli City.[51]

One of the most serious challenges to the Ottoman program was over the issue of land. Even after crushing the major tribal rebellions in 1855, the Ottomans could not be assured that the tribes would be willing to settle down and pay taxes. The Ottoman Land Code of 1858 was aimed at registering land to individuals so that taxes could be collected from landlords and private property owners. However, issuing a decree was one thing; enforcing it was another matter. Fearing taxation, many tribes resisted the state's demand that they register their land, or tribal land under individual holders, in the department of land registration, the tabu. Few people registered and most of the tribesmen, also fearing army service, declined to do so. Only at the end of the nineteenth century were large numbers of people registering their land because of other developments in the regency like the decline of the Sahara trade and the penetration of European capital.

Despite tribal resistance to the state, the Ottoman administration managed to make some changes in the region of Fezzan. The regional governors collected taxes from peasants and some tribes.[52] In 1900 taxes broke down as follows:

Types of Taxes	*Amount in Turkish Lire*
Taxes on animals	10,828
Ushur on agriculture	69,000
Miri land revenues	13,200
Courts	5,000
Others	7,000
Total	105,028

This table shows that the state had organized courts and claimed *miri* land revenues, which had never been recorded before. The relative expansion of the state was at the expense of the defeated Awlad Sulayman and the peasant-sharecropping population. As mentioned earlier, the Tuareg and some of the Wadi al-Shatti tribes either did not pay taxes or were exempted, as in the case of the Magarha. The Ottoman state increased its presence in Fezzan by first building a modern network of communication. In 1900 a telegraph line was built between Tripoli and Fezzan.[53]

The Decline of the Merchant Class

If Ottoman state-building made a relatively slight impact on rural Tripolitania, the decline of the Sahara trade during the second half of the nineteenth century was devastating. The decline began with the banning of the slave trade in 1860 and culminated in 1890 when colonial wars blocked trade in Bilad al Sudan; later, the French and the British diverted the trade in West African Atlantic ports.

The British had two vice consuls in Fezzan, one in Murzaq (1843) and another in Ghadamis (1849). These consuls were appointed to monitor the Sahara trade with an eye to exploring the Niger River. Several European travelers were sponsored by the British to achieve this goal. When the Niger River was explored in 1854, these British vice consuls departed.[54]

Though the slave trade through Fezzan was not big business, it was still viable. Even after the trade was banned in 1856, a small number of slaves continued to be smuggled to the north until this practice finally ended in the 1890s. Even European consuls at this time who exaggerated the slave trade agreed that it had become marginal. W. Gagliuffi, a Maltese trader who became the British vice consul in 1843 in Murzaq, reported in 1852 that "the caravan [from Bornu] brought 800 slaves."[55] The American consul in Tripoli, M. J. Jaimes, reported in 1856 that by "a decree recently published here, the slave trade, which has been very considerable in this country of late years, is now entirely prohibited."[56] Finally, by 1891 the British consul in Tripoli stated that "the slave trade was virtually extinct in this province."[57] In short, the slave trade, like other commodities of the Sahara, made a great impact on the population and social classes. The population of the region declined and the class structure dominated by merchants collapsed.

A look at population statistics in 1789–1900 and the class structure shows the magnitude of this change. Western travelers appraised the population of Fezzan as follows: Hornemann (1789)—75,000 inhabitants, Nachtigal (1869)—50,000,[58] De Agostini (1917)—31,600, of whom 27,400 were settled and 4,200 nomadic.[59] The town of Ghadamis had a population of 12,000 in 1804, which declined to 6,831 in 1911 and 3,000 in 1965, whereas Murzaq, the capital, which had a population of 5,000 in 1867, had only 1,000 inhabitants in 1911.[60] In short, the once populous, rich oases of the Sahara and Fezzan had become poor ghost towns by 1911. Banning the slave trade in 1840, and more important, blocking trade in the 1880s, led to the impoverishment of the region and the collapse of the class structure.

The biggest losers were the merchants, who returned to their towns and coastal cities in Jalo, Sukana, Misurata, Tripoli, and Ghadamis.[61] Many tribesmen and peasants migrated to Tripoli City and French Tunisia looking for better jobs created by both new European projects in Tripoli City and French agriculture in southern Tunisia.[62]

The decline of the Sahara trade was disastrous for the Fezzani economy, as well as the Tripolitanian economy. Many tribesmen who worked as guides and leased camels or received tributes, or merchants who invested in the trade, forced a crisis. The Sahara trade crisis coincided with Ottoman state building and the opening of European capitalist markets in Tripolitania and Tunisia. British capital invested in the esparto trade and the Italians, through the activities of the Bank of Rome, provided job opportunities in urban Tripolitania. Many tribesmen migrated there from Fezzan and rural Tripolitania and became wage laborers in mills, construction, esparto-collection concerns, or on farms.[63] Others migrated to colonial Tunisia to work in the olive tree projects. There were 20,000 Libyan emigrants in Tunisia in 1920.[64] The old tributary trading and pastoral economy of Tripolitania began to collapse as a result of integration into the European market economy. This integration was only partial, however. Tripolitania was in transition.

The Genesis of Class Formation in Tripolitania

By the turn of the twentieth century, the old tributary social structure began to change, a consequence of the development of capitalism either through Ottoman state reforms or direct European capitalist penetration. The decline of the Sahara trade pushed this process further, and four classes emerged in Tripolitania. At the top of the hierarchy was a compradore merchant class tied to British and Italian capital and a salaried *'ayan*, or urban notable class which owned land and was linked to the Ottoman state administration.[65] At the bottom other class formations were at work: the process of peasantization, that is, settling tribesmen on land, and proletarianization, or the rise of wage laborers in towns.[66] This process of class formation was not necessarily deep, nor can it be viewed as replacing the old agropastoral and mercantile groups; rather, it ushered in the genesis of changes. Among these changes was increased urbanization, especially the development of Tripoli City as the largest urban market of the whole Regency.

When the Ottoman army defeated the autonomous tribal chiefs of the hinterland in 1860, the balance of power began to tip. State authority was enhanced in the interior, especially as the cross-Sahara trade declined and European commercial investments provided jobs for peasants and tribesmen. Exports to Europe of esparto, wheat, and animals increased. Many tribes in eastern and coastal Tripolitania began to settle; for example, the Warshafana tribe settled along the coast between 'Aziziyya and Janzur. In eastern Tripolitania, some members of the Tarhuna and Misllata tribes had become settled by 1911.[67] However, the independent seminomadic tribes of the Gibla and Syrte regions, such as the Zintan, Rijban, Awlad Busaif, Mashashiyya, Magarha, Warfalla, Haraba, Riyyah, Gaddadfa, and Awlad Sulayman, continued to be self-sufficient and avoided the state army by withdrawing to the desert frontiers.

Thus, social differentiation increased during the second half of the nineteenth century. The population increases from 1883 to 1911 of Tripoli City and other major towns clearly prove this trend: Tripoli City went from 20,000 to 29,664; Zawiya from 8,000 to 28,842; al 'Aziziya from 9,000 to 26,899; Zlitan from 20,000 to 38,042; and Misurata from 20,000 to 39,029.[68]

Some Tripolitanian towns, particularly the city of Tripoli, began to develop a degree of hegemony over the countryside. Tripoli City had been the Regency's major market since Roman times as well as having been the capital of most of the states. The city had been the major port for the Sahara trade; by the late nineteenth century, it developed as the major market for the agropastoral products of the hinterland. Artisans, peasants, and pastoralists sold their surplus and bought tools, cloth, and manufactured goods in Tripoli or through Jewish traders who roamed the countryside.[69] Other towns grew as ports for the esparto export trade to England, as in the case of Zlitan, Khums, and Zawiya.[70]

Tripoli City, the capital of the Ottoman administration, grew as a major economic market of the Regency. The Ottoman state expanded into the hinterland and ensured security and trade more than it had in the previous century. European commercial projects and investments began to appear and offered jobs to local merchants, peasants, and landless tribesmen. By 1885, Tripoli City began to develop modern business institutions. The city had 20 bakeries, 22 mills, 1,019 shops, 40 wholesale stores, and 9 British and 11 Maltese firms.

By the end of the nineteenth century, the economic and political ties between the city of Tripoli and the hinterland strengthened. The city provided political and economic services to peasants, tribesmen, artisans, and merchants of the hinterland. The courts, banks, schools, and markets became important to the hinterland people. These new urban institutions began to replace tribal institutions, the result of military defeats and the extension of the Ottoman administration. The economic and political importance of Tripoli was aided by the decline of the Sahara trade through Fezzan. These changes led to the settlement of some tribes and the migrations to coastal towns of others. Migration was in the service of finding new jobs, especially in British and Italian businesses. Other tribesmen migrated to French Tunisia where the colonial administration needed wage laborers for the construction of commercial agriculture.

The Compradore Merchant Class

By the end of the nineteenth century most of the population was pressured to become more involved in agriculture. The merchants of Tripoli began to play major roles as creditors, moneylenders, and employers. Most of these merchants were either Libyan Jews or Europeans, mostly from Malta, Italy and France.[71] Some merchants were Tripolitanians who had become foreign citizens. During the early nineteenth century, the weakness of the Qaramanli and later Ottoman states allowed European consuls to favor Ottoman subjects who were European citizens.[72]

European merchants had their own courts, were exempted from some taxes, and protected from the state. These privileges attracted many Jewish and Maltese merchants to European citizenship. To defend their own interests, these compradore merchants defended European interests; some collaborated with the Italians before and after the occupation in 1911. For example, in 1910 most of the local and import-export trade was owned or managed by non-Muslim traders and artisans, who numbered around 18,903; of these, 2,600 Maltese merchants were British nationals, and 930 Jewish Libyan merchants were Italian nationals. In the city of Tripoli alone, 8,609 Jewish Libyan artisans and traders had Ottoman nationality, in addition to the 500 French nationals. There were many Jewish merchants in other towns, some of whom were Spanish nationals. Benghazi, for example, had 40 Spanish Jewish merchants.[73]

The compradore merchants benefited from the strong Ottoman state, since the state facilitated the development of capitalism through securing communication and trading with the hinterland. When European capital, mostly British and Italian, began to invest in Tripolitania, local merchants were attracted to British and Italian firms. Local Jewish, Maltese, and some Muslim merchants were employed in these firms not only because they had financial expertise and knew European languages, but because they were familiar with the local culture. Some of these merchants had become partners with or agents for British and Italian investors in the region prior to 1911.

Among leading Jewish Tripolitanian merchants who carried foreign nationalities were the following: the Arbib family had Italian and British nationalities, and managed the trade in foodstuffs, cloth, and hides; the Nahums, the Lavis, and the Hananas had Italian nationality, and were engaged in the trade of cotton, esparto, and wool, and in shipping; the Dabash, the Labis, the Baranes, and the Sarur were French nationals, trading in soap, cloth, cotton, and hides.[74] The Muslim merchant families, the al-Muntasir of Misurata and Tripoli, Ahmad al-Izmirli of Tripoli, and Mustafa Bin Gudara of Zlitan worked for the Bank of Rome in 1907, and hence were sympathetic to Italian influence.[75]

In addition to the merchant class, other classes emerged in Tripolitania at the turn of the twentieth century: an urban notable class, a peasant class, and a small working class, which emerged for the first time.

Tripolitanian private property became more stable in coastal areas and land began to be owned privately in many parts of the countryside. A comparison of Ottoman revenues in 1881 to those in 1906 makes it clear that the Ottoman administrator's ability to collect taxes increased (see Figure 3).

Figure 3
State Revenues, 1881 and 1906, in Piasters

Type of Taxes	*1881*	*1906*
Livestock	150,025	478,428
Production	500,000	11,291,858
Military	43,350	241,748
Property	—	9,104,088
Profit	—	79,770
Income from State Property	—	14,000
Court Fees	—	147,874

Source: Abdallah Ali Ibrahim, "Evolution of Government and Society in Tripolitania and Cyrenaica (Libya) 1835–1911," Ph.D. dissertaion (history), University of Utah, 1982, 348.

As the state's authority increased politically and a degree of economic integration was achieved through urban markets and the creation of the *'ayan* class, state taxes increased. Military taxes were imposed on non-Muslims like the Jews and Maltese. The state began to collect fees and taxes from newly founded courts, to expand private property, and to lease state land. Production taxes increased, a fact that may be linked to taxes collected by the newly founded municipalities, especially in Tripoli City. For example, in 1906 municipal taxes in the city of Tripoli reached 500,000 piasters, in contrast to only 80,000 piasters in the town of Benghazi.[76] This highlights Tripoli's growth in contrast to Benghazi's comparative marginality.

The *'Ayan*, the Bureaucratic Notable Class

Ironically, the Ottomans and local *'ulama*, Cologhli, and some tribal chiefs began to cooperate with the new state. That is, though Ottoman authority was set up originally to eliminate intermediaries and rule directly, many local notables either resisted or disliked the removal of their tax-exempt status in 1892. Yet the state and notables needed each other: the Ottomans needed to build a centralized state and collect revenues to defend against the advance of European states in their last regency, the gate to Muslim Africa; in turn, since the notables were the leaders, the most educated and the wealthiest among the population, they became intermediaries between the state and the local peasants, artisans and tribesmen, taking advantage of the new opportunities opened to them by the state and the penetration of European capital.

The Tripolitanian notables, the 'ulama, the Cologhli and tribal chiefs came from religious, military and tribal social bases. They registered tribal land under their names and began to settle in towns. Also, they were the only educated group—they sent their sons to neighboring universities in al-Azhar in Egypt and al-Zaytuna in Tunisia.[77] They provided the state Ottoman administration with authoritative religious interpreters, judges, court officials, teachers, and mosque shaykhs. Among these leading *'ulama* notables were the families of the Bishtis in Zawiya, the Barunis in the Jabal, the Bakirs, the Na'ibs, and the 'Alims in the city of Tripoli.[78]

Cologhli notables and some tribal chiefs owned large portions of land, as in the case of the Cologhli notable Muhamad of Saghir, who was administrator and landlord in the rich district of the Aziziyya in 1884–1885. The Adgham family controlled the district of Khums up to 1860 and the *Ka'bar* family administrated and dominated the district of Gharyan, where it owned 64 out of the 175 farms in the district.[79] In short, the notables filled most of the middle and low administrative jobs under the new system. The Regency *Wilayat* was divided into counties, districts and subdistricts—or *mutasarri-*

fiyya, *qaimmaqamiyya*, and *nahiya* respectively. Tripoli City, the Jabal, Khums, Fezzan, and Benghazi became counties. The notables were *mutasarrifs*, *qaimmaqams*, and *mudirs*, and some of them became members of the Regency's administrative council and the Ottoman parliament.

The Ottoman state bureaucracy provided the best means for attaining status and wealth in addition to generating trade. A good example illustrating this point is the case of the Warfalla clan chief Abd al-Nabi Bel Khayre. When 'Abd al-Nabi was appointed tax collector and *mutasarrif* in 1908 by some of his Turkish friends in Tripoli, he became wealthy and subsequently managed to become the undisputed chief of a Warfalla subdistrict in the town of Baniwalid.[80]

In summary, a commercial and administrative urban class emerged. Facing no serious challenge from below, the notables of the *'ulama* and Cologhli, as well as tribal chiefs, began to fight over land and positions in the state apparatus. This was the major cause of the internotable factionalism in the late nineteenth and early twentieth centuries, as can be seen in the cases of the Suwayhli-Muntasir of the town of Misurata and the Ka'bar-Baruni in the Jabal.[81] At the same time, some tribes began to fight over land, as in the cases of the Zintan-Awlad Busaif disputes in 1870 and 1910. Despite factionalism, however, notables tied to the state bureaucracy began to preach pan-Islamic ideology during the Young Turk rule (1908–1911) when many newspapers emerged in Tripoli City.[82] This pan-Islamic ideology did not replace tribal and religious affiliations but reflected the change in the balance of power in the towns' favor, a result of the rise of the urban class. The notables were conscious of their status and intermarried despite their interfactional conflict.[83]

The *'ayan* class dominated the bureaucracy of the new state. Among the Cologhli *'Ayan* were Hassuna Qaramanli, who was mayor of the city of Tripoli until 1911. Muhammad al-Saghair was the *agha* (military officer) and *mudir* (administrator) of the rich district of the 'Aziziyya, south of Tripoli, between 1884 and 1894. The Adgham family administered the district of Khums until 1860, and the Ka'bar family dominated the Gharyan district. Hadi Ka'bar, Farhat al Zawi from Zawiya, and 'umar al-Kikhiya of Benghazi were three Cologhli *'ayan* elected to the Ottoman parliament in 1908.[84]

Muslim merchants also became influential in the new administration. The Muntasir family of Misurata rose to power as a result of trade, replacing their rivals in the Adgham family in the district of Khums in the 1860s. 'Umar al-Muntasir and his sons Salim, Ahmad Diya al-Din, and 'Abd al-Qdir became administrators of the districts of Tarhuna, Syrte, and Gharayan. Diya al-Din became a member of the state council and the Ottoman parliament.[85] Hasan al-Faqih of the Faqih merchant family of Tripoli was a member of the state council.[86] In short, *'ayan* power continued through state bureaucracy, while the onus of taxes lay on artisans, peasants, ordinary tribesmen, and the urban poor.

A salaried urban notable class composed of bureaucrats emerged in Tripolitania. Compradore merchants, mostly Maltese nationals and Libyan Jews, became strong because of their ties to European import-export firms. These classes constituted the bourgeoisie. At the bottom of the social structure two other classes began to form.

Peasantization and Proletarianization

The push of the desert and the pull of the towns were two major forces behind peasantization and proletarianization. In the hinterland, the weakening of the major tribal confederation came as a consequence of state military expansion and the decline of the Sahara trade—first, the slave trade in 1860, and later the trade block in 1890. Many tribesmen and peasants lost their livelihood as guides, lessors of animals, and tribute recipients. Agriculture became the only remaining major activity besides herding. The State Land Code of 1858 had paid off by the end of the century. Land began to be registered individually and more tribes began to settle, especially along the coast, in the Warshafana, Jabal, Tarhuna, and Misallata regions, among others. New peasants either worked their own plot of land through extended family labor or worked as sharecroppers for rich peasants and landlords. Other tribesmen worked as shepherds for rich tribal chiefs.[87] The Ottoman state encouraged settlement through land registration, security, and the legal system to solve disputes in addition to introducing new crops such as potatoes, cotton, coffee, and rice.[88]

The new peasants had to pay state taxes; as a result, they became tied to the state administration and its courts. In addition to peasantization, small-scale proletarianization began. Landless peasants and tribesmen moved to urban towns and worked as wage laborers, particularly for British esparto companies and the Bank of Rome projects, or migrated to Tunisia to work for wages in the colonial olive tree projects. The new wage laborers worked 14 hours a day collecting and shipping esparto grass.

In conclusion, the Tripolitanian regional economy was in transition, from a communal and self-sufficient tributary trading economy to a mixture of a tributary and capitalist economy. Capitalist penetration was strong in coastal and eastern Tripolitania. Most seminomadic tribes continued to reproduce their tributary social relations and were not penetrated by capitalism. The tribes of the western Jafara plain and the Gibla and Syrte regions remained self-sufficient and militarized, continuing their seasonal migration and tributary relations.

The transition in Tripolitania, small as it was during the late nineteenth century, was significant. It explains the existence of contradictions and provides the context for the tribal, regional, and pan-Islamic ideologies that arose. The *'ayan*, who functioned as *'ulama*, or members of the Ottoman parliament, in the state bureaucracy, supported pan-Islamic Ottoman ideologies, as in the case of Sulayman al-Baruni, a member of the Ottoman parliament in 1908, and the Madani family, a famous Sufi order whose Shaykh was advisor to Sultan 'Abd al-Hamid. Regional ideology surfaced among independent *'ayan* of the towns, as in the case of the Suwayhli of Misurata and the Maryyid of Tarhuna. Along the frontier regions of the Gibla and among Syrte tribal chiefs, tribal ideology was still reflected, as in the case of 'Abd al-Nabi of the Warfalla, and Muhammad B. Hasan of the Mashashiyya. Yet the majority of the population identified with *Ummat Muhammad*, the larger Muslim community.

As the Tripolitanian political economy began to expand its periphery, Fezzan was undergoing a major crisis. The Tripolitanian economy managed to adapt to the Sahara trade's decline by turning to agriculture and capitalist investments forced by the Ottoman state and British and Italian finance capital. This transformation ushered in the process of class formation—compradore merchants, the salaried *'ayan* class, the settlement of some tribes, and the rise of wage labor in the towns. Tribesmen, the peasantry, and the urban poor, like artisans and porters, paid the price for changes—taxes, minimal wages, the loss of tribal land. The recovery of the Tripolitanian economy was a result of its relatively large population, better agriculture, and craft industry, in contrast to what the regions of Fezzan and Cyrenaica had. If the Tripolitanian tributary economy had begun to change and recover its peripheral regional economy, Fezzan would have been in a deep crisis.

The economic importance of Fezzan derived not only from its rich and strategic trans-Sahara trade markets, but also from its productive oasis agriculture. In 1900, Fezzan's agricultural land was irrigated by underground water. There were 2,079 wells and 213 springs. These wells and springs supplied the 3,066 small farms, or *swani* (in the singular, *Saniya*). Each *saniya* ranged from one-half to one hectare and the total *swani* land was 2,300 hectares.[89]

Fezzan's settled agriculture supplied the country with most of its dates, one of the country's basic foods. Indeed, Fezzan was the date basket of the Regency, with around 1,175,000 palm trees producing 1,600,000 *kayla* of dates. One *kayla* equaled 8 kilograms, with a value of 2,400,000 piasters a year.[90] Every year, many merchants bartered dates with nomadic tribes for their pastoral products, collected dates from their own groves, or received dates as tribute from client peasant sharecroppers.

As the Sahara trade declined during the nineteenth century, agriculture became more important than it had been before. A new class structure began to form. The merchant class declined as a result of migrations out of the region or impoverishment. The new Turkish authority reached Fezzan in 1842, but was still marginal in influence since it was limited to a few oases, such as Murzaq, Ghat, Sukana, and Brak. Seminomadic tribes continued to be autonomous, like the Arabs of Wadi al-Shatti, the Gibla, and the leading aristocratic tribal clans of the Tuareg. Some Sharifian Murabuti emerged as the landlords of most of the Swani because of their military force. For example, the Arab tribes of the Magarha, Awlad Busaif, Hasawna, Huttman, and Guwid conquered the oases of Wadi al-Shatti in the fourteenth century and then again in the eighteenth and nineteenth centuries. These tribes owned most of the palm groves in Wadi al-Shatti.[91] The northern tribes of the Gibla, such as the Zintan, Mishashiyya, and Warfalla, bartered with the peasants of Wadi al-Shatti, usually trading dates for cereal, animals, and their products. The tribes of the Syrte region, Awlad Sulayman and the Gaddadfa, owned their own palm trees. The Awlad Sulayman owned most of the palm trees in Sammnu and al-Zighan, in addition to half of Sabha's. The Gaddadfa owned palm trees in Zalla and Hun.[92] Finally, the Tuareg in the Tibesti mountain area and the Tibbu in the Ubari-Ghat region owned many palms and had their own clients and slaves, especially the Tuareg.[93]

By the turn of the twentieth century, the Fezzan population was divided into three major classes: a landowning class, a small peasantry, and sharecroppers. The landowning class came mainly from aristocratic tribal clans who were mostly composed of Arab, Tuareg, and a few Sharifian marbutic families. These clans owned most of the Swani and employed either freed slaves as sharecroppers or held slaves.[94] By 1913, out of 31,600 people living in Fezzan, 27,400 were settled and only 4,200 were nomads.[95]

A class of tribal and Sharifian origins owned most of the land. For example, the Guwid tribe owned 11 Saniya in the town of al-Dissa in Wadi al-Ajal, and 73 in Hatiya. Their neighbors, the Hutman of Bergen, owned 4 Saniya in al-Hatiya and 21 in al-Gharifa.[96] Land ownership followed the same pattern in the oases of Murzaq, Ghat, Ghadamis, and Sukana. In Ghadamis two major classes existed—the noble merchant Ghadamsiyya class, which owned the land, and the freed-slave, laboring peasant class which the Ghadamsiyya dominated.[97] In Sukana, the Riyyah and the Nujumat formed the landowning clans; sharecroppers and slaves emerged as the only two classes of the oasis.[98] Few shaykhs owned large *swani*. For example, one of the chiefs of the oasis of Ghraifa in Wadi al-Ajal owned 300 palm trees but only two *swani*; another chief in the oasis of Toush owned 900 palm trees, and a landowning chief from the Guwid of Wadi al-Shatti, Shaykh Mubarak, owned 30 camels, 60 goats, 20 donkeys, and eight *swani*, with a total of 3,000 palm trees.[99]

The sharecropping class was heterogeneous. Sharecroppers sold their labor in exchange for a percentage of the harvest with the landlord, while the landlord provided land, seeds, animals, clothing, and food for the peasant. These sharecroppers were either freed slaves, known as *shwashna*, or immigrant laborers from tribal backgrounds of low status. The relationship between the landlord and sharecropper was paternalistic. Many ex-slaves were fathered by Arab or Tuareg men; according to Islamic law, children of a free father and female slave are free. Accordingly, many *shwashna*, that is, children of Muslim fathers and black female slaves, were incorporated into the tribe of the father. This class of tenant-peasants of *jabbad* worked for 10–12 hours a day in the *swani*.[100] No reliable statistics are available on their numbers, but we do have statistics for the *shwashna* in Fezzan in 1917, indicating that they numbered 20,470.[101] In addition to sharecroppers, there were slaves in the oases and among the Tuareg nomads. But many peasants worked their own plots of land; others contracted with landlords as sharecroppers.

Sharecroppers were called *jabbad, sagai,* and *wabbar*. The *Jabbad* was a peasant who directed an animal to pull water from wells; the *sagai* was a peasant who watched over watering the fields; finally, the *Wabbar* was a peasant who cleaned palm trees and planted seeds. Sharecropping was not fixed in Fezzan; it varied according to the nature of the agreement between the landlord and the sharecropper as to the peasant's share of the crop, which might be one-fifth or one-half of the crop.[102]

CHAPTER 4

THE POLITICAL ECONOMY OF THE SANUSIYYA: RELIGION, TRADE, AND STATE FORMATION

"There are many paths to God."

—Muhammad B. Ali al-Sanusi, founder of the Sanusiyya

The previous chapter analyzed Tripolitanian and Fezzani tributary political economies in the context of three major developments: Ottoman state formation, European commercial penetration, and the decline of the Sahara trade routes. The Tripolitanian political economy became a mixture of tributary and capitalist relations, while in Fezzan the decline of the Sahara trade caused an economic crisis that forced many merchants and peasants to migrate to Tunisia and coastal Tripolitania. Equally significant was Ottoman state expansion into the hinterland through the use of military force followed by the creation of an urban bureaucratic class acting as a middleman between the state and the local population.

By 1911 major social forces in Tripolitania and Fezzan had shaped an Ottoman military elite, an urban notable class, and a class of compradore merchants. These forces had also left tribal chiefs of the hinterland in the Tripolitanian Jabal, Cyrenaica, and Fezzan independent.

Cyrenaica was separated from Tripolitania by a large desert barrier; hence, it developed a distinct regional character. The tribes of the hinterland were autonomous from the time of the Ottoman state up until the middle of the nineteenth century. The rise of the Sanusiyya perpetuated the region's old autonomy. In order to understand how this was the case, one must see that socioeconomic forces conditioned Sanusi history and politics—which, unfortunately, have been read only through textual and ideological interpretations of Islam at the expense of an understanding of social and economic conditions. Colonial historians and Sanusi apologists advanced this mainstream interpretation—the former of course focusing on fanaticism and the latter on religious achievements.[1] In order to trace the rise of Sanusi politics and ideology, this chapter devotes itself to examining the politics and economics of Cyrenaica during the second half of the nineteenth century.

During the second half of the nineteenth century, the administrative status of Cyrenaica, or *Barqa,* changed vis-à-vis Tripoli. Between 1836 and 1863, Cyrenaica was a subcounty, or *qaimmaqamiyya,* linked to the province, or the *iyala,* of Tarabulus al-Gharb. But in the period between 1863 and 1872, it became an independent county, or *mutasarrifiyya,* directly tied to the imperial capitol, Istanbul. Later, between 1872 and 1888, Cyrenaica became a fully independent province, or *wilayat,* like Tripoli. Finally, by 1888 and until 1911, it was reduced again to a county linked to Tripoli.[2]

Taxes were not collected easily from Cyrenaican tribes because these tribes, mobile and armed, resisted state intrusion during most of the second half of the nineteenth century. The Ottoman state did not have enough resources to wage a campaign against the tribes, nor did it have the motivation during times when the region had fewer economic resources than Tripolitania and Fezzan. In 1856, when the Sanusi order emerged as the most organized brotherhood in Cyrenaica, the Ottomans appeased the order by exempting its property from taxes.[3] This de facto autonomy of the region played a role in the changing status of its administration vis-à-vis the central state, which ruled only the marginal urban towns. The Ottoman empire's ability to spend money on a peripheral province like Cyrenaica became more limited in 1875, when the empire's foreign debt was so large that bankruptcy was declared. The power to impose taxes was limited by the new economic difficulties.

Consequently, the Ottoman administration's presence in the region was marginal. In 1881 there were only 1,100 troops in Benghazi; in 1890 the number rose to 3,500.[4] These small Ottoman garrisons were unable to control the powerful armed Cyrenaican tribes. In 1920 the British navy reported the number of firearms owned by major tribes in Cyrenaica and Syrtica as follows: the Bra'sa owned 14,000 firearms; the Drasa 8,000; the 'Abaydat 6,000; and the 'Awagir 14,000; the Zuwayya, the Magharba, and the Awlad Sulayman also possessed firearms.[5] When the Ottoman governors attempted to collect taxes from the tribes, the latter resisted by fighting back, as in the case of the Bra'sa tribe in 1888.[6]

Urban-Rural Relations

Between 1835 and 1911, the Ottoman state exercised its authority only over the small towns of Benghazi, al-Marj, Darna, and al-Qaiqab. These towns served mainly as stations for Turkish garrisons. Benghazi, in addition to al-Marj and al-Qaiqab, was revived by the Ottoman state from 1835 on. Darna was revived by Andalusian refugees in the sixteenth century after the exodus of the Muslims and Jews. (During the Greek and Roman periods, up to the fifth century A.D., Cyrenaican towns had flourished, declining after this time because of ecological changes and waves of nomadic invasions.) In short, the Ottoman presence in the region was limited to a few hundred small garrisons, unable to exercise the claim to state sovereignty, which involved collecting taxes, outside of these towns. Moreover, Cyrenaican towns did not have strong economic relations with the hinterland, unlike Tripolitanian towns.

As has been seen, Tripolitania's urban markets, especially those in the City of Tripoli, developed a degree of economic hegemony over the countryside of Fezzan. This economic dominance developed as urban markets in these towns attracted peasants and tribesmen or middlemen merchants to borrow money from creditors and moneylenders and sell their surplus products. Economic ties between the countryside and the merchants of Tripoli were not new. But the formation of a central Ottoman administration in the second half of the nineteenth century enhanced the importance of the towns politically and economically. First, many tribal chiefs were designated tax collectors, administrators, judges, and police under the state administration in rural Tripolitania. Second, this new administration ensured a degree of security for trade and exchange between the settling tribesmen and peasants; it opened trade markets in the towns of Gharyan, Misurata, Zawiya, and, of course, the City of Tripoli.

Most records from the last century agree on the demographic and economic marginality of Cyrenaica's coastal towns compared with Tripoli City and other cities in Egypt and Tunisia. In 1817 the Italian traveler Della Cella appraised the population of the region's major town, Benghazi, at around 5,000. Half of these were Jews.[7] In 1856 the British traveler James Hamilton visited Benghazi and confirmed Della Cella's description: "the town had few necessaries, and none of the luxuries of life to be found there, above all there is no kind of society."[8] Hamilton estimated Benghazi's population at 5,000.[9] In 1896 the Muslim traveler Muhammad b. 'Uthman al-

Hashaishi confirmed the earlier observations made of Benghazi.[10] The region's two other major towns, al-Marj and Darna, were even smaller than Benghazi.[11] In short, the demographic and economic marginality of the towns of Cyrenaica continued up to the Italian invasion in 1911. Only during the colonial period did Benghazi became the region's major urban market, its population rising to 10,000; Darna had 9,700 inhabitants, and al-Marj only 1,540 in 1922.[12] Until 1911 the towns of Cyrenaica were small trading posts for those engaged in the Sahara trade and for the Ottoman troops. These towns, more than Tripolitania, lacked an absentee-landowner class like the ones in Egypt and Greater Syria; they also lacked a settled peasantry.[13]

Inhabitants of the towns had weak economic ties with the tribesmen of the hinterland. During the second half of the nineteenth century, Benghazi's population was mainly made up of immigrants from Tripolitania, Tunis, Crete, and Europe. The towns had more commercial ties with Tripoli, Malta, Alexandria, and Crete than did the hinterland.

According to the Italian colonial demographer De Agostini, the total population of Cyrenaica was 185,400 in 1922. Only 24,920 people lived in towns; most of them were Muslims and Jews from Tripolitania. The oases' population was 8,000. As for the types of tribal social organization, De Agostini estimated the population of settled tribes at 130,640, seminomads at 34,940, and nomads at 16,170.[14] Among the settled tribes were the Drasa, Hasa, and most of the 'Abaydat and the Bra'sa. The settled tribes were transhumant; the seminomads moved between their tribal homelands and the oases of the interior. Only a few tribes were actually nomadic in the sense of moving continually to various places in search of pasture, as in the cases of the Murabtin tribes of the Huta, Minfa, and Fawakhir.[15] In other words, seminomadism was the dominant type both of production and social organization. The origins of this social structure are to be found in the middle of the eleventh century.

The migration of the Arab tribesmen of Bani Hilal and Salim, who numbered between 200,000 and 300,000 with their children, women and herds, changed the social structure of the region. The Bani Salim settled in Cyrenaica and the Syrte region, and the Bani Hilal moved to Tripolitania and parts of North Africa.[16] These tribes took over the best pastoral land and water resources and made Berber and Arab settlers, who had been defeated in the seventh century, their vassals. The client vassals in Cyrenaica were called *Murabtin,* and the conquering tribes were called the *Sa'adi,* a reference to their ancestress, Sa'da of Bani Salim. The division of tribes into the *Hurr,* or free Sa'adi tribes, and the client Murabtin has been traditional in the peoples of the region since the eleventh century.

Figure 4
Sa'adi Tribal Divisions in Cyrenaica, 1900

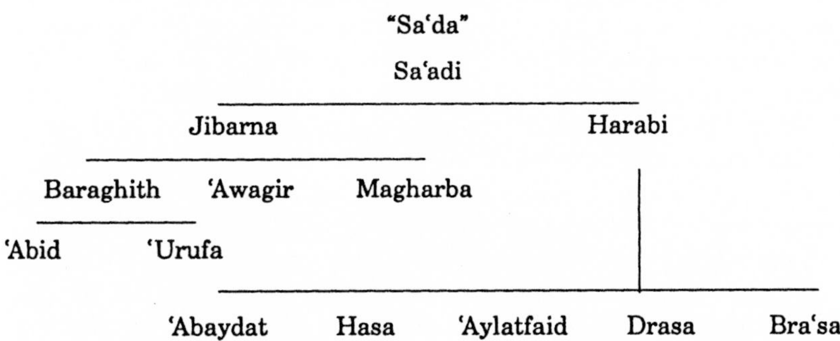

The Murabtin were composed of Berbers and descendants of the old Arabs who had arrived in the eleventh century. As clients of the Sa'adis, they were required to ask permission of the Sa'adi lords to use pastoral lands and water resources. In exchange, the Murabtin paid tributes of grain and animals to the Sa'adi, especially around harvest time and weddings; when a Sa'adi tribesman killed another tribesman, the Murabtin collected blood money.[17] The essence of this patron-client relationship was the economic dependence of the Murabtin on the conquering Sa'adi tribes. The privileged aristocratic Sa'adi ten clans legitimized their economic domination of the sixteen tribes Murabtin through prohibiting intermarriage and promoting their noble genealogy. Each Sa'adi tribe had its own Murabtin tribe. As a result, patronage and kinship ideology unified and legitimized this rudimentary class structure.

The Sa'adi needed the Murabtin to protect their wells and herds as well as to help fight other tribes in times of war. The Sa'adi need for the Murabtin raised the latter's vassal status above that of Sa'adi artisans and slaves. Collective ownership of land among the Sa'adi and the Murabtin weakened class antagonism since all tribesmen had a right to herd and cultivate a plot of tribal land. These two facts prevented the Murabtin, who carried weapons like most nomadic peoples, from aggression against or flight from the Sa'adi.

The vassal-client tribes were diverse and occupied positions depending on whether they were subordinated economically and militarily or performed religious services. The social implications of tribal names are important. The Murabtin tribes included the following: Murabtin *al-'asa* (the stick); Murabtin *al-zbal* (the manor); Murabtin *al-Sadaqa* (charity); and Murabtin *al-Baraka* (God's blessing); or *al-Fatha* (a verse of the Qur'an). Murabtin *al-'asa* referred to the fact that tribesmen were subject to beatings; Murabtin *al-zbal* to their low status; and Murabtin *al-Sadaqa* referred to the fee paid to the Sa'adi tribes by the Murabtin tribes such as the Minfa, Awlad Mariyam, 'Awama, Taraqi, Shwa'ir Alawana, and Hasanna.[18]

Murabtin *al-Baraka* or *al-Fatha*—that is, the Awlad al-Shaykh, the Massamir, and the Firjan—were accorded higher status because they either claimed a Sharifian descent, and therefore God's blessing, or they had a religious knowledge of the Qur'an and the Hadith. This group of Murabtin tribes was respected for its *Baraka*, and the educational service it provided to fellow tribes in the region. Its status was higher than that of the other Murabtin in the eyes of the Sa'adi.

This precapitalist patronage system was fluid, a consequence of the nature of the pastoral economy. Unpredictable rainfall made grain and animal surpluses fluctuate from one year to the next. Because the Murabtin tribes had the opportunity to flee their patrons, unlike the settled and dependent peasantry, the Sa'adi domination was not stable either. By the end of the nineteenth century, relations between the two became more a matter of status and less a matter of economic dependence. This was due to the demographic increase in the number of Murabtin, which gave them the ability to resist patronage successfully, and the rise of the Sanusi movement. The Sanusiyya Islamic religious ideology stressed brotherhood and education, regardless of tribal origins, which undermined notions of lower and higher status, subordination and domination.

In 1920, De Agostini appraised the Sa'adi population at 134,550 and the Murabtin at 40,600. This appraisal is misleading, however, if compared to the population within each Sa'adi tribe. De Agostini showed that many Sa'adi tribes contained a large number of Murabtin. Since the Sa'adi clans needed their Murabtin tribesmen to fight other tribes, the Murabtin were integrated into their clans. The following cases show the reliance of the Sa'adi on Murabtin clients. The first example is the clan of 'Aylat Haduth (of the Bra'sa Sa'adi tribe), which numbered 2,520. Only 630 actually were Sa'adi, whereas the rest were Murabtin linked to this Sa'adi clan.[19] A second example is the Sa'adi clan 'Aylat Sulayman of the 'Awagir tribe. This clan numbered 1,940, of whom only 740 were true Sa'adi with the rest Murabtin.[20] Another Sa'adi clan, Saghirin of the Drasa tribe, numbered 7,700, of whom 1,652 were Sa'adi and 6,050 were Murabtin.

Another important feature in forming the tribal social structure was the size of each tribe. The status of a Sa'adi tribe or clan was enhanced by its size and helped to defend its claim to land over other tribes. The need for Murabtin warriors raised their status. Thus, though some Sa'adi tribes were large—for example, there were 21,000 Bra'sa and 27,000 'Awagir—others were very small—for example, the 'Aylat Faid numbered only 400.[21] At the same time, some Murabtin tribes such as the Zuwayya and the Fawakhir grew, enabling them to refuse to pay tribute to the Sa'adi. By the middle of the nineteenth century, the relationship of the Sa'adi to the Murabtin changed from Murabtin economic dependence on the Sa'adi to a simple matter of noble status, especially after the rise of the Sanusi order in the second half of the fourteenth century. Both Sa'adi and Murabtin tribesmen became integrated into the Sanusi religious and trading order.

The basic unit of these Cyrenaican tribes was the household, or *bait*. *Baits* made a clan, or *'aylat*, and in turn many *'aylats* constituted a tribe, *qabila* or *gibila*. This elaborate tribal system was based on a yearly economic cycle, which impelled moving between the plateau, the plain, and the oases of Jalo, Awjila, Mirada, Zalla, Jaghbub, Kufra, Siwa, and Kharja in western Egypt. Economic self-sufficiency formed the core of the reproduction of pastoralism from the eleventh century until the turn of the twentieth century. The Ottoman state was unable to disturb the autonomy of the armed Cyrenaican tribes. Although the Ottomans conquered the country in 1551, they only reached coastal Cyrenaica in 1635, and even after 1835 their presence was limited to Benghazi, Darna, al-Marj and al-Qaiqab, which were the stations of a few hundred Turkish troops.

The Ottoman state in Cyrenaica could not exercise a de jure political authority over the tribes of the hinterland outside isolated coastal towns. In 1835 the Ottomans were occupied with the rebellion of the Mahamid and Awlad Sulayman in Tripolitania and Fezzan. After these rebellions were crushed in 1858, the Sanusi order began to exercise more and more influence among the tribes; by 1870, rural Cyrenaica had become capable of resisting the Ottoman state.

The Ottomans owed a large European debt and could not raise enough resources to penetrate the remote desert region of Cyrenaica's interior. Therefore, Ottoman state building did not affect rural Cyrenaica. For example, the Land Registration Code of 1858 applied only to the towns of Benghazi and Darna. In 1863, the Ottoman Land Committee declared that tribal lands were state lands leased to the tribes, and that all nontribal lands were state land. Regardless of the state's claim, the tribes believed they owned their land and indeed exercised full ownership of it.[22]

The Sanusi order did not emerge in a vacuum but against an elaborate social structure in Cyrenaica. The primary means of production such as water resources and land were controlled by strong Sa'adi tribes who leased them to vassal tribes. At the bottom of the social structure were slaves who provided most of the labor in the palm groves of the oases, especially Kufra.[23] The Sanusi success was rooted in building on and adapting to this tribal social organization.

Prior to the rise of the Sanusi order, rural Cyrenaica was commercially and socially tied to western Egypt and Wadai in the south. These ties, enhanced by the Sanusiyya, were by no means new in the second half of the nineteenth century. The coming pages address Cyrenaican tribal divisions, their commercial ties with western Egypt, and the development of the Sahara trade through Cyrenaica.

The social organization of the tribes was geographically divided along three major zones. Semisedentary or transhumant tribes, like the Hasa, the Drasa, and some of the Bra'sa and 'Abaydat, inhabited the north Green Mountain zone. These tribes cultivated grain and herded goats and cattle. The second zone was the middle plateau; here, seminomadic tribes moved between their homeland, or *watan*, on the plateau and the oases in the interior. Among these seminomadic tribes were the 'Awagir and the 'Abid.

The pastoral economy of the Cyrenaican tribes was part of a larger regional economy that included Wadai in the south and western Egypt. As in the case of Tripolitania, Cyrenaican tribes traded with peasants and urban dwellers, selling their surplus animals, products, and grain in exchange for equipment, cloth, and dates. The urban markets of Cyrenaica, however, were marginal and had weak relations with the hinterland. The question of where the hinterland tribesmen sold their surplus animals and grains, and bought their equipment, sugar, and tea, needs to be addressed by examining the larger regional economies beyond the borders of

Cyrenaica. This type of interregional connection was widespread prior to the colonial period and the rise of nation-states all over the Middle East and North Africa.

Cyrenaican tribesmen viewed western Egyptian towns such as Sallum, Umm al-Hamam, Matruh, and Alexandria as their "natural" markets during the nineteenth and the first quarter of the twentieth centuries. Usually, surplus animals were taken on foot by their owners to Egyptian towns with their large settled populations.[24]

From 1850 on, travelers and European consuls examined the economic ties between rural Cyrenaica and western Egypt. James Hamilton observed that the tribes of Cyrenaica sold their surplus animals in the markets of western Egypt.[25] The British consul in Benghazi, Justin Alvarez, provided some statistics on Cyrenaica's pastoralism and its ties with Egypt and Wadai between 1890 and 1902.

Through Alexandria, Egypt received large numbers of Cyrenaica's surplus animals, which were exported overland. For example, in 1891, Cyrenaican tribes exported 920 camels, 248 horses, and 53,131 sheep, worth a total of 51,600 pounds, in addition to 3,600 kilograms of butter worth 20,200 pounds to Egypt.[26] In contrast, in 1898–1899, the exports to Egypt were as follows: 2,000 camels worth 12,000 pounds, and 43,300 sheep, worth 21,600 pounds.[27] The exports in the following years to Egypt were 5,000 camels in 1900 and the same number in 1901; in 1902, the number increased to 6,000. In 1900, 160,000 sheep were exported to Egypt and Malta; exports of sheep increased to 200,000 in 1901 and 300,000 in 1902. As for butter, 195,000 kilograms were exported in 1902 to Egypt and the Ottoman empire; in 1908, 20,000 cattle and 34,000 sheep were exported to Egypt.[28] This dependence on Egyptian markets was enhanced by the rise of the Sanusi order in Cyrenaica. Thus, for example, successful rainy years like 1922 and 1923 in Cyrenaica led to the export of 80,000 sheep and goats and 75,462 kilograms of butter.[29]

In the years between 1800 and 1815, Cyrenaican tribes found a new market in British Malta. During the Napoleonic wars, the British navy in Malta could not get supplies from French-occupied southern Europe. But Tripolitania and Cyrenaica were close, and provided safe sources of food like grain and meat for the British navy. Cyrenaican trade with Malta continued after the defeat of Napoleon. Prior to 1911, Cyrenaica exported the following quantities of sheep and cattle to Malta: 6,800 in 1898–1899; 6,000 in 1900; 7,000 in 1901; and 5,000 in 1902.[30]

Nevertheless, it is necessary to remember that Cyrenaica's exports to Egypt and Malta were possible only in productive rainy years. When there was no rain, grain was usually imported. Severe drought years could lead to famine and consequently migration, as in 1881 when many tribesmen migrated to Tripolitania and western Egypt.[31] This unpredictable pastoral economy posed a continuous threat to the tribes during drought seasons. Also, war between tribes over land or against the central state in Tripoli forced defeated tribes to Egypt's western deserts, as in the case of the Jwazi and Awlad Ali, who lost a war in 1817 against their cousins, the 'Abaydat, who allied with the Qaramanli state in Tripoli.

This war is a good example of tribal politics in early nineteenth-century Cyrenaica. The Awlad Ali and the Jwazi were allied with Muhammad Qaramanli, the son of Yusuf Qaramanli, who was the governor of Darna. When Muhammad rebelled against his father in 1817, the Awlad Ali and the Jwazi supported him. The Awlad Ali and the Jwazi took advantage of their alliance and usurped the land of their cousins, the 'Abaydat, killing their chiefs. Yusuf Qaramanli sent the army led by his other son, Ahmad, who defeated his brother and his brother's tribal allies.[32] The Awlad Ali and the Jwazi were forced into the western desert of Egypt to join defeated Cyrenaican tribes such as the Bahaja, Awlad 'Una, Hanadi, and the Fawayd.[33]

In severe drought years, defeated tribes were forced to migrate. Tribes living on the edge of the desert, however, had to develop different strategies. One common strategy was to subjugate, or ally with, peasants from the oases, as in the case of many seminomads in southern Tripolitania and Fezzan. Another common strategy was for tribal members to join the caravans of the Sahara trade as guides, guards or investors, especially for the leading shaykhs.

The 'Aylat Ibrahim clan of the Sa'adi Magharba tribe lived in Ijdabiya and eastern Syrtica. Their tribal land and that of their neighbors, the Zuwayya, an independent Murabtin tribe, received less rain than did the other Sa'adi tribes of northern Cyrenaica. The 'Aylat Ibrahim adjusted to their need for dates by intermarrying with the dominant clans of the oases of Mirada and Zalla. This alliance allowed the Magharba clan access to a yearly share of the date harvest.[34]

The Zuwayya tribe chose a more aggressive strategy. They conquered the richest oasis of the interior, Kufra, in 1840, and brought the indigenous Tibbu tribes under their patronage.[35] The Zuwayya tribe owned most of the palm grove dates of the Kufra oases, ideally located between Wadai and northern Cyrenaica, by virtue of conquest. Consequently, the Zuwayya tribe received a yearly date harvest from the Tibbu tribesmen who labored in the date groves. The Zuwayya and the Majabra of Jalo began to trade with Wadai; by 1870 they dominated this trade. Without a doubt, the conversion of these two tribes into the Sanusi order allowed the Sanusiyya to spread their ideology into Wadai and Chad and receive large tributes and revenues from the trade.

In 1900 the Sanusi order spread among Ghadamsi merchants, the Awlad Sulayman, the Tuareg, and the Tibbu, who were all Sanusi followers. But the spread and influence of the Sanusi in Fezzan was not as strong as in Cyrenaica, the home base of the order. The Sanusi enjoyed success among tribes, oasis dwellers and merchants. In this sense, Fezzan was similar to Cyrenaica, though the Ottoman presence in Fezzan was stronger than that in Cyrenaica; in addition, intertribal alliances had an impact on Fezzan, unlike the well-organized Cyrenaicans under the Sanusiyya after 1870.

The Sahara Trade

The route between Wadai and Cyrenaica gained importance during the late nineteenth century as a consequence of two major events. The first was the decline of the Sahara trade routes through western Libya, which resulted from French and British colonial expansion in north and West Africa. This expansion shifted trade to the colonially controlled economies of West Africa, especially after the opening of the Kano-Lages railway. Added to this was the fact that the Mahdiyya war against the British in the Sudan blocked trade through Egypt. The fact that the Cyrenaican hinterland was outside the war zone of Chad and the Sudan contributed to the importance of the Wadai-Cyrenaica route.

The commodities passing through Cyrenaica consisted mainly of re-exports of ivory, ostrich feathers, goatskins, and slaves; the imports were British cotton goods, tea, and equipment. The commodities of the trans-Sahara trade route came from Wadai and Darfur, re-exported from Cyrenaica to Egypt, the Ottoman empire, England, France, Italy, and Malta. In 1890 one of the re-exports was 325 bales of ivory, worth 29,500 pounds, that went to England and France.[36] In 1898–1899, France imported 500 bales of goatskins worth 14,000 pounds, 150 bales of sheepskins worth 5,600 pounds, and 8,260 bales of wool worth 26,840 pounds, all of which passed through Marseilles.[37] In 1900–1901, among Cyrenaican exports and Sudanese re-exports were 9,000 pounds' worth of wool, 10,000 and 3,000 pounds' worth of which went to France and Malta, respectively. In 1902, 24,000 pounds' worth of ivory went to Malta and England and 10,000 pounds' worth of ostrich feathers went to France.[38] These trade figures indicate the growth of regional trade in Cyrenaica, which had begun after 1870.

Cyrenaica and the central Sudan became major markets for British cotton goods, the predominant imported commodity. By the end of the nineteenth century, cheaply priced British cotton goods made up 50 to 64 percent of the total cargo of the caravans returning to Cyrenaica.[39] The Sanusi order organized and protected the Saharan caravans through its network of lodges all over the Sahara. Sanusi merchants such as the Majabra of Jalo became wealthy and prosperous in 1875.[40] According to Miege, some Cyrenaican merchants made a 600 percent profit from their Sahara trade investments.[41]

This examination of the details of the political economy of Cyrenaica refutes the erroneous image of pre–Sanusi-Cyrenaican tribal structure as primitive, feuding and anarchic, an image popularized by travelers such as the Egyptian Ahmad Hasanain, and some historians such as Fu'ad Shukri and, to a lesser degree, Ahmad S. Dajani.[42] Contrary to this image, Cyrenaica actually had an elaborate, well-organized tribal social structure. In fact, it was this very developed tribal structure that facilitated the spread of the Sanusi order among the tribes of Cyrenaica. The Sanusi adopted the tribal segments as units of the order Zuwayya.

Tribal alliances were also common in Cyrenaica. A number of intertribal wars, usually over land, led to tribal alliances. The Sa'adi patrons split generally into two divisions in Cyrenaica, the Harabi in the center and east and the Baraghith in the west. The Harabi division included the Drasa, 'Abaydat, Awlad Ali, Bra'sa, and the 'Aylat-Faid. The Baraghith included the 'Urfa, 'Abid, 'Awagir, and the Magharba.[43]

During the nineteenth century, many wars were waged over land claims and against state policies, which created tribal alliances. In 1811–1812, the alliance of the Magharba, the 'Awagir, and the Bra'sa defeated their cousins, the Juwazi and the Fuwaid. Some of the Juwazi and the Fuwaid were pushed into the western desert in Egypt. Another tribal war was fought in 1817 when Muhammad Qaramanli rebelled against his father, Yusuf.

After 1835 the Ottoman administration tried to incorporate the

Cyrenaican tribes into its administration, pursuing strategies to recruit leading tribal chiefs. Some of these chiefs were appointed head of a subdistrict, *mudir*, or head of a district, *mutasarrif*, or head of a county, *qaimmaqam*. This policy was pursued as a compromise to avoid a long, expensive war like the one that occurred during the Mahamid and the Awlad Sulayman's rebellions.

Despite the policy of compromise, Ottoman officials failed to collect taxes from the tribes. In 1872 the county of Benghazi's tax records showed a debt of nonpaid taxes between 1843 and 1871.[44] This debt seems to be the result of tribal evasiveness and opposition to the state, even though incentives to pay were offered. However, along the coast, Ottoman policy succeeded in recruiting some town notables to serve in the state administration.

Notables from Benghazi and Darna and some tribal chiefs were appointed to the administration. Among the urban notables were Mansur al-Kikhiyya, a Cologhli from Benghazi who became the Drasa mudir in 1867 and later a member of the Ottoman parliament in 1908. Ramadan Amnaina, also from Benghazi, was the mudir of the 'Awagir in 1878; Salim Dghaim from Benghazi became a *qaimmaqam* of the 'Awagir in 1870.[45] Some tribal chiefs also joined the state regional bureaucracy; in a particularly ironic case, Abu-Bakir Haduth of the Bra'sa was appointed the mudir of his own tribe in 1871. The al-Ataywish family, a leading Magharba clan, filled administration posts in Syrte and Kufra in the second half of the nineteenth century. Ali Basha al-'Abaydi, of the 'Abaydat tribe, was the *qaimmaqam* of al-Marj. The Kizza and the 'Abar clans of the 'Awagir were also given administrative posts.[46] But even this policy of coopting the small urban notables and some of the tribal chiefs did not guarantee a "safe" state administration. Many tribes resisted tax collecting and their resistance became well organized as a new force unified the region. That force was the Sanusi brotherhood.

The Sanusiyya

The Sanusi order emerged as the most influential socioreligious movement in North Africa and the Sahara during the second half of the nineteenth century. In Tripolitania it had limited success—18 lodges in 1920—but only among the Gibla and Syrte seminomads.[47] The limited success of the Sanusiyya was due to the new Ottoman bureaucracy and the court systems, which encouraged the rise of an urban salaried alama class. Fearing a potential conflict with Sufi Islam, this class blocked the spread of the Sanusiyya into Tripolitania. Also Tripolitanian *'ulama* looked down at the "tribal" Sanusi order contemptuously, as in the case of Shaykh Tahir al-Zawi, the 'Alim and historian, who claimed superciliously that the Cyrenaica of the Sanusi had no science or culture.[48] It seems, then, that the difference between the urban Tripolitanian *'ulama* and the Sanusi order arose mainly from social bases, the Sanusi ideology representing tribal and trading oasis dwellers and the Tripolitanian *'ulama* representing reformist *salfi* urban bureaucracy.

The preceding analysis of Cyrenaica's social history underscores the inaccurate and ahistorical depictions and representations of the tribal social structure in Cyrenaica by some Western travelers and Sanusi historians, who represent tribal social relations in the pre-Sanusi period as consisting mainly of feuds, wars, and lawlessness.[49] Other Muslim and Sanusi historians perpetuated such images of the pre-Sanusi period, but at the same time glorified the socioeconomic and cultural impact of the Sanusiyya during the second half of the nineteenth century.

Also equally flawed were the colonial, that is, French and Italian descriptions of the order as fanatical and a menace to progress in the Sahara.[50] Indeed, the Sanusi order contributed tremendously to the cohesiveness, literary standards, and settlement of the tribes of Cyrenaica. Yet the order did not operate in a vacuum: it built its organization on an already elaborate and complex tribal social organization.

The Origins of Sanusi Ideology

The Sanusi order was founded by an urban Sharifian scholar from Algeria, Muhammad b. Ali al-Sanusi (1787–1859), better known as "the Grand Sanusi." He was a scholar who had studied in Algeria, Morocco, Egypt, and al-Hijaz in Arabia. His order, the Sanusiyya, became one of many resistance movements that appeared in the Middle East and North Africa during the eighteenth and nineteenth centuries. Among these movements were the Wahhabiyya in Arabia, the Mahdiyya in Sudan, and the Sanusiyya in Cyrenaica and the Sahara.

The rise of these resistance movements came as a reaction to the decline of the Oriental trade, as in the case of the Wahhabi movement in the eighteenth century. The Mahdiyya and the

Sanusiyya emerged as a reaction to the weakening of the Muslim states (Ottoman and Egyptian) to counter the colonialist British in the Sudan and the French in North Africa. Just as Sufi movements had led the anti-Iberian attacks on Morocco in the sixteenth century, new Sufi reformist movements such as the Sanusiyya and Mahdiyya took the initiative to organize local resistance against European imperialism in the late nineteenth century.

European imperialism in North Africa began with the French occupations of Algeria in 1830, Tunisia in 1881, and Morocco in 1912. The British began to occupy Egypt in 1882 and the Italians invaded Libya in 1911. The resistance movement took the Islamic model of the state to organize its followers, as in the case of Amir 'Abd al-Qadir in Algeria (1830–1847), the Sanusi in Cyrenaica, and 'Abd al-Karim's Rif Republic in Morocco (1920–1925).[51]

Islamic historical experience provides a model of state building based in the Sharia, especially the charismatic period of the Prophet and the first four Califs (610–661). Yet, like other ideologies, Islamic ideology could be interpreted either for the purpose of preserving the status quo (dynastic Islam) or for changing it, as in the cases of the Shiite concept of leadership, or *Imamat*, and the radical Khariji principle of revolution against unjust rulers. Furthermore, the Islamic doctrine of *jihad*, or holy struggle, is a powerful moral and judicial doctrine against corruption, unjust rulers, infidels, and invaders of Dar-al-Islam, or Muslim land.[52]

The Grand Sanusi was a committed intellectual influenced by his education and his travels in the Muslim world. His commitment was combined with a remarkable ability to simplify his ideas so that he was widely understood. This conversation not only demonstrates his effective and simple method of explaining ideas to his followers but also a keen awareness of the Muslim world on the eve of colonialism: During the building of his headquarters at Jaghbub, a remote oasis in the interior which became the capital of the Sanusiyya in 1856, al-Sanusi asked his followers, "Does a bird have a mind or not?" They replied, "No." Al-Sanusi went on: "Yet, he puts his eggs on the top of a remote mountain so no fox or wolf can get them. Does the Yarbu' [a big desert rat] have a mind or not?" His followers replied: "No." Finally, al-Sanusi answered: "Yet he digs many routes in his tunnel to escape snakes. Thus, be aware of the black snake which will come to you and point in an east-west direction."[53] Al-Sanusi's decision to move to Jaghbub was a good strategy to avoid Ottoman surveillance near al-Bayda. The "black snake" was an allusion to the Ottoman state and a metaphor for European colonialism.

Sayyid Ahmad al-Sharif, al-Sanusi's grandson and the third leader of the order, told another interesting story about al-Sanusi. In 1854, at the town of Darna, the Grand Sanusi predicted that European powers would invade Muslim countries, British Alexandria (Egypt), and the "Napoltan" (people of Napole, later Italians) Tripoli. The reference to Italy came from al-Sanusi's experience in the late eighteenth century. He passed by Tripoli City during a siege by ships of the Italian kingdom of Napoli. Al-Sanusi stated that the people of the Green Mountain (Cyrenaica) would fight the European invasion headed by his son al-Mahdi. Sayyid Ahmad reported that his grandfather stressed that when the Europeans attacked the country, people must be ready economically and militarily.[54] Such statements prove, as Abd El-Moula El-Horeir argued, that Sanusi leaders were well aware of the colonial threat to the region.[55] The Grand Sanusi had a long-term plan to prepare the people in Cyrenaica slowly in all aspects of morality, society and economics, to defend against the coming invaders from Europe. After all, Algeria had been occupied in 1830. Al-Sanusi's vision proved to be true.

Al-Sanusi's travels and studies in all parts of the region gave him well-rounded knowledge and political experience. Cyrenaica became the best choice for him in comparison to the political conditions in other Muslim countries, such as Hijaz, Egypt, and Tripolitania.

Al-Sanusi first studied at Sufi Zawiya in Algeria, and then attended the Qarawiyyin University at Fez in 1805. At al-Qarawiyyin he became aware of Sufi and Shahi'a studies. He received graduate certificates (*ijazas*) which gave him recognition as a scholar. In 1824 he visited al-Azhar University in Cairo on his pilgrimage to Hijaz. In Hijaz he met his teacher, Ahmad b. Idris al-Fasi (1749–1837), a famous scholar who believed in reform and *ijtihad*, free scholarly interpretation of the Shari'a, a return to the original principles of Islam in the Qur'an and the Hadith, and who criticized rigid *taqlid*, imitation, of the four Sunni schools of Islam.[56]

The Hijazi *'ulama* disliked al-Fasi's and al-Sanusi's critique of the Sunni schools and the call for free interpretation of the Shari'a. Al-Fasi was pressured to take refuge in Yemen with his students, including al-Sanusi, who remained in Yemen until the death of his teacher in 1837, whereupon he decided to return to North Africa. Yet Algeria, his birth place, was already occupied by the French and Egyptian *'ulama* like the one in Hijaz, which was hostile to his ideas.

One Egyptian scholar at al-Azhar University even wrote a book denouncing al-Sanusi's ideas regarding the Sunni schools and free interpretation.[57] Tunisia was not on his agenda, perhaps because the French had already planned a takeover, which occurred in 1881.

Tripolitania already had a centralized state bureaucracy, including a salaried urban *'ulama* class. These Tripolitanian *'ulama* filled the positions of Muftis, judges, teachers, court officials, and mosque shaykhs. The Grand Sanusi thought he could not compete with the established bureaucracy of these 'ulama. For all these reasons, Cyrenaica seemed a good choice for settlement, since it was remote from the central Ottoman authority in Tripoli and its tribes and merchants were virtually autonomous.

The Grand Sanusi and his associated *'ulama* from Algeria, Tunis, Hijaz, and Sudan arrived in Cyrenaica in 1842. In that year, he built his first lodge, or *zawiya,* in northern Cyrenaica near the town of al-Bayda. He traveled to Mecca in 1846, and after four years there returned to Cyrenaica, where he lived until his death in 1859. Northern Cyrenaica was still under the surveillance of the Ottoman state in 1856, so al-Sanusi moved to the remote but strategic oasis of al-Jaghbub. Al-Jaghbub was far from Benghazi and Darna, the center of Ottoman garrisons, and was located on the main pilgrimage route to Mecca and on the trade route to Wadai in the south.

Ottoman-Sanusi Relations

Relations between the Ottomans and the Sanusi, though not negative or hostile, were mutually mistrustful. The Grand Sanusi was critical of the weak Ottoman response to European colonialism, as demonstrated in the case of his birth place, Algeria. Furthermore, al-Sanusi, like Ayatuallah Khumayni of the Iranian revolution, believed that the *'ulama* were the most qualified to lead the Muslim community because of their knowledge of the Shari'a. To use al-Sanusi's own words, *"al-ulama warathatu al-Anbiya"* [the *'ulama* are the successors of the prophets].[58]

The Grand Sanusi believed in Quraishi kinship (only descendants of Qurayshi must lead the Muslim community) as a major qualifying condition for political leadership, or *khilafa,* in a Muslim state. Moreover, he traced his ancestors to the Prophet's family. As a sharif, he claimed to have *Baraka,* or God's blessing, which was similar to the Shi'i belief in the Prophet of Islam's descendants who have God's grace and hence are qualified to lead the Muslim community.[59]

Al-Sanusi's claim to be a sharif and his belief in the Qurayshi kinship qualification meant he saw Ottoman sultans as illegitimate leaders of the faithful. Moreover, he was aware that the Ottomans would not accept a rival social movement among rebellious tribesmen like the one in Cyrenaica, which could threaten Ottoman sovereignty. He tried to remain on good terms with the Ottomans through his representative in Benghazi and moved away from their sphere of influence. For example, in 1856, he moved his center to the remote oasis of Jaghbub. In 1895, his son, al-Mahdi, decided to move the capital of the order south. Al-Mahdi's decision to go to Kufra, deep in the Sahara, was made after a visit by an Ottoman delegation led by the courier Sadiq Mu'id al-Azm. After the visit, al-Mahdi said to his aides, "The visit of this person [al-Azm] is dubious."[60] He meant that behind Ottoman gifts and diplomacy lurked a plan to observe Sanusi activities.

Indeed, Ottoman policy toward the Sanusi was suspicious, as some reports made by Ottoman governors indicate. A major worry for the Ottomans was armed rebellion. However, most Ottoman reports to the Porte were favorable. They praised their religious piety and indicated the Sanusis' pedagogic role among the "ignorant" tribesmen.[61]

The Porte policy was to appease the Sanusi, as it had other Sufi shaykhs before, by granting Sanusi *waqf* land exemption from taxes in 1855. The Sanusi in turn sent a delegation to Istanbul to thank the Sultan and maintain good relations with the Ottoman empire. Yet, when the Italians invaded the country in 1911, Sanusi and Ottoman forces fought a mutual enemy. This alliance resulted in arms, money, and training for the Sanusi; when the Ottoman empire fell in 1913, the Sanusi declared their own state.

The Grand Sanusi was an eclectic and innovative theologian. He combined elements of the reformist ideas of urban *'ulama*, such as the belief in the individual's positive moral engagement in social life, with Sufi institutions and methods of organization. In other words, he criticized both rigid limitation of the four schools of Sunni Islam and also the withdrawal of some Sufi orders from social life.

His goal was clearly to unify the Muslim *umma* or community. He opposed any disunifying doctrine. Therefore, he accepted only the Qur'an and the Sunna, and criticized rigid beliefs in the four schools of Sunni Islam. Instead, he called for a renewal of Islamic theology. The title of one of his 44 books is *Iqaz al wisnah fi al-*

Amal biil al-Hadith wa-al-Qur'an [Awakening the Sleeping to Work with the Hadith and the Qur'an].[62] He called for free scholarship in interpreting the Shari'a. He argued that the Hadiths were written 200 years after the death of the Prophet; hence, no one could possibly know all of the Hadith. In addition, some of the Hadiths are contradictory and possibly fabricated; others did not survive. Hence, he argued, we know more than did people before us and we need to keep free thinking and interpretation of the Shari'a alive.[63] It seems logical, then, for him to have disregarded the Sunni schools and to have focused instead on the Qur'an and some of the Hadith because they are the original bases of Islam, accepted by all Muslims.

Al-Sanusi, despite his long association with Sufism, nevertheless was critical of some of its practices and claims. In his book *al-Masa'il al-'Ushr* [The Ten Matters], he disputed some Sufi claims of having to reach God-like perfection and the importance of withdrawing from daily life. He argued that there are many paths to God and that no one must claim the ultimate truth.[64] Instead, he believed in simple religious practice and stressed work, production and commitment to daily life. He reminded his followers once that "the essence of Islam is intention, prayer and other basics. If you do these things, nobody can be a better Muslim than you."[65] This simple and reformist vision of Islam, combined with patience and sensitivity to tribal conditions, made the Grand Sanusi successful in building a strong social movement in Cyrenaica.

The ideology of the Sanusiyya stressed austerity, moral commitment and anticolonial resistance. The main goal of the Sanusi was to build a coherent, unified community through education, work, self-reliance, and reliance on local resources. The order was built on an Islamic model of the state—taxation, law, education, and mobilization for *jihad*. The Sanusiyya relied on the North African Sufi institute of *zawiya* or lodge, which began to emerge in the fourteenth century as Sufi orders assumed the leadership of the resistance against the Iberian crusade in Spain and North Africa. The *zawiya* was a place for worshiping, a center for the followers of a given brotherhood, a sanctuary, and a shrine where the *murabuks* or founders of a brotherhood were buried. Al-Sanusi built his order around the important Sufi institution of *zawiya*.

Al-Sanusi built his lodges in strategic places, either between tribal boundaries or along trading routes. He preached Islam to tribesmen and indicated the need for learned teachers. For example, in a letter to Salih Latawish of the Magharba tribe, the Grand

Sanusi stated, "We built you a *zawiya* with a shaykh to lead the prayers and teach the Qur'an so people can go back to their religion and so agriculture and settlement will flourish."[66] When the Sanusi built the "mother" lodge at al-Bayda, he provided education for children, a place to arbitrate disputes, and allocated land around the *zawiya*. These services began to attract tribes to him.

The Grand Sanusi succeeded in attracting people to his cause because he was a religious man, a scholar, and a descendant of the Prophet. Equally important, he was not linked with any of the tribes of Cyrenaica. Preaching simple Islam and social reforms in a peaceful way, he began to gain attention. Tribes began to ask him to build Zawiya in their homelands. For example, the tribe of Awagir asked him to build a Zawiya on their land. He replied, "I sent your brothers to build you a Zawiya so you and your children can learn about the Qur'an and the Shari'a."[67] One has to remember that the Ottoman state provided no basic services inside the Cyrenaican hinterland, which made the Sanusi call very persuasive.

The Grand Sanusi made his lodges not only places of worship and schools, but also sanctuaries and places to solve tribal disputes. He reconciled the tribes of Zuwayya and Tibbu in the region of Kufra; both tribes became devoted Sanusi. His skill was apparent in his letter to the Tibbu tribe:

> People from the Zawiya tribe came to us and asked for forgiveness and asked us to build a Zawiya in Tzir. We want to be your neighbours, to teach you and your children the book of Allah. We want to reconcile you with the Arabs [the Zuwayya tribe], who used to attack you and take your money and children, by turning to the Qur'an, which demands reconciliation among Muslims.[68]

The Grand Sanusi succeeded because he called for simple religious practice—to be a Sanusi was not a very different matter. He did not require a high degree of reading and writing skills, but simply that his followers learn how to pray and how to recite religious formulae, or *dhikr*. Any tribesman could satisfy these requirements.[69] Young children could study at the local *zawiya* and then finish their higher education at the University of Jaghbub, which offered classes in religion, the Arabic language, and mathematics, in addition to crafts and military training. The University of Jaghbub had a large library containing 8,000 books.[70]

Al-Sanusi turned his attention to missionary activities and trade. He once bought a caravan of slaves, freed them, and sent them back to Bilad al-Sudan as preachers.[71] Merchants such as the Ghadamsiyya and Majabra became Sanusi, since the order provided security and sanctuary for them, and eventually missionaries. In short, the Sanusi contributed to the Islamization of many tribes in the region of Lake Chad.

Al-Sanusi adapted his reformist call to the needs of tribesmen and merchants. His call for simple Islamic practice appealed to many poor tribesmen, and his emphasis on *ijtihad* and individual morality was attractive to the merchants of the Sahara. Therefore, many seminomadic and trading tribes became Sanusi followers, like the Zintan, Rijban, and Awlad Busaif of the Gibla, the Awlad Sulayman of Syrte and Fezzan, and some of the Tibbu and Tuareg of Fezzan and Chad. Among the merchant clans in the Sahara who became Sanusi were the Zuwayya, Majabra and the Ghadamsiyya (see Map 3).

By 1870 a Sanusi lodge was more than a place to worship. It was a mosque, a children's school, a residence of the shaykh of the lodge and his family, a guest house for travelers, an accommodation for caravans and refugees, and a storehouse for supplies and caravan goods.[72] The management of each lodge consisted of a head ikhwan, a shaykh, or *muqadam*, a Sanusi administrator or *wakil*, and a third aide or *aqha*. This staff educated people and led prayers, collected religious taxes from tribes and caravans, invested in the Sahara trade on behalf of the order, and acted as judges and arbitrators among tribesmen.[73] The Sanusiyya, comprising a de facto state, provided an elaborate socioeconomic and legal organization for the tribes and the Sahara trade. The Sanusi network of lodges became an alternative communicational and administrative structure equivalent in strength to the Ottoman state bureaucracy and its town markets in Tripolitania.

The order unified both tribal divisions of Cyrenaica as well as the oasis dwellers of Jalu, Awjila, Siwa, and other Saharan oases. A general policy of its leaders was to avoid Ottoman strongholds along the coast. The three capitals of the order were all major stations of the trans-Sahara trade between Wadai and Cyrenaica: Jaghbub (1856–1895); Kufra (1895–1899); and Quru, in today's northern Chad (1899–1902). The Sahara trade became a crucial source of revenue for the order after the 1870s and a network for its missionaries in the Greater Sahara.

To ensure the security of the Sahara trade, the Sanusiyya divided the shaykhs of the Sahara into two major trading tribes, the Majabra and the Zuwayya. The Majabra of Jalo had a merchant

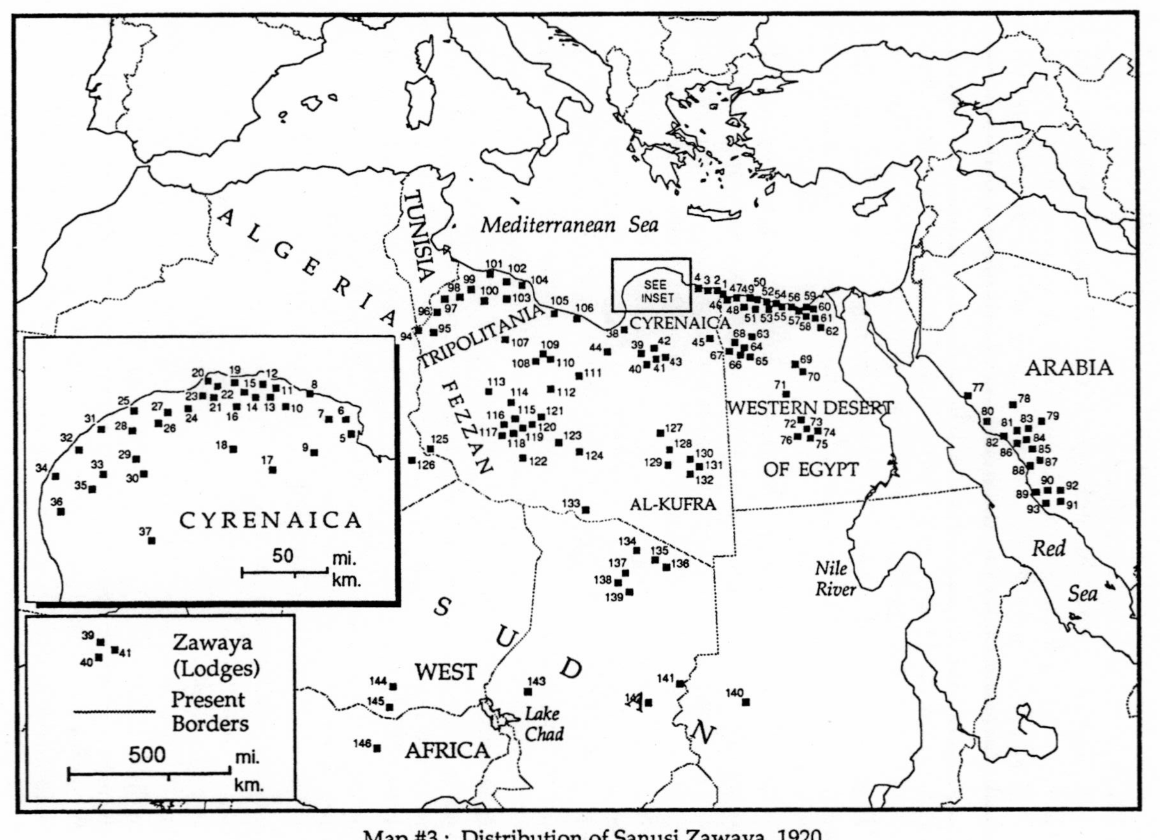

Map #3 : Distribution of Sanusi Zawaya, 1920.
Source: E. E. Evans-Pritchard, "The Sanusi," 24.

network in Wadai, Egypt, and Benghazi. They were as influential as merchants as the Ghadamsiyya of western Libya. The Zuwayya, a powerful Murabtin tribe, conquered the rich oases of Kufra in 1840.[74] These two merchant tribes controlled the most important oases in the Sahara of eastern Libya—Jalo, Awjila, Jikhra, and Kufra. Finally, they made an alliance with the sultans of Wadai during the residence of the Grand Sanusi in Hijaz in the 1830s.

Muhammad al-Sharif, a prince from the sultanate of Wadai (today's Northern Chad), met the Grand Sanusi in Hijaz when both were students there. Al-Sharif became a friend of al-Sanusi and was persuaded by his ideas. Strong ties continued between them when Muhammad al-Sharif became the Sultan of Wadai. The alliance persisted in part because all of Wadai's sultans from 1838 to 1909 were Sanusi followers.[75]

The Sanusiyya's success as the major religious social movement in late nineteenth-century North Africa and the Sahara resulted from the Sanusi's ability to transcend ethnic and local tribal identifications. The order provided a supratribal and ethnic institution for the Sahara trade. It supplied the trade with a network of communicational and bureaucratic structures through its lodges and missionaries.[76] This unity became a key to anticolonial resistance—moreso than in Tripolitania, where factionalism among the notables in the nineteenth century weakened the resistance and led to its defeat in 1922. In Cyrenaica the resistance continued till 1932.

During the Grand Sanusi's leadership, until to his death in 1859, there were 52 Sanusi lodges.[77] By the late 1920s their number had grown to 146, located as follows: 45 in Cyrenaica, 31 in western Egypt, 7 in Hijaz, 18 in Tripolitania, 15 in Fezzan, 6 in Kufra, and 14 in the Sudan and Chad (see Map 3), administered by the Sanusi brothers, or *ikhwan*. The Sanusi lodges constituted the order's socioeconomic and administrative structure, forming the core of a de facto state. The Sanusi bureaucracy replaced the Ottoman administration as well as replacing the role of Tripolitanian towns. Finally, the Sanusi lodges consolidated the old commercial ties between Cyrenaica and western Egypt. Map 3 shows that 31 Sanusi lodges were located among the Cyrenaican tribes in the western Egyptian desert, such as Awlad Ali Jmay'at, Fuwayd, Haraba, Hanadi, and Awlad'una. In 1928, Murray and Evans-Pritchard estimated the number of these tribes at 70,000, of whom 30,000 were Haraba and 40,000 Awlad Ali and their vassal Murabtin.[78]

Class Formation: Cyrenaican Tribesmen in Egypt

The transformation of Cyrenaican tribesmen into landlords, peasants, and wage laborers was a result of tribal wars, droughts, and state recruitment. Yet this process occurred mainly within the regional economy of Cyrenaica, the western desert, and the Nile Valley, rather than inside Cyrenaica itself. Understanding class formation requires looking beyond colonial and nation-state boundaries, which, after all, came into existence only at the turn of the twentieth century.

Severe drought and intertribal wars forced some Cyrenaican tribes to migrate to Egypt. The western desert frontiers became regions of refuge for defeated Cyrenaican tribes. Exiled tribes fought each other over the best pasture land and water resources. In turn, defeated tribes were pushed farther east into the Nile Valley, where they settled as *fellahin,* or peasants. The pattern of migration from Cyrenaica, intertribal wars in the western desert, and, finally, settlement along the Nile Valley occurred from the eighteenth through the middle of the twentieth centuries.

The first migration occurred in the eighteenth century when the Bani 'Una and the Hanadi were forced to leave Cyrenaica. By the middle of the eighteenth century, the Hanadi tribe had defeated Awlad 'Una near the Nile Valley. The Hanadi, in turn, were defeated by Awlad Ali, who lost the civil war against the 'Abaydat in 1817 in northeastern Cyrenaica.[79] By the turn of the twentieth century, most Cyrenaican tribes had located segments of their clans in the western desert or the Nile Valley. Tribes such as the Bahaja, Fawayad, Hanadi, and the Awlad 'Una, who had been defeated earlier, became settled peasants; some of their chiefs became landlords. Muhammad Ali and his descendants, who ruled Egypt during the nineteenth and the first half of the twentieth centuries, used policies of force when they could not buy off armed Cyrenaican tribesmen in the western desert. Some tribesmen were recruited as soldiers in Muhammad Ali's army in the 1830s and 1840s.[80] However, the most successful policy seems to have been buying off the chiefs of the tribes. Some chiefs became wealthy landlords: the chief of the Fuwayd Shaykh Mahjub B. 'umar Kishar owned 481 acres; in the Minia district during Muhammad Ali's reign and 865 acres during Ism'ael's; the chief of the Jwazi, Shaykh Ali al-Basil, owned 481 acres and Shaykh 'Umar al-Masri, also of the Juwazi, was given 961 acres in the Minia district during the period of Muhammad Ali; the chief of al-Hanadi, Shaykh Mahmud Sultan, owned 4,050 acres in the Sharqiyya province during the period of 'Abbas. By the end of Ism'ael's reign in 1879, there were 207 landlords who were bedouin tribal shaykhs. In 1902, Lamlum al Sa'di, a shaykh of the Fuwayd, owned 4,000 acres in the Minia district, and his brother Muhammad owned 3,000 acres. In 1903, Hamad al-Basil of the Jwazi owned 1,191 acres in Fayyum.[81]

The Awlad Ali who came to the western desert in 1817 did not settle the land until the 1950s. The western desert environment was similar to their tribal land in Cyrenaica. The Awlad Ali aided the reproduction of their social relations as seminomads through a yearly cycle of herding animals along the coast in the winter and harvesting dates from the oases of Siwa and Kharja in the summer.[82] The Awlad Ali and most of the Cyrenaican tribes in the western desert were Sanusi followers.

In short, the Sanusiyya had an elaborate network of lodges across the Sahara. These lodges grew to replace the weak coastal towns of Cyrenaica. The lodges were useful to the population in many ways: they served as stations for trade, cultivation, education, worship, and the courts. Furthermore, the lodges began to provide military training for tribesmen faced with an expanding French army in 1900 in central Sudan and the Italian invasion of Libya in 1911. Shukri appraised the total number of armed Sanusi men at 54,000 when the army became a force to be reckoned with in the Sahara in the 1870s.[83]

It should be stressed once again that the success of the Sanusiyya stemmed from the ability of its founders to integrate the elaborate tribal system and the merchants of the Sahara into a de facto state. The order began as an anticolonial resisting revivalist movement in the age of imperialism, developed through the Sahara trade into a rich organization and became a state in 1913. The Sanusi state was built on indigenous tribal and Islamic state traditions prior to the Ottoman conquest in the sixteenth century.

The Sanusi brotherhood began as a religious movement that slowly won the adherence of many tribesmen in the 1870s. The consent of these tribes was consolidated by the lodge system. The location of Sanusi lodges was between tribal lands, a natural location which transcended tribal affiliations. The Sanusi religious ideology won the support of Sa'adi and Murabtin tribesmen. Not only Arabs, but also Tibbu and Tuareg tribes gave their support. The Sanusi brotherhood unified many tribal, regional, and ethnic loyalties. This religious ideology integrated these ethnic groups under the banner of trade and Islam.

The Sanusi order became deeply rooted as a state and a religion. It organized trade, led prayers, and solved disputes. It comes as no surprise to see Sanusi followers voluntarily giving the Muslim *'ushr*, tithe, to the Sanusi shaykhs while refusing to pay taxes to the Ottoman state. In 1880 the Turkish governor of Awjala angrily reported that Cyrenaican tribesmen sent caravans of 4,000–5,000 camels loaded with grain as a tribute to the Sanusiyya in Jaghbub, their center.[84] The tribesmen resisted the Ottoman state mostly during times of tax collection.

The Sanusi State

Although the Sanusi did not declare their state officially until 1913, under the leadership of Muhammad al-Mahdi, in a practical sense they had already developed an elaborate infrastructure by 1890. First, there were the Higher Majlis of the Ikhwan, or the senior *'ulama*, headed by al-Mahdi's brother, Muhammad al-Sharif, and the leading shaykhs of the *zawiya* in Cyrenaica, Tripolitania, Egypt, the Sudan, and Hijaz. Majlis met once a year to decide the general policies of the order. After their meetings, the Mahdi would modify and then enact the decisions of the Majlis (see Figure 5).[85]

The second Majlis was called *al-Majlis al-Khas*, or the private Majlis. It functioned as an executive body, meeting daily and supervising the application of the decisions of the higher Majlis. Among its duties were supervising university education with its religious and scientific schools, providing services to trade caravans and missionaries, collecting taxes and training the military.[86]

Education became the core of the Sanusi state. In 1897 there were 5,000 Sanusi students, 2,000 of whom were in Jaghbub alone. By 1900, according to El-Horeir, the Sanusi had around 15,000 students.[87] The Sanusi educational system allowed many non-Sa'adi tribesmen to become prominent when they excelled in their studies. Later on, many leaders of the anti-colonial *jihad* came from a Murabtin background, as in the cases of 'Umar al-Mukhtar, Yusif Bu-Rahi, Fadil Bu-'Umar, and Fadil al-Mahshhash, or from Muslim countries such as Palestine and Chad.[88]

Sanusi religious ideology helped reconcile intertribal hostilities. A good example of this is to be found in the all-Cyrenaican tribal conference arranged by the Sanusi to reconcile the exiled Jawazi, Hanadi, and Awlad Ali of western Egypt with the cousins in Cyrenaica. This conference was headed by Sayyid Ahmad al-Sharif, the third leader of the order, in Sallum in 1910.[89]

Figure 5
The Sanusi State, Jaghbub, 1890

Imam Muhammad al-Mahdi al-Sanusi

Higher Majlis leading Ikhwan General Policy (Judicial and Legislative authority)

Tashrifat Special advisor to the Imam

Private Majlis (executive authority)

Military training

Housing for caravans and guests

Missionary

Mail

Education

Major Regional Lodges

Fezzan: Zawiya, Zawiya

Kufra: Zawiya, Zawiya

Egypt: Zawiya, Zawiya

Arabia: Zawiya, Zawiya

Tripolitania: Zawiya, Zawiya

Maqadam
Waqil
Agha

The Sanusi state was financed by *'ushr* and *zakat* taxes and trade tributes. Sanusi followers donated land and work in the Sanusi *waqf* land. Yearly revenues provided the state in Jaghbub and later in Kufra with its major source of funding.

Since its beginning, the order of the Grand Sanusi had aimed at moral and social education for resisting the European colonial advances into North and central Africa; such advances also made military training an integral policy of the order. The *zawiya* system in Jaghbub University taught students how to use arms and ride horses in classes that met on a weekly basis. The Sanusi bought arms from Egypt and even Tripoli. In 1890 there were 400 guns in Sanusi *zawiya* and 200 in Jaghbub alone.[90] The Sanusi emphasis on military training demonstrates their political awareness of European colonial schemes and international politics.

The Sanusi leadership bought arms from Egypt. Ironically, Italian intelligence men in Cairo tried to appease the Sanusi who were fighting French armies in Chad by sending them arms as gifts in 1905. The Sanusi's response was an illustration of the order's militant, anticolonial ideology. Sayyid Ahmad al-Sharif responded to the Italian gift in a long letter, which reads in part:

> There is nothing dearer to us in life than arms and books. With arms we can defeat our enemies. With books we increase our knowledge and this is the most valuable thing for Muslims. . . . We need, if you do not mind, four small artilleries . . . and a thousand guns.[91]

Sayyid Ahmad was not naive about the motives of the Italians, who wanted him to fight French armies; he was aware of the Italian interests in North Africa. Nevertheless, he needed arms to fight the French in Chad, whom he referred to as "our and *your* enemies" (the enemies of the Sanusi and the Italians). Sayyid Ahmad knew that the Italians had interests in Libya and was therefore opposed to French expansion in the Sahara.

Class Formation in Cyrenaica

Sanusi social structure was by no means egalitarian. The Sanusi hierarchy reflected processes of class formation that deserve some explanation.

The Sanusi brotherhood was dominated by two classes whose members were the Sanusi family, the Ikhwan class, and the merchants of the Sahara, especially the Zwayia and the Majabra. These two classes received most of the surpluses from trade and agropastoral products. The merchants profited from their investments in the Sahara trade, and the Ikhwan received yearly *'ushr* alms, and *zakat*, tribute in kind, such as wool, sheep, and grain.

In 1902 the French army defeated the Sanusi resistance and occupied the lodge of Bir 'Alali in Kanem, stealing Sanusi goods. The French took 3,000 loaves of sugar, large quantities of tea, and piles of cloth and carpets.[92] The Italians estimated the order's yearly revenues, excluding Jaghbub and Kufra, at around 200,000 Italian lire,[93] while Sanusi *waqf* property in Cyrenaica reached 500,000 acres in 1930.[94]

The Sanusi family and the Ikhwan *'ulama* class received most of the tribesmen's yearly tributes. Leading Ikhwan headed different lodges, as did their sons after them. Among these Ikhwan families were the Dardafi, the Ghmari, the B. Baraka, and the Khattabi. The elite *'ulama* intermarried with the Sanusi family but not with members of other groups.[95]

The Sanusi family was at the top of the class hierarchy. They received a yearly tribute from their *waqf* land, which was exempted from Ottoman taxes. It originated as a tribute from tribesmen for the building and services of the Sanusi lodges. Sanusi tribes worked this land without compensation and gave the Sanusi family gifts, such as skins, wool, grain, butter, and honey, and imported goods, such as rice, tea, sugar and cloth.[96]

By 1916 the Sanusi family divided the administration of Cyrenaica and Fezzan among themselves. Sayyid Muhammad al-Rida, the brother of Sayyid Muhammad Idriss, was in charge of the Cyrenaican plateau. Sayyid Hilal was in charge of Marmarica, Sayyid Safi al-Din of Syrtica, Muhammad al-'Abid of Fezzan, and Ali al-Khattabi of Kufra. The Sanusi family, the senior Ikhwan and Egyptian merchants claimed most of the economic surpluses in Cyrenaica.

The Sanusiyya was becoming a rich and powerful trading organization, and by the end of the nineteenth century the order had grown from its humble reformist beginning into a state. Obviously, the Sanusi relied heavily on the Sahara trade and on their followers' tributes to finance their network of lodges, their missionaries, and their bureaucracy. Prior to 1913 the Sanusi had not declared an independent state for fear of conflict with the Ottomans. There was no serious threat to the Sanusi until 1900. Nevertheless, the order developed a class structure, an infrastructure in the form of lodges, and a distinct ideology. In other words, the Sanusiyya had all the characteristics of a state, ranging from territory to support for their followers and a judicial and bureaucratic structure.

The coming of European colonialism tipped the balance of power in the Sahara. First, French expansion into Bilad al-Sudan posed a threat to the Sanusi influence. The Sanusi fought the French army in what is today's Chad from 1897 to 1910. Second, the Italians invaded Libya in 1911. Third, the Sanusi fought with the Turks against the British in western Egypt in 1916. The Sanusi leadership faced these new threats with two strategies.

The first strategy was to invite the Ottomans to Sanusi territory in Cyrenaica so as to benefit from the Ottoman empire's legal, diplomatic and military status. Therefore, when the Sanusi forces were defeated in Chad in 1902 at Bir'Alali, Sayyid Ahmad al-Sharif, the head of the order, asked the Ottoman authorities to send a governor to Kufra, the center of the order.[97] This policy was effective—the French army did not expand into Kufra.

The real threat to the Sanusi order came from the north, beginning with the Italian invasion of Libya in October of 1911. When the Ottoman empire signed a peace treaty with Italy in 1912, the threat became even greater. The Ottomans, after the Italian attack on Ottoman strongholds, were too weak to wage a full-scale war against Italy. They signed a peace treaty, left Libya, and to avoid embarrassment granted independence to Libyans. Left alone, the Sanusi declared *jihad* the ideology of their own independent state in 1913.[98] This was part of the second strategy.

CHAPTER 5

REACTIONS TO COLONIALISM: THE POLITICS OF COLLABORATION AND RESISTANCE, 1911–1932

> *"I leave you with peace my beloved homeland but I envy those who could stay behind."*
>
> *—Poet, Ahmad Rafiq al-Mahdawi, on his way to exile, 1923*

The Italian military invasion of Libya on October 4, 1911 decisively disrupted the competition between the Ottoman, Sanusi, and tribal confederations over state formation and consolidation. This invasion rapidly changed the balance of power and led to a new phase of Libyan history, in which collaboration with and resistance to the Italian colonizers played a major part. Understanding these reactions to colonialism, particularly the factors leading to Libyan resistance, is crucial to understanding Libya today. It is not the intention in this chapter to narrate the history of resistance movements chronologically, but rather to interpret and reread aspects of collaboration and resistance from new theoretical and sociological perspectives.

Modern capitalist colonization has two basic characteristics. First, colonialism is, as Indian scholar Bipan Chandra stated, "a social growth that is part of a distinct social formation—capitalism—and which is imposed from outside on other societies."[1] The European scramble over Africa was accelerated after the economic depression of the capitalist system in 1880. Colonialism was basically sought as a solution to limited European markets in terms of investments, raw materials, and new markets, in addition to giving the capitalist ruling class a means to export peasants to the colonies instead of solving the agrarian question at home as in the case of the peasants of Southern Italy. Second, modern capitalism is not just a European invention, but existed in other regions of the world as early as the thirteenth century. Furthermore, capitalist classes and local elites have operated and collaborated with colonial states to enhance their wealth and power. Yet modern capitalist colonization transforms self-sufficient tributary economies or dominates them, in part by means of a new set of social relations conducive to capitalist production.[2]

Aside from these basic characteristics, modern colonialism's tactics and strategy range from allying with the local upper classes in order to extract surpluses to allying with settler types. An example of the former can be seen in the British policy of indirect rule; French Algeria provides an example of the latter. These strategies not only differ from precapitalist strategies; they also vary from one capitalist country to another and can be pursued by the same colonial country in various periods and various colonies.[3]

The Italian colonization of Libya between 1886 and 1911 was motivated by ideological and socioeconomic forces. As early as 1886, Italian nationalists, industrialists, and the Catholic church had called for colonial expansion.[4] These groups advanced a number of justifications for colonialism, including the promise that Italy could achieve the status of other European powers and the hope that the so-called problems of Italian overpopulation and mistreatment of Italian immigrants to America could be solved.[5] Furthermore, Italy had a "civilizing" mission, similar to that of other European colonialists in Africa.[6] Finally, the advocates of colonialism argued that modern Italy, as heir to the Roman empire, had a historical right to claim the Mediterranean as a sphere of influence.[7]

Advocates of colonialism argued that Italy would also gain from it economically. The creation of Italian colonies in East and North Africa was expected to be a prelude to the larger goal of settling Italian nationals and controlling the Sahara trade.[8] Italian nationalist journals depicted Tripolitania as a future El Dorado. "Bella Tripolitania" would be the strategic gateway to West Africa's trade, as well as a good source of grain and olives for Italy.[9] Also, a colony in North Africa would allow Italy to "breathe" in a Mediterranean dominated by the great European powers of Britain and France.[10]

Yet behind all these ideological arguments lay the most crucial determinant: the agrarian question in the south during the 1890s. The Italian ruling classes, mainly the industrial bourgeoisie of the north and the big landlords of the south, were being pressured by the landless and sharecropping peasants of the south for land and voting rights. But the landlords of the Italian south refused these demands.[11] After many riots and rebellions in the south, the ruling classes began to look for a way to rid themselves of this problem by settling Italian peasants in colonies, thereby easing social tensions inside Italy and putting an end to the revolutionary dreams of Italian nationalists. The notion of an overpopulated Italy was nothing more than an ideological myth created by the Italian bourgeoisie to divert attention from the "peasant question" in the south. Indeed, the population of Italy today is far greater than that in 1900, but no longer appears to be a problem.[12]

Italian territorial colonialism began in 1882 in Eritrea in East Africa. It started through the commercial purchase of lands and expanded as Crispi, the Italian prime minister, campaigned for the colonization of Eritrea and Ethiopia. But this phase ended when the Ethiopian army, led by Emperor Menelik, defeated the Italian army at the Battle of Adawa on October 26, 1896. The Italian defeat in East Africa led Italian policy makers to pay attention to Tripolitania, the last Ottoman regency in North Africa.[13]

Italy began to prepare for the conquest of Tripolitania beginning in the 1890s. Italian banks, schools, and newspapers began to flourish, especially in the city of Tripoli; powerful Jewish and Muslim merchants were contacted by Italian consuls in Tripoli as early as 1890. Finally, in 1907, the Bank of Rome became the vehicle for buying land, investing in trade, and employing key people to work for the Italian cause.

Italian colonial policy faced strong resistance, which led to colonial compromises, especially when Italy entered World War I in 1914. Between 1914 and 1922 autonomy and self-rule were granted to the Libyans because of their resistance. But in 1923 this policy was changed by the fascists. The Italian fascist government pushed the colonial plan of the liberals to full scale, declaring that Libya was essential for settling Italian peasants and thus that there was no room for compromise on this point; only force would succeed in clearing the land for settlement. Fascist imperialism threatened all noncollaborating groups, especially autonomous states, tribal confederations, and peasants. Yet the fascists' goal of conquering the hinterland was not as easy to accomplish as had been expected.

The Italian conquest began in 1911; only in 1932 did the Italian armies succeed in controlling the whole country. That period is divided into three phases according to the conquest of territories: 1911–1914, 1915–1922, and 1923–1932. The first phase began with the successful conquest of Tripolitanian Jabal in 1913 and Fezzan in 1914. Yet a rebellion began in November 1914 in Fezzan and Jabal, and spread throughout Tripolitania. In 1914 Syrtican, Tripolitanian, Fezzani, and Sanusi forces managed to defeat the

Italian army. Consequently, Italian armies withdrew to the coast and Italian authority became limited to the coastal cities of Tripoli and Khums.

The second phase of Italian colonization began in 1915 and lasted until 1922. Colonial policy makers, defeated by a highly motivated and well-equipped resistance and burdened economically by their entry into World War I, made many concessions to the resistance, such as recognizing the autonomy of the Sanusi order in interior Cyrenaica in the treaties of 1915, 1917, and 1920. These treaties gave the Sanusi leader Idris the title of prince in the Sanusi government, paid salaries to him and his family, and granted Cyrenaica a parliament in 1920. In exchange, Idris al-Sanusi agreed to eliminate Ottoman officers from the army and remove his militant cousin Sayyid Ahmad al-Sharif, the head of the Sanusi order from 1902 to 1916, from power. Al-Sharif led the Sanusi forces against the French in Chad in 1902, the Italians in 1912, and the British in 1915–1916. Idris agreed in principle to disarm and disband Sanusi military camps.

In Tripolitania the defeat of the Italians in 1914 and the flow of Ottoman and German aid up until 1918 laid the groundwork for the rise of many small governments. Each major notable or chief became the head of a "government" in his own region or domain. Among the most important states were the Sulayman al-Baruni government in the Jabal and western Tripolitania in 1912 and 1916; the Ramadan al-Suwayhli government in Misurata and eastern Tripolitania from 1915 to 1922; the Shaykh Suf al-Mahamudi government in 1915; the government of Tarhuna in 1915; and the government of Khalifa al-Zawi in Fezzan from 1916 to 1926. When the Ottoman empire withdrew from Libya in 1918, Tripolitanian leaders found themselves without either aid or strong allies like those of the British-Sanusi alliance. Thus, they decided to form an all-Tripolitanian government in 1918, the Tripolitanian Republic, which managed to negotiate a peace settlement with the colonial authorities in 1919. The fundamental law granted Tripolitania autonomy, a parliament, a free press, and citizenship for the Muslim population. But interfactional conflict, bribery, and exploitation of local feuds by the Italians led to the collapse of the Republic and Tripolitanian resistance during the two major civil wars in 1920.

Between 1910 and 1920 interfactional conflict among Tripolitanian notables and chiefs weakened resistance and eventually led to the Italian reoccupation of Tripolitania in 1923. The causes of interfactionalism were complex. A combination of socioeconomic differences between settled tribes and autonomous armed tribes, as well as competition among notables for power and revenues, led to frequent hostilities and even small civil wars. Ottoman and Italian arms and aid contributed to still more conflict among the notables and chiefs of Tripolitania.

In short, by 1924 the region of Fezzan had become a refuge for most of the resisting Tripolitanian tribes who, with the Awlad Sulayman, engaged in a successful guerrilla war against the Italian armies. They fought the Italian armies in a number of surprising battles such as Tagrifit, on March 24, 1928, and 'Afiya on October 31, 1928.[14] The resisting tribes of the Awlad Sulayman, Warfalla, Gaddadfa, Zintan, Awlad Busaif, and the Mashashiyya succeeded in blocking the Italian advance inside Fezzan until 1930, when modern airplanes and poison gas finally overcame them.[15] The tribes fled to Chad, Niger, Egypt, and Tunisia.

By 1930, Cyrenaican tribesmen were well organized; led by 'Umar al-Mukhtar, they continued guerrilla resistance from 1923 until 1932. To crush this resistance, Italian military leaders used tactics unmatched in brutality at any other time during the colonial wars in Africa, such as sealing wells, confiscating herds, closing Libya's borders with Egypt, dropping rebels from airplanes, and, finally, forcing 85,000 tribesmen and their families to leave their homes, consigning them to horrifying concentration camps in the desert of Syrtica. In 1933 there were only 35,000 survivors of these camps. The colonialist goal was to separate the resistance from its social base. Toward this end, al-Mukhtar was eventually captured and hanged in 1931, and in January of 1932 four of his commanders were trapped along the Egyptian borders; one died, two were captured, and one escaped into Egypt.

This is, in brief form, the hitherto untold story of the Libyan resistance to Italian occupation. What follows is a discussion of the issue of collaboration and of the resistance movements that serves to elaborate on this story.

Types of "Collaboration"

The subject of collaboration has been one of the most complex issues of the colonial and postcolonial periods. This is due to the fact that postindependence Libyan nationalism drew its stock of heroes, martyrs, and legends from the anticolonial resistance . History was used socially and politically by postcolonial states in both the monarchical years of 1951–1969 and the republican eras. Sources on collaboration, such as memoirs and other documents, are still retained by concerned families; only after 1970 did new material become available to researchers, such as the personal letters of Sayyid Ahmad al-Sharif and the correspondence of the Jabal notables during the civil war of 1920.[16]

Reactions to colonialism took many complex forms ranging from armed resistance, trade, negotiation, invasions, emigration, accommodation, and collaboration. The reactions of various factions of Libyan society differed from one region to another as well as inside each region. This diversity stemmed from the unequal socioeconomic development of each region in relationship to urban markets and the degree of capitalist penetration. Whereas Tripolitania was partially penetrated by finance capital and portions of its hinterland became integrated into Tripoli City, the major market, the tribes of Cyrenaica, even after the rise of the Sanusi order, had a weak socioeconomic relationship with the coastal towns. Instead, western Egypt continued to be the natural market of the hinterland. By the 1890s, Fezzan had lost its economic vitality as the largest market of the Sahara trade, and tribal confederations competed with the Ottoman administration.

Each region had distinct social classes due to the changes that occurred in the nineteenth century. Tripolitania had an urban notable class, a peasantry, and a tribal confederation. Fezzan was dominated by tribal confederations, landowning clans, and sharecropping peasants. Cyrenaica had no peasantry and the formation of the Sanusi state integrated tribal factions into one cohesive social force. This constituted the socioeconomic structure of the three regions in 1911.

The Italian colonial policy makers tried to buy off local notables and merchants as early as the 1890s. All in all, various socioeconomic factors determined the collaboration of classes, tribes, and some ethnic groups. To understand resistance movements, one must first examine why these groups cooperated and collaborated with the colonial state as guides, soldiers, and informants.

Tripolitania

Big compradore merchants, especially those tied to the Bank of Rome, sided with Italy to protect their economic interests. Collaborators of this class, such as Hassuna Qaramanli, the Mayor of

Tripoli, powerful Muslim merchants like the Muntasir clan and Jewish merchants such as the Halfuns family, not only facilitated Italian economic and cultural interests in Tripoli City, but even aided the Italian army in occupying the city.[17]

Through the Italian consulate in Tripoli, Mayor Hassuna was in contact with the Italian government from 1890 on.[18] His motive for collaborating with the Italians was his ambition to become the ruler of Tripoli like his grandfather, Ali Qaramanli. Believing the Italians would install him as ruler of Libya in the same way the French alliance had installed the local Hussaynid dynasty in Tunisia after 1881, he helped the Italian army by collecting Ottoman-distributed guns from the city's people and guiding the Italians in their occupation of the city on October 4, 1911.[19] However, the colonial authorities did not appoint him ruler since he had no influence outside the city, instead awarding him the vice governorship of the city.[20]

Another example of upper-class collaboration is to be found among the members of the Muntasir notable merchant class. They were motivated by a combination of economic interests and the desire for revenge against their rivals in Tripolitania.[21] Ahmad Diya al-Din al-Muntasir was in Rome just before the invasion, consulting and advising the colonial officials on Libyan affairs. His father, 'Umar, used his influence to aid the army in occupying Tripolitania, the city of Syrte, and later Fezzan.[22]

The Muntasir clan and other urban merchants and notables working for the well-paying Bank of Rome sided with Italy against the government of the Young Turks in 1908. Mansur Gudara of Zlitan, Sharif Ganaba, Ahmad Gurgi, Yusuf Bel-Haj, Ahmad al-Azmarli, Muhammad Abd al-Rahman al-Busayri, and the judge Shans al-Din, all from Tripoli City, collaborated with the Italian government; but the Muntasirs were the most conspicuous and enthusiastic in their collaboration with the Italian occupation.[23] There were specific reasons for their enthusiasm. A brief background of the Muntasirs is crucial for understanding why they sided with the Italians.[24]

The Muntasir clan emerged as merchants in the coastal town of Misurata during the second half of the nineteenth century, replacing their rival clan, al-Adgham, after the defeat of the latter in the rebellion of 1835–1858. 'Uthman al-Adgham, the Agha of Misurata, allied with the rebels against the Ottoman state.[25] By the end of the nineteenth century, 'Umar al-Muntasir and his sons Ahmad Diya al-Din, Salim and 'Abd al-Qadir became wealthy and rose to the top of the newly organized local bureaucracy.[26] The wealth they accumulated from trade allowed them to build clientage and to intermarry with members of other prominent clans in the region, such as the Marriyads in Tarhuna and the Ka'bars in Gharyan.[27] These kin connections with other notables help to explain why until 1908 the Muntasirs were accepted locally by other notables as administrators of Gharyan, Tarhuna, Misurata, and Syrte.[28] The Muntasirs, as part of the notable establishment, became partisans of Sultan 'Abd al-Hamid II. When the Young Turks took power in Istanbul in 1908, they appointed other notables to the state bureaucracy and removed the old pro-'Abd Hamid elite, including the Muntasirs. The saga of the Muntasirs is best summarized in the testimony of Ahmad Diya al-Din al-Muntasir, found in the colonial archives in Rome:

> The young Turks came, and because of their hatred of the partisans of 'Abd al-Hamid, pounced on our family. First, when there were elections [for the reopened Ottoman parliament], I, who was elected deputy for the Sanjak of Khums and Tripoli, was not confirmed by the government of the young Turks on the pretext that I did not know the Ottoman language well, while there were many others confirmed who knew less than I. Then I was unjustly dismissed as a *qaimmaqam* of Tarhuna, and they lured some murderers to kill my brother 'Abu al-Qasim, who was barbarically killed in the street, after protection had been promised to the murderer. . . . Fortunately for us, we came to know Italy had decided to occupy Tripoli, and my brother Salim and I joined with . . . the Banco di Roma in denouncing publicly the actions of the young Turks committed against us. We offered them our cooperation in the occupation of the City of Tripoli.[29]

Like most collaborators, the Muntasirs justified their actions as a reaction to what they saw as harassment and a bias against their interests. As a merchant family, they wanted to retain their fortune and influence in the region. This is why they aided the Italians in occupying Tripoli City, Misurata, and Fezzan in 1914.[30] In exchange, the Italian colonial authorities kept them on as advisors and administrators.[31]

In addition to Muslim merchants, Jewish middleman merchants tied to Italian interests also welcomed and collaborated with the Italians prior to and during the occupation. Many merchants such as the Halfuns, the Hassans, the Labis, the Arbibs, and the Nahums dominated the import-export trade with Italy and spoke

Italian.[32] When Italy began its policy of cultural and economic penetration, the Jews in Tripoli were eager to enroll in Italian schools, work in the companies of the Bank of Rome, and write in Italian newspapers. In 1907 the first newspaper in a European language was the Italian *Eco di Tripoli*, edited by Gustavo Arbib.[33] In sum, economic interests motivated many merchants to collaborate with the colonial Italian state. Poor Jews were less enthusiastic than rich merchants; however, it seems most Jews welcomed the Italians.[34]

This reaction was due to the fact that more than half of Libya's 20,000 Jews were living in the city of Tripoli, which was occupied as early as October 4, 1911.[35] Also, as a distinct and small minority, the Jewish community believed they could better protect themselves by allying with the conqueror. The Libyan Jewish rabbi, Mordachi Hakohen, described the Italian invasion as "the reconquest of Libya by Rome as in ancient times," and dismissed anti-Italian resistance fighters as a bunch of thugs and bandits.[36]

The collaboration of some old-class notables and compradore merchants was not the dominant pattern in Tripolitania. Unlike the urban notables of Cyrenaica, most of Tripolitania's urban notables, especially those who were pro–Young Turks (such as Sulayman al-Baruni and Farhat al-Zawi, both elected to the Ottoman parliament in 1908, and Ramadan al-Suwayhli of Misurata), emerged as the main leaders of the resistance.

There were also collaborators, whom one could call "waverers" in the Tripolitanian interior. Tribes that still lived on the periphery and had been rivals of the Ottoman administration, or that had been active in the resistance at other times, either did not view the Italian expansion into other areas as inimical or accepted Italian money and arms and fought on the side of the Italian army. These tribes saw their action not as collaboration but as a matter of getting even with their rivals. Other tribal leaders fought the Italians until they were killed or forced into exile. The explanation of such diverse actions depends on the issue of tribal politics in late nineteenth-century Tripolitania.

A review of collected oral histories reveals a persistent trend: many notables and chiefs, composing the local ruling classes, were eager to retain their administrative positions even after the Ottoman empire signed a peace treaty with Italy in October 1912 and withdrew from Libya. These positions gave local notables access to state salaries, as well as the ability to offer favors to their kin groups by using their influence in the bureaucracy. As the Ottomans withdrew from Libya and local government emerged in

Tripolitania, local notables began to make alliances, rewarding certain notables over others. These alliances affected some notables and chiefs who became bitter and wanted to "get even," or preserve their influence with those who threatened and imperiled their power by excluding them from bureaucratic leadership. Some of these notables and chiefs, such as Harb al-Naili of the Nuwail and Muhmad B. al-Haj Hassan of the Mashashiyya, joined the Italian side to correct what they saw as injustices committed against them. The politics of these tribes were linked to the *sufuf* political alliances discussed in Chapter IV. Some of these peripheral tribes in the Gibla and Syrtica had no strong ties to the Ottoman central state, and hence acted as independent socioeconomic and political organizations.

There were two major *sufuf*: the alliance of the Ibadi peasants with the Arab Mashashiyya, Awlad Busaif, and Nuwail tribes, versus the *suff* of the Zintan, Rijban, Mahamid, and Haraba tribes. These *sufuf* emerged as a result of conflict over land rights and alliances with or against the Ottoman state, mainly over taxation policies. As late as 1910 a war over tribal land was waged between the Zintan and Awlad Busaif and their allies, the Mashashiyya. The Ottoman army aided the Zintan who defeated the other two tribes. This is the main reason that the Awlad Busaif and the Mashashiyya developed hostility toward the Ottoman state.[37]

When Ottoman officers organized the resistance movements during 1911–1913, some chiefs of the Mashashiyya and Awlad Busaif were reluctant to join, especially when their local rival chiefs and notables held most of the leadership positions in the resistance. The chief of the Mashashiyya, Shaykh Muhammad Hassan al-Mashai, fought against the Italians in 1912–1913, but then joined the Italians who exploited his tribal rivalry with the Zintan and the Rijban. Only in late 1926 did al-Mashai reconcile with the Zintan and fight the Italians from then until 1930 in Fezzan.[38]

Another notable was Muhammad Jalban of the Riyyana tribe in Gharyan, who fell out with Shaykh Muhammad Fkayni of the Rijban; Fkayni had appointed Jalaban's intratribal rival, 'Abdallah al-Rhaybi, as administrator of the Riyyana tribe in 1918. When al-Rhaybi put Jalban in jail, Jalban joined the Italians to get even, regaining his administrative position from his rivals.[39] Ahmad al 'Ayyat of Awlad Busaif defected to the Italian side after he was defeated in Fezzan between 1918 and 1926.[40] Khalifa al-Zawi allied with two tribes, the Magarha of Wadai al-Shatti and the Riyyah of al-Jufra; both were rivals of the Awlad Sulayman. When Khalifa al-

Zawi was defeated by the Awlad Sulayman in 1926, he went to Tripoli and joined the Italians, advising them on their occupation of Fezzan in 1928–1930. Al-Zawi's tribal allies, the Magarha and the Riyyah, cooperated with the Italians as a means of counterattacking the Awlad Sulayman.[41] In short, the Italian army was not the main enemy; many chiefs regarded rival chiefs as more urgent threats to their status and power.

By 1911, in the district of Gharyan, the Cologhli Ka'abra clan had become the most prominent. Using the power of their office, they registered most of the agricultural land in the Jafara plain under their names. The Ka'abra increased their power in the district, state, and even the Ottoman parliament, when Hadi Ka'bar was elected as one of eight parliamentary representatives in 1908. Other notables of the town of Gharyan felt threatened by Ka'abra domination and hence some of them, like 'Akif Msayk, al-Mabruk al-Gu'ud and Nafi' al-Mabruk, joined the Italians.[42]

Since many chiefs and notables did not have religious or nationalist goals, but cooperated with the Italians to protect their tribal or economic interests, they had no difficulty collaborating with the colonial state. This pattern was not unique to Tripolitania and was echoed in many colonies. Colonialism was, for these chiefs and notables, a pragmatic way to preserve their interests and positions.

In 1916, Shaykh Suf al-Mahmudi was appointed regent in Tripolitania by the Ottomans. He used his position to distribute Ottoman money and positions to his own tribe and members of its alliances at the expense of other chiefs and notables. Shaykh Suf appointed Farhat Busahmain as administrator of the town of Zuwara, an act that angered the dominant clan of B. Sha'ban. The appointment of Muhammad Belqasim al-Mahmudi as the administrator of the Nuwail tribe and Muhamad Bash al-Mahmudi of the Yefran angered Shaykh Harb, the chief of the Nuwail, and Sasi Khzam, the notable of the Yefran. Consequently, both joined with the Italians.[43]

Factionalism in the Jabal between the chiefs of the Yefran, Jadu, Rijban, and Zintan tribes in 1915–1916 and 1920–1921 was due to the complex structure of that region. The Ibadi tribes and peasants had inhabited the Jabal from the time that the tribes of Bani Hilal and Salim forced them to leave the Jafara plain in the eleventh century. In the Jabal the peasants lived in fortresslike villages, which protected them from rival tribal confederations and the Ottoman army. The armed Ibadi peasants and transhumants intermixed racially and socially with other groups in the Jabal.[44] They were organized into *sufuf*, which included Ibadi and non-Ibadi tribesmen. For these reasons, it would be erroneous to treat them as a racially distinct ethnic group, as did the Italian colonial demographer, De Agostini, by classifying the population of Tripolitania as comprised of Berber, Arab, Arab-Berber, Ashraf, Jews, and Cologhli. Whereas Jews kept their distinct character as a religious and ethnic minority, there no "pure" Arabs or "pure" Berbers, since all were mixed and had mixed with each other for centuries. The notion of a pure Berber, for example, is a colonialist construct designed to separate peoples hierarchically so as to facilitate domination. Further, the Cologhli were a distinct ruling group only in the nineteenth century. The Ashraf were any Muslims who claimed descent from the Prophet's family. In short, Ibadi and Sunni Tripolitanians, like other Muslims, were organized into various alliances rooted in specific socioeconomic conditions rather than racial or ethnic ones.

Therefore, it would be misleading to interpret the conflicts in 1916 and 1920 as mere racial or ethnic rivalries of Arabs and Berbers, since most of the Jabal tribes were descendants of Arab-Berber mixing.[45] It is necessary to remember that the great rebellion of Ghuma al-Mahmudi in 1835–1858 was supported by a wide confederation of "Arab" and "Berber" peasants and tribesmen.[46] Perhaps the most appropriate way to understand factionalism in the Jabal is to view it as part of the local phenomenon of *sufuf*. There is ample evidence disputing racially based "Arab-Berber rivalry," since many Arab tribes allied and fought on the side of the Berbers, as in the cases of Awlad Busaif, the Mashashiyya, and segments of the Riyyana.

Some tribes shifted sides, "wavering" between collaboration and resistance, or vice versa. This was true of the chiefs of tribes such as the Mashashiyya of the Gibla and the Warfalla in eastern Tripolitania, who viewed their relations with rival tribal chiefs as the most important issue. This attitude meant that the Italian army was, for them, not the most urgent enemy. An analysis of the politics of the tribe of Warfalla and its chief 'Abd al-Nabi Bel Khayre provides a good illustration of the "wavering" pattern of local reaction.

We have as an example 'Abd al-Nabi's rise to power as a tax collector in the Ottoman bureaucracy around 1908. His position allowed him to build his patronage until he became the sole leader of the Warfalla tribe in eastern Tripolitania.[47] Yet, with the coming of Italian colonialism, some tribal chiefs from Gibla and Syrtica acted either in coordination with their tribal allies or remained neutral when the Italian armies did not attack them. These tribes had not been as affected as the coastal communities by Ottoman state reforms nor by capitalist penetration. They acted as collectives according to their chief's definition of local interests.

In 1913, 'Abd al-Nabi, facing the advance of the Italian army into the interior, decided to collaborate with Colonel Antonio Miani. Abd al-Nabi became an advisor to Miani, whose troops occupied Fezzan in the middle of 1914.[48]

The shrewd and pragmatic 'Abd al-Nabi, however, remained neutral during the revolt against the Italian occupation, which began in Fezzan on November 28, 1914, and continued in the Jabal. When the resistance crushed the Italian army in the battle of Gardabiyya on April 18, 1915, he joined the resistance and attacked the Italian garrison in Bani Walid. All his life he stayed faithful to his tribal interests. Although 'Abd al-Nabi became one of the leaders of the Republic in 1918, he viewed with caution the expansion of his rival notable, Ramadan al-Suwayhli, into his sphere of influence. Al-Suwayhli, one of the major leaders of al-Gardabiyya, became the most powerful notable in eastern Tripolitania. His power came from looting Italian garrisons and receiving Ottoman and German ones that arrived through the port of Gasar Hamad near Misurata between 1916 and 1918.

Al-Suwayhli founded a local government and became the most committed anti-Italian leader in Tripolitania.[49] But as Ottoman and German aid increased, his influence began to expand to his neighbors, especially to the government of the Tarhuna and Warfalla. 'Abd al-Nabi accepted money and arms from the Italians, who began to exploit feuds among the notables and chiefs.[50]

By the summer of 1920, Ramadan decided to attack 'Abd al-Nabi, but bad planning and lack of water led to his defeat and death. 'Abd al-Nabi became isolated from the resistance until 1923. As the fascists began their "reconquest," 'Abd al-Nabi had either to surrender or fight. He joined the resistance when his tribe's autonomy was threatened. 'Abd al-Nabi fought the Italians in Fezzan from 1923 to 1930. After the defeat of the resistance, he withdrew to the Algerian desert frontiers. He disappeared in the Algerian desert in the summer of 1932, and his body was never found.[51]

In summing up the issues surrounding collaboration in Tripolitania, there are a number of points to be stressed. To begin with, changing attitudes and the various types of collaboration make collaboration a complex issue.

As in other peripheral societies, factionalism led to collaboration. Each faction sought allies, especially in the context of colonial rule. Many chiefs viewed alliances with the colonial state as the safest means to protect their authority and interests. The best way to make sense of collaboration in Tripolitania is to relate the political actions of notables, chiefs, and tribes to the larger political economy of Tripolitania. The coastal areas were penetrated by finance capital and Ottoman state and land reforms; hence, merchant and upper-class collaboration was conditioned by economic and political interests. However, the Tripolitanian interior, especially in the Gibla and Syrtica, kept its socioeconomic independence and political organization (*sufuf*). The departure of the Ottoman army and bureaucrats after 1912 and 1918 led to competition among the notables and chiefs over taxes and Ottoman and German aid. Thus, class and tribal hierarchies surfaced in Tripolitania. The transitional political economy inhibited the rise of one unified leadership, since many independent tribes in the interior refused to give up their autonomy, and many notables competed with each other over the leadership of the region. Against this background emerged several types of collaboration, motivated by class interests, the political ambition of upper classes, getting even with rivals, ethnic divisions of labor, and "wavering."

Fezzani peasants and tribes reacted to the colonial conquest in similar ways. Like the tribes of the Gibla and Syrtica, the Awlad Sulayman, the Tuareg, and most of the Arabs of Wadai al-Shatti fought the Italians who threatened their autonomy (except the Magarha and Riyyah, who had long-standing feuds with the Awlad Sulayman and sided with the Italians).[52] Fezzani peasants were too impoverished and isolated to engage in broad political action.

In Cyrenaica the coastal urban population had weak ties with the hinterland and became the target of Italian propaganda. Most of the urban notables collaborated with the Italian colonial state and did not cooperate with the Sanusi resistance in the hinterland, a result of the weak socioeconomic ties between the hinterland and the towns during the nineteenth century.[53]

The town notables, lacking similar economic and social ties with the hinterland, became isolated under the Italian occupation. The Italian colonial officials in turn offered these notables jobs and salaries. For all these reasons, many notables decided to make peace with the Italians.

These are some of the social and regional forces that influenced some groups in the three regions to collaborate with the Italians.

Collaboration surfaced after 1918 as contradictions among Tripolitanian notables became exacerbated by the Italian exploitation of these contradictions through money, arms, and promises to appoint these notables as administrators. Collaboration, especially in Tripolitania, led to the early crushing of the resistance and the 1923 occupation of that region, bringing us to the issue of anticolonial resistance.

Types of Anti-Colonial Resistance, 1911–1932

Italian policy makers expected to occupy Libya with limited military operations, thinking that the natives hated "Ottoman tyranny and backwardness." Instead, they faced one of the longest and most militant anticolonial movements in the history of Africa in that period. To address the social and ideological bases of this long resistance, it is important first to examine the Mujahidins' own reasons for resistance, and then to view these reasons in light of practical political action.

Anticolonial resistance was organized by major political institutions: the Ottoman empire between in 1911–1912 and later from 1915 to 1918; local states, the Sanusi states, and the Tripolitanian Republic; and finally, tribal confederations that operated on their own as local states. Essentially, however, the lack of funds and interfactional war aided the Italian army in defeating the resistance in Tripolitania and later in Fezzan and Cyrenaica.

The Young Turk officers, motivated by their aims of revitalizing and strengthening the Ottoman empire against European colonialism, organized the resistance in 1911–1912. Nash'at Pasha in Tripoli and Anwar Pasha (later the defense minister), Mustafa Kemal (later Ataturk), and 'Aziz Ali al-Masri in Cyrenaica cooperated with the Sanusi leadership of Sayyid Ahmad al-Sharif. The Ottoman government sent arms, money, and supplies through Tunisian and Egyptian borders to the resistance fighters. This aid was essential in helping the resistance to organize.[54] Yet after the Ottoman empire signed a peace treaty with Italy on October 18, 1912, Libyan notables and tribesmen found themselves virtually on their own, with few Ottoman officers remaining behind.

A peace treaty between Italy and the Ottoman empire was a result of Italy's increasing its territorial threat on the Ottoman empire by attacking the Ottoman Dodecanese Islands and the Dardanelle Straits in October 1912. The Ottoman empire decided to withdraw from Libya, but to abandon its Muslim subjects was embarrassing, especially since the Italian conquest of Libya became a major Islamic issue. Aid and volunteers from India, Tunisia, Egypt, Algeria, and Chad began to arrive in Libya. Further, Islamic and Arabic newspapers began to mobilize Muslims against the Italian crusade in Libya.[55]

The peace treaty was very ambiguous: Ottoman officials agreed to withdraw from Libya and recognize Italian claims. But at the same time, the Ottoman government granted "independence" to Tripolitania and Cyrenaica in a different declaration to Libyans. Thus, Italy was given a free hand to occupy Libya and withdrew from the Ottoman Straits. This two-faced Ottoman policy was the means by which the empire attempted to preserve its status temporarily in the eyes of its Libyan Muslim subjects.[56]

Sayyid Ahmad al-Sharif met with Anwar Pasha, who gave him arms and supplies before the Pasha left Cyrenaica. Sayyid Ahmad declared the formation of a Sanusi state and called on his followers to fight for the *jihad* against the invading Italians in 1913. The Sanusi leadership was able to declare *jihad* because it had well-integrated economic, social, and religious institutions, developed during the second half of the nineteenth century. The situation in Tripolitania was different.

Sulayman al-Baruni and Farhat al-Zawi, two Tripolitanian members of the Ottoman parliament, called for all Tripolitanian chiefs and notables to meet in ʿAziziyya to discuss action subsequent to the Italian-Ottoman peace treaty. Two opinions surfaced at the conference: some coastal notables such as Farhat al-Zawi and Ali B. Tantush wanted to negotiate with the Italians for their independence; a group led by Sulayman al-Baruni, a notable from the Jabal, was in opposition. The tribal chiefs who composed this latter group, including Shaykh Suf al-Mahmudi of the Mahamid and Shaykh Muhammad B. Abdallah al-Busayfi of Awlad Busaif, were determined to fight the Italians as the only way to preserve their independence.[57]

The pronegotiation faction met with Italian colonial officials outside Tripoli but failed to reach an agreement with them and hence decided to join the opposition. Al-Baruni formed his own state of Tripolitania at the conference in 1913 and relied on the other notables and chiefs to administer the region. The Ottoman government provided him with money and arms.[58]

During the first phase of conquest, the Italian colonials had no plan for local autonomy or cooperation with the local leadership.

This policy pressured some reluctant coastal notables to join the interior leadership. When the Italian army occupied Syrte with the aid of 'Umar al-Muntasir, most of the coastal notables lost hope of achieving independence from Italy. Shaykh Farhat al-Zawi, a French-educated judge, had been a member of the Ottoman parliament since 1908. He advocated negotiating with Italian officials to preserve Tripolitanian independence. But al-Zawi soon realized that the Italians wanted total occupation of the country. He and other coastal notables changed their strategy and joined the armed resistance in the hinterland.

When the war continued in 1913, the anticolonial resistance numbered 31,000 fighters. The Sanusi forces stood at about 16,000, while in Tripolitania they numbered about 15,000.[59] The social base of the resistance was the tribe, which provided a certain number of fighters with food and supplies.

The Sanusiyya, with their well-integrated sociopolitical system, managed to mobilize and keep the Italian armies inside the coastal towns of Cyrenaica. Tripolitanians in the interior resisted the Italian army until the battle of al-Asab'a on March 23, 1913. Plagued by a lack of supplies and arms, the resistance was defeated and the Italian army occupied the Jabal.[60] Consequently, leaders of the resistance such as al-Baruni, Shaykh Suf al-Mahmudi, and Shaykh Harb al-Naili went into exile, and 3,000 fighters escaped to Tunisia and turned their arms over to the French. Another group of 600 fighters withdrew into Fezzan; they were mainly from the Gibla and were led by Shaykh Muhammad B. Abdallah al-Busayfi, Salim 'Abd al-Nabi al-Zintani, and the Sanusi Shaykh Muhammad al-Sunni, head of the Mizdah Zawiya in the Jabal.[61]

The Italian army began to advance into Fezzan after it took over Syrte. Colonel Miani led a force advised by two Tripolitanian notables, 'Umar al-Muntasir and 'Abd al-Nabi Bel Khayre. This force reached Wadi al-Shatti, where it was faced with the al-Busayfi and 200 fighters. The resistance was overwhelmed by the number and arms of the Italians. Shaykh al-Busayfi was killed at the Battle of Mahrugah on December 24, 1913.[62] Miani advanced into Fezzan until he occupied Ghat on August 12, 1914, at which time colonial officials in Tripoli completed the occupation of Tripolitania and Fezzan.[63]

The Italian occupation did not last very long, however. A rebellion began on September 28, 1914, in Fezzan and the Jabal and culminated in an Italian defeat in the battle of Gardabiyya on April 28–29, 1915. Obviously, something had gone wrong with the Italian policy and military strategy. Colonel Miani had made a fatal mistake; specifically, he had advanced into Fezzan and left his garrisons vulnerable to the many mobile tribes of the Fezzan and the Gibla, whose territory ranged from Syrtica to the Haruj mountains. Tribal bands led by Salim 'Abd al-Nabi in Fezzan, and by Awlad Busaif and Awlad Sulayman in Syrtica, began to apply hit-and-run tactics, but the first major victory of the tribal resistance occurred in Fezzan.[64]

On November 27, 1914, a 280-man guerrilla group that had survived the battle of al-Shab, led by Salim B. 'Abd al-Nabi al-Zintani, surprised the Italian garrison of al-Gahara near Sabha, killing most of the troops and capturing arms, ammunition, and food.[65] The success of the attack was due to the defection of a Libyan soldier from the Italian army, who provided information to the guerrillas. Also, the cooperation between the tribesmen of the Gibla (Wadi al-Shatti, Tuareg, and the Sanusi Shaykhs) led to the liberation of Fezzan by the end of the year.[66]

Italian garrisons fell to the guerrillas one after the other: in Murzaq on December 6 and Ghat on December 23. Colonel Miani and his troops fled to Syrtica and reached Misurata on December 25, 1914. Italian troops in Ghat and Ghadamis fled to the protection of the French in Algeria and Tunisia. By the end of the year, Fezzan was liberated and the revolt in Fezzan had spread to the Jabal and Syrtica.[67]

A similar revolt occured on al-Jabal al-Gharbi, when Khalifa B. 'Askar marched against an Italian army caravan near Kabaw and took most of its supplies. This victory ushered in another uprising against the Italians in the Jabal. Here peasants and tribesmen of the Jabal became active in the uprising. The Italians withdrew their troops from Sinawin and Ghadamis on December 1, 1914. On January 15, 1915, the garrison of Waddan fell to the resistance, and by the end of February, the region of Jufra was also liberated.

Colonel Miani tried hastily to halt the revolt in Fezzan and the Jabal. He offered money and arms to many notables who were under Italian control in Tripolitania. But this policy led to disaster for the Italians and ended his military career. Miani sent two armies to reoccupy Ghadamis and Fezzan, but these were defeated. Thus, he focused on Syrtica in order to crush the most active pocket of resistance.

Miani recruited around 3,000 Tripolitanians through their notables by giving them money and arms. Again, the notables' and the chiefs' major concerns were their own interests, and perhaps they did count on the Italians having different agenda from the

Ottomans. These notables agreed to side with Miani, but many were planning to defect to the victorious side. Ramadan al-Suwayhli of Misurata, for example, ordered his followers to shoot the Italian soldiers in their backs during a battle. Defection aided the 2,000 bands of the resistance movement led by Ahmad Saif al-Nasir and Safi al-Din al-Sanusi. The Italian army was almost eliminated at the battle of Gardabiyya on April 19, 1915.[68]

The Italian army lost 500 officers and soldiers as well as 232 Libyan collaborators. Misurata's opportunistic notable Ramadan al-Suwayhli took most of the battle's spoils, putting him at odds with the Sanusi. The loot included over 5,000 rifles, several million rounds of ammunition, machine guns, 11 pieces of artillery, money, and food supplies.[69]

The victory of the resistance in the al-Gardabiyya battle resulted in part from al-Suwayhli's defection, but it ought chiefly to be attributed to the unity of the resistance in Fezzan, Cyrenaica, and Tripolitania. This unity was, however, exceptional since each region normally organized its local forces independently.

The Italian defeat at Gardabiyya had very serious consequences for the political balance in the hinterland. It ended Colonel Miani's military career. But this was not to take place without revenge when the outraged and desperate Miani ordered 700 Libyan civilians hanged, and 11,300 more in Italy exiled. But the atrocities did not slow the momentum of the revolt. Relentless attacks against Italian troops resulted in 1916 in the constriction of the sovereignty of the colonial state to the cities of Tripoli and Khums. Fezzan was already liberated and in Cyrenaica the Italian army was blocked by Sanusi-organized tribes inside the towns of Benghazi and Darna.[70]

Anticolonial resistance was organized by Ottoman officers and supported by Ottoman aid until 1912, but up until 1915 the Ottoman presence was limited to a few officers, and local leaders relied on their own autonomous organizations to fight the Italians. In 1915, when the Ottoman empire entered World War I on the side of Germany, it renewed its ties with the Libyan resistance through German submarines at the port of Gasar Hamad near Misurata. Ottoman aid was also smuggled overland across Egyptian and Tunisian borders. The local resistance movement received military advisors, arms, and money in this manner between 1915 and 1918.

Exiled leaders of Libya and some Arab volunteers remained active and several were ready to return to the country. As the Ottoman policy required more involvement from the exiles in the resistance, many of these leaders joined up. The Ottoman policy was to engage the Libyan resistance to fight the British in Egypt as well as the Italians. Al-Baruni returned from exile in Istanbul, Shaykh Suf al-Mahmadi from Syria. They joined with 'Abd al-Rahman 'Azzam, an Egyptian Arab nationalist, and Nuri Pasha (brother of Anwar Pasha, by then a defense minister in the Young Turk government) in Cyrenaica.

The Ottoman policy sought to persuade Sayyid Ahmad al-Sharif to use Sanusi influence in Cyrenaica, Chad, and the western desert of Egypt against the British. Sayyid Ahmad was reluctant to oblige. He knew that most of his supplies came mainly through Egyptian borders and thus saw no urgency to fight the British in Egypt.[71] Pressured by his Ottoman allies, Sayyid Ahmad attacked in late 1915. At the beginning, the Sanusis advanced inside the desert, but finally the superior 60,000-man British army defeated their forces of 20,000.[72] Sayyid Ahmad's army was forced out of Egypt, and was left nearly starved in Syrtica.

The Sanusi-British war had far-reaching consequences for the resistance in Cyrenaica and Tripolitania. Sayyid Ahmad al-Sharif was opposed by his cousin Idris al-Mahdi, who blamed him for the disastrous war against the British.[73] In the 1916 peace talks, the British insisted that Idris al-Sanusi, the new leader of the Sanusiyya, oust Sayyid Ahmad al-Sharif and all Ottoman officers from Cyrenaica, Idris al-Sanusi having made clear to the British his intention to have good relations with them. The British had been aware of Idris's willingness to ally with them since 1913, when they had contacted him in Cairo on his way to Arabia.[74] Apparently, Idris al-Sanusi wanted to preserve the order's influence, which had been weakened by military defeats against the French in Chad in 1902 and the British in 1916. Thus, the elimination of the militant pan-Islamic Ahmad al-Sharif paved the way for a Sanusi-British alliance.[75]

The British feared that a hostile state in Cyrenaica could pose a potential threat to their control of Egypt. The Sanusiyya had followers not only in Cyrenaica, but in western Egypt and the rest of the Sahara. Idris agreed to get rid of Nuri; 'Azzam and the rest of the Ottoman officers reacted by banning his cousin Sayyid Ahmad from entering Cyrenaica.[76] The British then became Idris's patrons. They arranged for truce with the Italians at the Sanusi-Italian treaties of al-Zuwaytina in 1916, 'Akrama in 1917 and al-Rajma in 1920.

Those responsible for the failed attack on Egypt were asked to leave Cyrenaica. Nuri, 'Azzam, al-Baruni, and the rest of the Ottoman officers went to Misurata, where they found in al-

Suwayhli an ambitious and determined anti-Italian leader. T helped him organize his army and administration.[77] Sayyid Ahm and his starving army were banned from reentering Cyrenaica. He left Libya to go into exile, first in Istanbul from 1918 to 1923. After Ataturk declared his secular republic in Turkey, Sayyid Ahmad left for Arabia, where he lived until his death in 1933.[78] Sayyid Ahmad continued to have contact with his followers between 1924 and 1933. His newly discovered personal papers indicate that he did not change his anticolonial ideology and kept in touch with his followers through pilgrims from Cyrenaica to Arabia.[79]

Between 1916 and 1922, Italian colonial policy, unable to crush the resistance, shifted its course to make peace with the Sanusi, who had become stronger as a result of their alliance with resistance fighters. The Sanusi, under the leadership of Idris, who allied with the British, signed three major agreements with the Italian government. In an April 1916 meeting with the Italians and British, arranged by the British, a Sanusi delegation signed the Agreement of al-Zuwaytina. This treaty was later ratified in another agreement made on April 17, 1917, at 'Akrama. According to these two documents, the Italians and the Sanusis agreed to cease hostilities, to recognize Italian sovereignty along the coast and Sanusi sovereignty in the hinterland, to allow free trade, to remove "troublemakers" from Cyrenaica (like Ahmad al-Sharif and the Ottoman officers), to exempt Sanusi land and *zawiya* from taxes, and to grant the Sanusi family and the senior Ikhman monthly salaries from the Italian government in exchange for a Sanusi agreement to disarm and disband their tribes. They also agreed to meet in the future to reevaluate the results of their compacts.[80]

Idris al-Sanusi could not convince the tribes and middle-level commanders to give up their arms. Shaykh 'Umar al-Mukhtar, a senior Sanusi Shaykh, led the opposition to these agreements. The leaders of the opposition were veterans of the anticolonial wars with the French in Chad and the British in Egypt. Many of them believed in Sayyid Ahmad al-Sharif's pan-Islamic anticolonial ideology and came from lower-status Murabtin tribal backgrounds. These commanders, like 'Umar al-Mukhtar and his deputies Yusuf Bu-Rahil and al-Fadil Bu'umar, all from Murabtin tribal backgrounds, led the guerrilla war against the fascist army between 1922 and 1932.

In Tripolitania, Ottoman and German aid came with Nuri, 'Azzam, and al-Baruni, who were expelled from Cyrenaica after 1916. Between 1916 and 1918, Ottoman arms and money that came through the port of Gasar-Hamad near Misurata strengthened the power of Tripolitanian notables and chiefs, particularly the government of al-Suwayhli in Misurata and Shaykh Suf al-Mahmudi in western Tripolitania. Both of these leaders used Ottoman arms and money not just to fight the Italians but also to reward their allies and expand their influence and authority over local rivals.

Al-Suwayhli became stronger than other notables when he took most of the Gardabiyya spoils and hosted Nuri, ʻAzzam and other Ottoman officials. He collected taxes, ran a military school, and had his own army, aided by Nuri and ʻAzzam. Ramadan's ambition went beyond Misurata's; his aspiration to influence over most of eastern Tripolitania brought him into conflict with neighboring notables, especially of the Tarhuna in 1916 and the Warfalla in 1920.[81]

In 1915, Shaykh Suf al-Mahmudi returned to Tripolitania as Ottoman vice governor and formed another state in western Tripolitania. He was concerned about his own tribe. He favored his own kinsmen and tribal allies, which forced disgruntled notables (like Sultan B. Shaʻban of the town of Zuwara and Shaykh Harab al-Naili, Chief of the Nuwail) to join with the Italians. In turn, Sultan B. Shaʻban aided the Italian army in its occupation of Zuwara in 1917; after this he was appointed a *qaimmaqam* of the town.[82] These two notables were interested in their own interests regardless of any difference between the Italians and the Ottomans.

The coming of ʻAzzam and al-Baruni to Tripolitania slowed down internotable conflict in 1916. Al-Baruni reconciled Tarhuna with Misurata by declaring the disputed town of Misallata a neutral zone. Up until that time, no major defection occurred, aside from that of the Nuwail and B. Shaʻban in the town of Zuwara. The call for national unity worked especially well, with Ottoman and German aid and arms continuing to arrive in Tripolitania until 1918. Once again, the Ottoman empire was defeated and forced to withdraw from Libya. Tripolitanian leaders knew the threat of Italian colonial policy and, watching the Sanusi in Cyrenaica securing political autonomy, decided to form an all-Tripolitanian government, which delayed the occupation of Tripolitania until 1923.

The Tripolitanian Republic, 1918–1920

Al-Baruni called for an all-Tripolitania conference, which was attended by most of the notables and chiefs in the region. After deliberation, the conference agreed on November 16, 1918 the first republic in the Middle East, with two capitals, A and Gharyan;[83] it would reflect the balance of po Tripolitania.[84] The conference elected a collective council of the four most prominent notables, al-Suwayhli, 'Abd al-Nabi Bel Khayre, al-Baruni, and Ahmad al-Marriyad of Tarhuna; another 24 notables and chiefs were elected to the parliament. A judicial and religious council was formed made up of leading *'ulama*; a police force and an army were also appointed. The leaders of the Republic sent letters to the Italian, British, French, and American governments asking for recognition. But the Italians had already secured their claim to Libya through treaties with England and France and their allies in World War I. The Republic was not recognized by none.

The leaders of the Republic insisted that peace with the Italian government required meeting a number of conditions: a peace based on the status quo; the restriction of Italian warships and airplanes to areas under Italian occupation; the cessation of propaganda inside the interior; and the granting of full authority to the Republic inside its territory. Italian colonial officials refused these demands, yet for reasons still unclear there was some disagreement between colonial military leadership and the authorities in Rome. The Italian delegation met again with a delegation from the Republic and reached an agreement at Khalat al-Zaytunah on April 18, 1919. A peace treaty was signed, known as the *al-Qanun al-Asasi*, or fundamental law, of Swani B. Yadim.[85]

The fundamental law of 1919 was an achievement for the leaders of the Republic. The Italians agreed to grant native Tripolitanians full citizenship and allow them representation in the government in Tripoli, to elect a parliament, and to respect local customs and traditions. The Republic's officials immediately nominated eight notables to represent them in Tripoli. This achievement was remarkable compared to the achievements of other anticolonial movements in the Middle East and Africa around this time. The formation of a unified republic was a major force in effecting the agreement.

The Tripolitanian Republic, however, lacked powerful allies like the Sanusi order's British allies. In the Period of Accords (1916–1920), the British pressured the Italians to reach a compromise involving a dual Sanusi-Italian rule over Cyrenaica. In 1920 a parliament was elected in Cyrenaica with a Sanusi majority; it met only three times. Italian officials realized the Tripolitanian Republic lacked a strong ally and that it was plagued by divisions its leaders. Because of this awareness, the colonial delegation insisted in their negotiations with the Republic that the parliament have only consultative authority.[86] This colonial divide-and-rule manipulation opened a rift between the two sides and a de facto truce continued between the two sovereignties designating Italian sovereignty along the coast and Republican sovereignty over the hinterland. This situation lasted until 1920.[87]

Colonial policy makers were aware of the fragility of the Republican coalition, which was due to the conflicting interests of its notables and chiefs, and began to exploit these weaknesses. They sent arms and money to the notables who were on the side of the Republic. This policy paid off, as interfactional conflicts disrupted the unity of the Tripolitanian resistance, allowing the Italian army to reoccupy Tripolitania in 1922.

Factionalism and the End of the Resistance in Tripolitania, 1920–1922

Factionalism between Tripolitanian notables and chiefs must be reinterpreted not merely as personal rivalry, as many nationalist Libyan historians such as al-Zawi, Fushayka, and al-Gashshat have argued, but as the result of specific structural socioeconomic forces. Ottoman state reforms and British and Italian finance capital integrated the coast and parts of Tripolitania's hinterland under the system of capitalist relations. At the same time, Ottoman arms and money strengthened local notables and chiefs. Eventually, notables competed over land and bureaucratic positions, and chiefs adjusted to these forces through reviving tribal alliances vis-à-vis the Italians and their local rivals. For these reasons, Tripolitania's transitional economy did not allow a single unified leadership after the destruction of the Ottoman state in 1912.

Notables and tribal chiefs allied to fight the Italians from 1911 until 1915. After 1915 many political differences began to emerge between them as a result of competition over land, tax collecting, and Ottoman aid. Some notables received more aid and arms, like the Suwayhli, who used these resources to expand at the expense of rival notables. The notables' and chiefs' reactions to colonialism and the causes of interfactionalism are significant in that they offer partial reasons for the end of Libyan resistance in this period. The two civil wars between the Warfalla and the Misurata tribes in eastern Tripolitania and the civil war in the Jabal in 1920 are especially important in this context.

Between 1911 and 1916 only urban merchants and notables tied to the Bank of Rome or dissatisfied with the Young Turk government in Istanbul (1908–1918) collaborated with the Italians. The remaining urban notables joined the hinterland resistance and organized local states to mobilize the population. In 1918, when Ottoman officers left Libya, Tripolitanian urban and rural leaders formed their own republic. Here, urban notables such as Farhat al-Zawi, Ali Tantush, and Ramadan al-Suwayhli joined the notables of the hinterland—al-Baruni Bel Kayre, al-Mariyyad, and the Ka'bar brothers. This cooperation resulted from the strong economic and political ties between the hinterland and urban towns. The growth of Tripoli City as a market enhanced by the incorporation of the notables as middlemen-bureaucrats strengthened social and political ties with the urban towns of Tripolitania at the end of the nineteenth century.

The relationship between the ideology of resistance and its reality is a complex one. The memoirs and oral histories of resistance fighters voice two motives for fighting the Italians: *al-Din wa al-watan*, or religion, and nationalism.[88] Tripolitanians and most Libyans viewed the war as a struggle to protect Islam from attack by a Christian power, Italy.[89] Further, various resistance groups stressed nationalism, land, and honor.[90] In action, the meaning of religion and nationalism was conditioned by class and tribal and regional interests.

An urban notable, Shaykh Farhat al-Zawi, merged as one of the main ideologues of the Tripolitanian resistance until his death in Fezzan in 1925. Educated in France, he returned to Libya and was appointed judge and elected to the Ottoman parliament in 1908. In 1912 he was interviewed by the French journalist George Raymond and asked what he would do if the Ottomans decided to leave Libya. Al-Zawi answered, "We shall declare that the Ottoman government has no right in our country and we shall declare the Tripolitanian Republic."[91] Al-Zawi's statement shows the determination of Tripolitanian leaders to resist the Italian army regardless of Ottoman policy. It also demonstrates the limits of Ottoman influence on Tripolitanians, who were willing to accept Ottoman political legitimacy only if it was linked to anticolonial resistance.

Al-Zawi's familiarity with French political life was made clear when Raymond asked him if the war was a holy war. He replied, "A holy war: do not write this phrase in your article, say we are citizens wearing ragged clothes and as bare-footed as the soldiers of the French Revolution, but do not say we are religious fanatics."[92]

Al-Zawi's statements seem to be geared to the sensibilities of the French reader; nevertheless, they voice a specific, materially based interpretation of religion and nationalism. In words and deeds, al-Zawi fought the Italians until he himself was killed in Fezzan in 1925.[93]

The shaykhs of a large tribe such as the Warfalla tribe in eastern Tripolitania interpreted nationalism differently from al-Zawi. In 1915 they wrote a letter to the British consul in Tripoli stating their position in regard to the Italian colonial state:

> We are the notables of the district of Warfalla, still keeping our independence which was given to us by our lord the Sultan. And in case any power attacks us, we are obliged to defend our dear homeland to the last soul. Thus we urge you to inform the Italian government that we are protecting our independence and if Italy decides to attack us, we will be forced to fight her.[94]

Here nationalism or the notion of homeland is interpreted as the Warfalla tribal homeland. And the shaykhs of this tribe were willing to fight the Italians only if they invaded their homeland, and not necessarily that of other tribes or towns. Indeed, the Warfalla remained neutral under Bel Khayre's leadership during the war against the Italian army until they reached the Warfalla. Only then did they fight the Italians. Yet in other cases, tribes not attacked by the Italians allied with those who were answering the call of the Tripolitanian Republic to resist the Italian invasion.

Different tribes from the Warfalla such as the Awlad Busaif, Tuareg, and Awlad Sulayman came from Fezzan to fight for *jihad* as early as 1912.[95] However, many of these tribes and peasants belonged to certain tribal confederations and traded with coastal peasants and thus had socioeconomic interests to defend. In short, Islam and nationalism were interpreted variously according to the socioeconomic interests of the urban classes and tribes in the Gibla and Syrtica. Such diverse backgrounds were integral to factionalism in Tripolitania. The Misurata-Warfalla conflict in eastern Tripolitania and the devastating civil war in the Jabal are cases in point.

As explained earlier, Ramadan al-Suwayhli, the head of the town of Misurata, emerged as an influential notable in eastern Tripolitania as a result of the huge tribute he collected from the Italian army at the battle of Gardabiyya. In 1915 he founded his own government in the coastal town of Misurata. Also, he received most of the Ottoman and German aid between 1915–1920. The defeat of the Ottoman-Sanusi campaign against the British in Egypt led to the departure of all Ottoman officers from Cyrenaica as stipulated by the British in their negotiations with Idris al-Sanusi. Nuri, 'Azzam, and the rest of the Ottoman officers discovered in Ramadan al-Suwayhli their best ally, since both sides were interested in fighting the Italians. The Ottomans were at war with Italy and Ramadan's role in the Italian defeat in 1915 was decisive.

Ramadan al-Suwayhli's ambition increased as money, expertise and arms came to him via German submarines at the port of Gasar Hamad near Misurata. His army grew and he began to extend his control to his neighbors in order to collect more taxes and increase his force. In 1918 he claimed the town of Misallata, which belonged to the government of Tarhuna. A war was waged between the two towns, but the coming of al-Baruni to Tripolitania led to a compromise, making Misallata a neutral town in 1916.[96]

Ramadan had had differences with the Sanusi since 1915 over dividing the spoils of the Gardabiyya, which he had appropriated. Following that dispute he did not tolerate the Sanusi presence, fearing the Sanusi might turn people against him. Thus, in 1916 Ramadan arrested three Sanusi shaykhs, accused them of plotting against him and had them executed in Misurata.[97] These Sanusi shaykhs were guests of Ramadan's neighboring chiefs from the Tarhuna and Warfalla tribes.[98]

Ramadan did not like the attitude of 'Abd al-Nabi Bel Khayre, the chief of the Warfalla, who hosted these Sanusi shaykhs, members of the Muntasir clan, his old rival clan in Misurata. As mentioned before, Ramadan killed Abu al-Qasim al Muntasir in 1910, but he was cleared by the Young Turk court in Tripoli. The Muntasirs did not forget their vendetta. 'Abd al-Qadir al-Muntasir, brother of Abu al-Qasim, began to attack Misurata's caravans and herds from a Warfalla camp in 1920.[99] Ramadan began to collect taxes from around Warfalla, which angered 'Abd al-Nabi, who saw this move as a threat to his influence. British reports mention that the Italian authorities in Tripoli shipped arms to 'Abd al-Nabi, who collaborated with them in their campaign to occupy Fezzan in 1913–1914.[100] It seems that 'Abd al-Nabi encouraged the Muntasirs and the Sanusi to counter Ramadan's ambition and expansion. Finally, on August 20, 1920, Ramadan organized a force of 2,000 men and planned a surprise attack on the Warfalla. Ramadan took a shortcut but made the fatal mistake of not securing water resources. By the afternoon, many of Ramadan's men collapsed in the hellish summer heat, which led to their defeat and his own death,[101] thereby removing one of the Italians' most ardent enemies. Further, 'Abd al-Nabi was blamed for Ramadan's death, and because of this became isolated from the resistance leaders. Worse than the Misurata-Warfalla war was the civil war between the tribes and peasants of the Jabal from 1920 to 1922.

Because of the deaths of many key actors in the Jabal civil war and the nationalist belief after independence that it should be condemned as a shameful affair—it led to the collaboration of defeated peasants and tribes with the Italian colonial state and the reoccupation of Tripolitania—the full story of the war has not yet been told. Shaykh Tahir al-Zawi, the major historian of that period, refused to elaborate on the war and bitterly lamented its disastrous outcome for the anticolonial resistance.[102] Recently, Muhammad Said al-Gashshat has published important letters and documents of the notables of the Jabal al-Gharbi. These new documents provide information on this ambiguous phase of Libyan history.[103] However, there is still room for further research on this subject when more data becomes available.

In 1911 the population of the Jabal was divided into peasants and tribal communities. Most of the peasants followed the Khariji Ibadi faith; because of long intertribal wars and the threat from the central state in Tripoli, they lived in fortresslike villages in the Jabal. The rest of the population was composed of seminomadic tribes such as the Rijban, Zintan, Asab'a, Haraba, Mushashiyya, Awlad Busaif, Riyyana, and the Mahamid.[104]

The Jabal's peasants and tribes retained their autonomy from the central state, partly because of their distance from Tripoli. They exchanged and traded with each other and whenever there was a tribal invasion or a war against the state, political alliances, or *sufuf*, emerged. Precolonial Ottoman policy, unable to generate enough resources to wage a military campaign against the armed population of the Jabal, often preyed on tribal and peasant divisiveness either by granting selective tax exemptions, as in the case of the Mahamid, or aiding some tribes militarily, as in the case of the Zintan.

By 1911 most of the Ibadi peasants and tribes, the Mashashiyya, the Awlad Busaif, and some of the Riyyana tribes belonged to one *suff*, which battled the Rijban, the Zintan, and the Mahamid. The Mahamid had been the dominant tribe in Tripolitania since the fourteenth century; they became tax exempt during the reign of Yusuf Qaramanli in the nineteenth century. The Awlad Busaif and the Mashashiyya had a number of disputes with the Zintan over tribal land in 1870 and 1910.[105] The Ottoman state supported the Zintan, which alienated the Mashashiyya and the Awlad Busaif and brought them closer to the Berbers. Yet it would be a mistake to read the history of the Jabal as consisting of ever-feuding tribes and peasants. In times of state over-taxation or military conquest, as in the period between 1835–1858, most of the population united against the Ottoman government. In 1835 the Jabal tribes and peasants supported the rebellion of Ghuma al-Mahmudi, fearing taxation and the loss of political autonomy. Again, after the Italian conquest in 1911, they allied to fight an outside enemy. Later, in 1915 and 1920, the people of the Jabal waged civil wars.

The causes of the civil war in the Jabal were mainly the notables' competition for political offices in the Tripolitanian Republic, aided by the Italians who poured more fuel on the fire through money, alms, and promises to rival notables on both sides. For example, in 1916, Shaykh Muhammad Suf al-Mahmudi, who founded a state in western Tripolitania aided by Ottoman money, favored his own tribe. He appointed his kinsmen and friends as officials over other tribes—for example, the Nuwail and Zuwara.[106] These appointments alienated old prominent notables who were contacted by the Italians. Factionalism among notables and chiefs impelled them in different directions. Those who had lost to their rivals in local government easily joined the Italians. These collaborators believed they could keep their autonomy under colonialism.

In 1915, Sasi Khazm, the notable of Yfrin, declared his loyalty to the Italians but was defeated and killed by members of the resistance. His followers, under the leadership of Yusuf Kharbish, fled to the coast. In the town of Zuwara, Sultan B. Sha'ban, another disgruntled notable, aided the Italian army in its occupation of Zuwara. Finally, disgruntled Shaykh Harb al-Naili of the Nuwail tribe, became angry at Shaykh Suf when he appointed his own cousin as administrator of the Nuwail Tribe. Shaykh Harb killed Shaykh Suf's cousin and then joined the Italians.[107] In short, by 1917 there were already Libyan recruits (known as the Banda) fighting for the Italians. When the Tripolitanian Republic and the colonial state made peace in 1919, the Italian delegation insisted that refugees return to their homes in the Jabal. They did, but armed with Italian guns.[108] Yet many local leaders, who did not know the Italians' intentions, discovered that cooperation was a tactic to control the population and not to give them autonomy. Italian fascists followed a scorched-earth policy as one of their main strategies to defeat the resistance in 1921.

The conflict resumed when Shaykh Mahammad Fkayni, the chief of the Rijban, bypassed a prominent Ibadi notable active in the resistance, Khalifa B. 'Askar, in favor of a friend of Fkayni named Abu al-Ahbas from the tribe of Haraba, who had no leadership qualifications except for his friendship with Shaykh Fkayni. When, for uncertain reasons, Abu al-Ahbas took the animals of an Ibadi man, his Ibadi kin rallied and took Abu al-Ahbas's animals in return. Abu al-Ahbas rode his horse without a proper saddle, a symbol of disgrace, and went to his friend Shaykh Fkayni; Shaykh Fkayni sent a force to attack Khalifa B. 'Askar at Nalut. From this point on, the war spread and engulfed most of the population of the Jabal. First the Zintan and the Mahamid, and then the Asab'a tribes, joined their allies, the Rijban, and the population of Nalut and Fassatu rallied the Mashashiyya, the Awlad Busaif and some of the Riyyana.[109]

First, Khalifa B. 'Askar led the Ibadi tribes and peasants of Yefran and Jadu and their allies to a victory over the Rijban and the Zintan, killing the son of Shaykh Fkayni, Hasan, and sacking the Rijban town of Tardiyya on September 23, 1920. But the Rijban, Zintan, and the Mahamid returned and defeated the B. 'Askar and their allies in the battle of Siyah. Fassatu was burned, and B. 'Askar and al-Baruni fled to the coast with their followers, taking refuge in the town of Zuwara.[110]

At the time, even the leading notables of the anticolonial resistance, such as B.'Askar and al-Baruni, became involved in the conflict. Al-Baruni convinced B. 'Askar to cooperate with the Italians through the head of the Italian-Libyan bands, Yusuf Kharbish. Yet General Rodolfo Graziani did not forgive B. 'Askar for his role in the rebellion of 1914 against the Italian garrisons in the Jabal. He tricked B. 'Askar by promising him a pardon, later arresting him and then ordering his execution. Thus, Tripolitania lost another militant anticolonial leader.[111]

The Conference at Gharyan, November 1920

The deaths of Ramadan and B. 'Askar and the war in the Jabal alarmed the other notables and leaders, who urgently called for a conference. The Tripolitanian leaders tried to regroup, to reconcile the Rijban and the Ibadi and think of a new strategy. They sent invitations to most notables and chiefs and met in Gharyan in November 1920, but 'Abd al-Nabi Bel Khayre and Sulayman al-

Baruni refused to attend. Shaykh Ahmad al-Mariyyad was the only member of the four leaders of the Republic who attended. 'Azzam and other notables also came to Gharyan.[112]

After deliberation, the conference elected a committee of 21 members headed by al-Mariyyad and advised by 'Azzam. The Association of Central Reform became a new government, replacing the Republic's previous executive council.[113] The conference called for the formation of an all-Libyan government led by an elected Muslim leader according to a constitution consented to by the Libyan people. The conference sent a delegation to Italy to inform the Italian government of its decisions. The colonial authority in Tripoli formed its own Libyan delegation, made up of collaborating notables, and sent them to Rome.[114] Because of this, the Gharyan delegation failed to meet with any Italian official aside from those in the socialist party.[115] After six months, its members returned to Gharyan, except for Khalid al-Gargani, who went to the USSR, where he attended the Muslim revolutionary conference in 1921.[116]

The leaders of the conference of Gharyan, unable to build a strong front, turned to Idris al-Sanusi, who had already been recognized by the Italian government as ruler of interior Cyrenaica in 1920. In January 1922 a delegation arrived in Syrte to meet with Idris. Idris found himself in a dilemma: if he accepted the delegation's terms, he would anger the Italians, and if he did not, he would anger the Tripolitanians. Shrewdly, he accepted the *Bay'a*, a Muslim term for consent, and left Cyrenaica for exile in Egypt.[117] When, on January 26, 1922, another delegation came to Syrte to arrange a Tripolitanian-Cyrenaican front, the Italian army occupied Misurata.[118] After taking over in Rome, the fascists decided to abrogate all treaties with the local leadership and conquer Libya by force. Thus, the *politica dei Capi* ended when the new governor Volpi stated, "our policy is not with the notables, not against the notables, but without them."[119]

The fascist campaign to occupy Tripolitania was aided by many refugees from the Jabal civil war who were eager to return to their homes in the Jabal. They fought with Italian armies, but the resistance collapsed, and by 1923 Tripolitania was reoccupied by the Italians. Some leaders surrendered to the Italian army but General Graziani, who had become the chief strategist of military operations, executed Hadi Ka'bar, Ali Tantush, 'Abaida al-Mahjubi, and Ali al-Shanta. The rest of the leaders of the conference of Gharyan were either killed later, like Farhat al-Zawi, or went into exile in Egypt, Tunisia, and Turkey, like Ahmad al-Mariyyad, 'Abd al-Hadi al-Muntasir (no relation to the other Muntasirs), Bashir al-Sa'dawi, and Mukhtar Ka'bar.[120]

Tribes that had resisted, such as the Zintan, Mashashiyya, Warfalla, and the Awlad Busaif joined the Awlad Sulayman in Fezzan. 'Abd al-Jalil Saif al-Nasir and 'Abd al-Nabi Bel Khayre allied against Khalifa al-Zawi, who ruled western Fezzan from 1918 to 1926. Khalifa al-Zawi relied on the Awlad Sulayman's rival tribes, mainly on the Magarha and the Riyyah, defeating Sanusi forces and establishing a government in Murzaq.[121] When the Italians occupied Tripolitania, 'Abd al-Jalil and 'Abd al-Nabi, both descended from the nineteenth-century tribal *suff*, defeated al-Zawi in 1926 after a six-month siege of Murzaq. Al-Zawi was allowed to leave Fezzan. He went to Tripoli and joined the Italians; in the following year, he advised them in their campaign to occupy Fezzan.[122]

From 1926 to 1930 the Awlad Sulayman and their allies led a brilliant guerrilla war against the Italians, pursuing hit-and-run tactics; this resistance delayed the Italian advance until 1930. But the use of airplanes and poisonous gas gave the Italians superior power over the tribes. In 1928, Italian planes bombed Wawu and Kufra.[123] 'Abd al-Jalil Saif al-Nasir and his brothers went into exile in Chad and Egypt, Salim B. 'Abd al-Nabi into Tunisia; 'Abd al-Nabi died of thirst in the Algerian desert in 1932, and his body was never recovered.[124] By 1930, Fezzan was occupied again by the Italians; only Cyrenaica still managed to resist until 1932.

The cohesion of the Cyrenaican tribes resulted from seventy years of education and mobilization by Sanusi leaders. The Sanusiyya created a state based on trans-Sahara trade and anticolonial, pan-Islamic ideology. This unity allowed Cyrenaican tribes to resist the Italians for 20 years; only after 1932 did the Italians penetrate into the hinterland of Cyrenaica.

Further, when the Italian fascist Party took power in Italy, they dismissed the "liberal" Italian policy, the *politica di Capi*, as a failure.[125] The fascist government replaced it with military force to clear and "pacify" the natives for what Mussolini called the "Second Roman Empire." The task of pacification was given to the architect of the reoccupation of Tripolitania and Fezzan, the brutal General Rodolfo Graziani.[126]

The shift in colonial policy reflected changes that had taken place in Italy when the fascists took power in 1922. The "liberal" colonial policy pursued the occupation of Libya as a means to avoid land reform in southern Italy. It was a political solution to the problems of continuing the Italian state, which existed in part because the bourgeoisie of the north controlled the state at the expense of the southern landlords. A compromise was made: the northern bourgeoisie continued to control the Italian state, while the landlords of the south were promised that no land reform would be exercised there.

From 1911 to 1922 Rome's "liberal" colonial policy encouraged collaboration with local leaders, as in the case of the French in Tunisia or the British in Nigeria. This colonial policy attempted to Italianize Libyan natives. Libyan Muslim students had to follow a course of study according to the Italian curriculum, which stressed Italian history, culture, and language. The Italian language was the main language in educational institutions.

In 1922 the fascists decided to abandon what they named a "weak" liberal policy in the colonies. They pursued a supremacist colonial policy, like the South African apartheid policy of today. Fascist ideology stressed hierarchy and force—specifically, that Italians are a superior race and because of their racial superiority have a duty to colonize the inferior Africans. Mussolini planned to settle between 10 and 15 million Italians in East and North Africa.

This new policy meant the forced subjugation of the natives. The fascists denied the natives national or individual rights—rights that had been accepted as such by the liberal government prior to 1922. Their racial policy was exemplified in educational policies. Instead of trying to Italianize the natives, for example, the fascists wanted to keep pure Italian culture away from the natives. Arabic was the language for education and Italian was only optional. The natives were offered education only up to the sixth grade; beyond this time, they were used a laborers.

The fascists also pursued a brutal policy unmatched in the colonial history of Africa against native resistance fighters. They recruited civilians en masse, locked the whole of Cyrenaica's tribes in concentration camps, and destroyed tribal herds, causing the starvation of thousands of people. Thus, it is not a gross error to compare German fascism with the "benign" Italian type. The only difference between them was that the Italian holocaust did not occur in Europe but in the colonies, especially in Libya.[127]

General Rodolfo Graziani, who was given the task of crushing native resistance, quickly discovered that this task was difficult to accomplish. He faced a well-organized, mobilized Cyrenaican resistance, the result of a half-century of Sanusi education and socioeconomic organization. The Sanusi had managed to integrate different tribes and ethnic groups in anticolonial solidarity through pan-Islamic ideology. After all, the founder of the order, the Grand

Sanusi, had long been aware of European intentions; his son, al-Mahdi, and after that his nephew, Ahmad al-Sharif, fought the French in 1899–1913 and the British in 1915–1916. Sayyid Ahmad al-Sharif's declaration of *jihad* in 1912 shows that the anticolonial spirit was deep and strong.[128] On September 12, 1931, the trial of the legendary leader of the Cyrenaican resistance, 'Umar al-Mukhtar, illustrates the strength of anticolonial sentiments. When al-Mukhtar was 73 years old, he was questioned by General Graziani: "Why did you fight us?" Al-Mukhtar replied, "For my homeland and religion." Graziani then asked, "Did you really think you could win this war?" Al-Mukhtar answered: "War is a duty for us and victory comes from God."[129]

Clearly, al-Mukhtar's actions prove that the strong belief in religion and nationalism were the major motivating forces of the Cyrenaican resistance. He refused Italian money, Idris's compromise with the Italians, and even exile, which was the option other active guerrillas took in the 1920s. Although al-Mukhtar's movement was centered in the region of Cyrenaica, by "homeland" he meant Libya in general and Cyrenaica in particular.[130] His militant, anticolonial ideology was rooted in a specific socioeconomic organization that enabled the resistance to continue for 10 years in the face of a brutal, modern, fascist army.

'Umar al-Mukhtar and the Cyrenaican Resistance, 1923–1932

In 1923 the Italian fascists abrogated all agreements with the Sanusi and began their military operation by occupying the town of Ijdabiyya, the capital of the Sanusi state. A split occurred among the Sanusi elite between advocates of diplomacy, such as Idris al-Sanusi, his brother al-Rida, and the notables of Benghazi on the one hand, and advocates of resistance, such as 'Umar al-Mukhtar as the only means of protecting Cyrenaica's independence on the other. Al-Mukhtar and the rest of Sayyid Ahmad al-Sharif's disciples and commanders led by al-Mukhtar rejected Idris's agreements with the Italians and refused to surrender their arms between 1916 and 1920.[131]

When the Italian fascists nullified these agreements and declared war, the position of al-Mukhtar proved to be correct for many tribesmen. Idris al-Sanusi fled into exile on December 21, 1922; other Sanusi princes gradually made peace with the Italians.

Brutal fascist tactics such as execution, the burning of harvests, and the confiscation of herds further motivated many tribesmen to fight. In 1930 the Norwegian traveler Knud Holmboe visited Cyrenaica and encountered some of al-Mukhtar's men. He summed up the situation: "I do not know your country, but just imagine that it was occupied by an entirely different race who treated the inhabitants like animals and shot everybody who resisted, would not you react against them?"[132]

Idris al-Sanusi, before he left Cyrenaica, appointed his brother al-Rida as head of the order and 'Umar al-Mukhtar as its military commander. In 1924, 'Umar al-Mukhtar and his deputy, Yusuf Bu-Rahil, visited Idris in Alexandria to request aid, but Idris informed them there was nothing he could do. Al-Mukhtar and his aides returned to Cyrenaica and wrote a letter to the deposed head of the Sanusiyya, Sayyid Ahmad al-Sharif, reflecting their disappointment with the Sanusi families:

> You left the homeland and stayed in Turkey, and al-Sayyid Idris escaped to Egypt and left us in red hell [*al nar al-Hamra*]. We swear in God's name to make you accountable at the hands of God for your actions. By God, you took it [Cyrenaica] when it was sweet and left it when it became bitter. . . . We tell you that when we could not get help [from Idris] we relied on God and returned to the homeland. We made a pledge not to surrender to the enemy, and defend our lives, religion and homeland to the last drop of our blood.[133]

A social revolution occurred inside Cyrenaica. The ordinary tribal commanders rebelled against the compromising Sanusi elite. A new leadership emerged to represent the majority of tribesmen willing to fight, composed of those from a nonelite social background. 'Umar al-Mukhtar himself came from the Murabtin Minifa tribe. His two deputies, al-Fadil Bu-'Umar and Yusuf Bu-Rahil, were from the Murabtin Masamir tribe. Some commanders came from outside Cyrenaica, such as Gaja Abdallah from Chad and Ibrahim al-Shami from Palestine. There were also commanders from a Sa'adi background such as Hussain al-Juwayfi and 'Abd al-Hamid al-'Abar. The non-Sa'adi leaders rose to power as a result of excelling in education and military skill, an indication of the non-sectarian nature of the Sanusiyya.[134]

As Italian military pressure continued to increase, Sanusi princes began to surrender in order to preserve their privileges, such as their estates and salaries, from the Italian government. Thus, on February 7, 1926, Sayyid Hilal al-Sanusi aided the Italian army in occupying Jaghbub, the important old capital of the Sanusiyya, and Sayyid al-Rida al-Sanusiya made peace with the Italian state after a period of exile in Italy. He made a declaration to Cyrenaica asking its inhabitants to surrender to the "merciful and compassionate General Graziani," and aided the colonial army in their occupation of other important oases, like Jalu and Awjila on November 25, 1928.[135] Sayyid 'Abid al-Sanusi did not participate in the defense of Kufra, fleeing to Egypt in late 1928.[136]

On the side of the resistance, 'Umar al-Mukhtar and his aides showed ample organizational and military skills. In 1924, 'Umar al-Mukhtar founded a unified military council and a number of tribal base camps or *'adwar* [in the singular, *duwr*]. Each tribe volunteered a number of fighters with arms and food. In case they were killed, the same tribe vowed to replace them.[137] Al-Mukhtar appointed al-Fadil Bu-'Umar to head the *duwr* of the Hasa and 'Abaydat tribes, Hussain al-Guwayfi of the Bra'sa and the Drasa *duwr*, Yusuf Bu-Rahil of the 'Abid and the 'Uruffa, and Gaja Abdallah and 'Abdal-Hamid al-'Abar as leaders of the 'Awagir *duwr*. Further, al-Mukhtar coordinated with Salih Lataywish, the chief of the Magharba tribe in eastern Syrtica.[138]

The resistance received supplies from *ushr* taxes on grain and animals and taxes on all caravans that traded with Egypt.[139] It had a well-mobilized population and a network of spies even inside Italian-controlled towns.[140] The active guerrillas numbered 3,000; Cyrenaican tribes owned 20,000 guns, according to General Graziani.[141] From 1924 to 1931 the guerrillas effectively used hit-and-run tactics. Their success was due to their knowledge of the Italian army's movements and the geography of the Green Mountain valleys, caves and trails. In 1931 alone, the guerrillas engaged in 250 attacks on and ambushes of the Italian army.[142]

Colonial Italian officials attempted at first to buy off 'Umar al-Mukhtar. They offered him a good salary and retirement. He replied very clearly, "We have deep faith in our religion and our Prophet's deeds which call for *jihad*."[143] Then General Graziani decided to crush the resistance by any means necessary. Not only did he pursue a scorched-earth policy, but he cut the guerrillas' supplies by first building a 300-kilometer fence stretching along the Libyan-Egyptian borders and then organizing a campaign to occupy Kufra, the capitol of the Sanusi order deep in the desert.[144] Graziani's army included 20 airplanes and 5,000 camels, which aided the occupation of Kufra after fierce resistance by the Zuwayya tribe. Finally, Graziani cut off the guerrillas' supplies in the south by occupying Kufra on February 20, 1931.[145] The resistance weakened, but managed to continue, after which Graziani decided to uproot the whole population and incarcerate them in concentration camps.

Between 85,000 and 100,000 tribesmen with their families and herds were moved to concentration camps stretching from Sulug near Benghazi to the 'Agayla in the desert of Syrtica.[146] By 1933 only 35,000 still survived in these terrible, genocidal camps; the others had died as a result of executions, diseases, and hunger.[147] Prisoners' oral histories and bedouin poetry recorded moving aspects of the genocide. One of the best-known poems is Rajab Bu-Huwaysh al-Manifi's epic, *Dar al-'Agayla,* which captures the suffering and agony of the victims of colonialism:

> Oh I was fine but now I am ill in the 'Agayla Camp
> Jailing our tribe away from our homeland
> I am homesick in this hellish summer
> for "'Akrama 'Adam and Saqaif" [his tribe's homeland]
> and the rainy seasons
> I am ill watching merciless guards cursing and
> slashing our women naked
> Oh I am ill.[148]

Elsewhere in the poem the poet contrasts the happiness and joy of his life before the Italian occupation with the horrors of the concentration camp.

General Graziani eventually won the war by closing the frontiers with Egypt and occupying Kufra, locking most of the tribes in Cyrenaica in guarded camps. He isolated the guerrillas, and severed their ties with their civilian social bases. One of the guerrillas told the traveler Knud Holmboe in January 1930, "We are getting fewer and fewer, our villages are bombed and destroyed, our women are taken away. We can do nothing against the devilish machines of the Italians."[149]

On September 12, 1931, the aged charismatic leader al-Mukhtar was captured. Graziani came quickly from Rome. After a short trial, al-Mukhtar was executed in front of 20,000 Cyrenaican tribesmen and tribeswomen on September 16, 1931. He was 69 years old.[150] Al-Mukhtar's aides tried to resist the fascists, attempting to withdraw into Egypt, but Hamad Bu-Khayralla and Yusuf Bu-Rahil were killed, 'Uthman al-Shami was injured and then captured, and only

'Abd al-Hamid al-'Abar escaped into Egypt, on January 24, 1932.[151] On that day, the colonial governor of Libya, Marshal Badaglio, announced the fascists' complete conquest of Libya after 20 years of local resistance.

CONCLUSION: TOWARD THE RECOVERY OF LIBYA'S CIVIL SOCIETY

In this study I have unearthed the buried social history of Libya between 1830 and 1932, a period filled with many severe challenges which Libyan society attempted to meet: political upheavals, rebellions, colonial conquests, disease, and hunger. And I have specifically traced patterns of social transformation during this period, as well as anticolonial resistance and strategies of survival pursued by local merchants, notables, peasants, and tribesmen. A number of conclusions must be drawn from this, particularly the need to study the socio-political changes brought about by colonialism, resistance movements, and the need for a new methodological agenda to recover the social history of Libya's indigenous society.

A comprehensive study of the colonial situation requires a realization that colonial policies were shaped by politics and economics specific to each European colonial state and to each colony as well. The Libyan experience must be differentiated from the colonial experience of other Maghribi countries. In addition, one must account for the changes in colonial policy over time. The "liberal" colonial policy in Libya from 1911 to 1922 pursued by a regime quite different from the fascist one from 1922 to 1943 offers one example of these changes.

The liberal Italian colonial policy recognized the local states of the resistance, whereas the fascists refused any collaboration, substituting for it total Italian supremacy. The difference between the liberal and the fascist colonial policies was rooted in the crisis of Italian capitalism—a crisis due to the competition of other capitalist countries in Europe and also to the weakness of labor movements in the north and the landless peasants of the south. Settler colonialism became a solution to the problems stemming from late industrialization and social conflict in Italy.

Too, French colonial policy in Algeria differed from its manifestations in Tunisia and Morocco. The French destroyed the precolonial state in Algeria while preserving the Husayni and the Alawite states in Tunisia and Morocco. The answer to the question of why

France pursued these various policies is to be found in the configuration of its state economy and politics in 1830, 1881, and 1912. French capitalism changed during these periods; hence, by the end of the nineteenth century a nonsettler form of colonialism became more efficient and profitable than military conquests and the need for land.

A civil society's social and political organization is outside the state bureaucracy. Modern civil institutions are, for example, trade unions, political parties, and civil associations.[1] However, the concept of civil society needs to be extended to non-Western, noncapitalist societies, as in the case of Libyan society between 1830 and 1932. Nonstate civil institutions in Libya were merchant corporations, guilds, Sufi orders, and tribal organizations. Yet, colonial policies and transformations did not occur in a vacuum, but rather against a living and dynamic indigenous society with states, merchant corporations, clans, Sufi orders, and political ideologies. The weaknesses of the Algerian military state and its isolation from the larger Algerian society was the crucial cause for its quick defeat. Also, the collaboration of the Husayni and Alawite elites with the French led the latter to pursue a policy of indirect colonization in the name of the old precolonial states. However, despite colonial policies and the collaboration of the upper elite, the hinterland tribes and peasants resisted colonialism and so delayed its penetration of the interior, as in the cases of Amir 'Abd al-Qadir in western Algeria (1830–1847), 'Abd al-Karim al-Khatabi in northeast Morocco (1921–1926), and the Libyan resistance (1911–1932).

Focusing exclusively on the state level does not reveal the real impact of colonialism. French colonial policy in Algeria and Italian policy in Libya eliminated the precolonial states. Yet noncapitalist relations persisted in the Libyan hinterland while in Algeria they were destroyed, leaving Algerians to become wage laborers in agriculture, pressuring some Algerians to join the urban proletariat, some to become wage laborers in agriculture, and still others to become migrant laborers in Algerian cities, and, by the 1960s, in France. French colonial policy in Tunisia and Morocco incorporated precolonial states; yet by the end of the colonial era Tunisian society was transformed in the manner of Algerian society, except for the creation of a Tunisian bourgeoisie. In Morocco, noncapitalist relations continued to persist into the 1960s.

The colonial experience of Libya from 1911 to 1943 led to limited social transformation because of the nature of Italian colonialism and the longevity of anticolonial resistance. By the year 1943 there were only 5,000 Libyan workers employed in the construction of colonial agricultural settlements, roads and ports. An additional 20,000 Libyans were recruited as a cheap labor force to fight during Italy's conquest of Ethiopia. Most of the arable land along the coast was expropriated by the colonial state. The hinterland in the south became a refuge for thousands of tribesmen and peasants who engaged in herding, sharecropping and bartering to survive colonial uprooting and displacement. Here one must realize that noncapitalist systems resisted and survived the violent onslaught of colonialism, especially in the hinterland. But along the coast and especially in Tripolitania, capitalism became dominant, as is true of the Algerian experience. In short, the study of colonial transformation requires an analysis of the basis of political power from below: production, labor relations, and land tenure systems. Only then can one grasp the whole impact of colonial state policy.

The ultimate failure of modernization theories applied to Libya is their inability to account for the persistence of noncapitalist relations, economic dependency, dynastic rule, and military regimes. Because of this failure, for modernization theorists the role of Islam as a revolutionary ideology in the Iranian revolution came as a surprise. The failure to account for social change stems from ignoring local dynamics, which looked either "chaotic" or "traditional." Furthermore, the indigenous civil society became "absent" or "weak." For modernization, orthodox Marxist theorists and the economistic dependency school, precolonial society is either traditional, tribal, or ruled too powerfully by patrimonial Asiatic or core capitalist states. It seems to these theorists that there was no civil society as there was in the West.[2] Further, alternative state formation is not well understood, because of the narrow focus on the Western nation-state. This focus was adopted by middle-class Arab nationalists who read local history through this anachronistic perspective.

An alternative research agenda would involve recovering the social history of the indigenous society, particularly the history of resistance and various strategies for survival. This recovery is crucial for interpreting both historical transformations and contemporary politics. We need to look at history from below and understand groups such as peasants, tribesmen, women, and outcast groups.[3] A social history from below requires focusing on production, class formation, gender, and popular culture. In short, this focus could help to overcome the Eurocentricism and anachronistic nationalism still predominant today.

This agenda requires moving beyond conventional sources such as colonial and state archives. These sources reflect the interests of European councils and colonial administrations. Other sources shed fresh light on indigenous social history—oral traditions, poetry, folklore, songs, and indigenous archival material.[4]

APPENDIXES

Appendix A
The Rates of Exchange of Other Currencies
(All equivalents are given in British pounds sterling)

1 Franc-	France	
1 Franc-	Belgium	1830–1859 = 0.03937
1 Lira -	Italy	1860–1913 = 0.04
1 Drachma-	Greece	
1 Kroner-	Austria	1897–1913 = 0.0417
1 Rouble-	Russia	1830–1839 = 0.0442
1 Mark-	Germany	1880–1900 = 0.05
		1901–1913 = 0.0492
1 Dollar-	U.S.	1830–1913 = 0.917
1 Lira-	Egypt	1850–1883 = 0.917
		1884–1893 = 1.0417
		1894–1913 = 1.0256

Source: Sevket Pamuk, "Foreign Trade, Foreign Capital," in *The Ottoman Empire and European Capitalism, 1820–1913* (Cambridge: Cambridge University Press, 1897), p. 202.

Appendix B
Libya's Major Trading Partners, 1885–1910
(value in pounds sterling)

Year/ /Country		*England*	*Ottoman Empire*	*France*	*Italy*	*Austria*	*Tunisia*	*Germany*	*Belgium*	*Egypt*	*U.S.A.*	*Other Countries*
1885	Ex	242,000	20,600	126,560	—	—	1,500	—	—	—	—	1,500
	Im	180,000	74,000	42,000	60,000	51,000	30,000	15,000	—	—	—	11,950
1886		183,000	10,000	22,500	—	—	5,000	4,000	—	—	—	6,500
		64,800	85,000	36,000	38,000	13,000	30,000	7,000	—	—	—	26,000
1887		198,000	3,500	17,000	—	—	—	—	—	—	—	6,000
		66,500	61,300	68,000	27,000	11,000	55,700	10,000	—	—	—	45,000
1888		242,500	27,000	58,000	—	—	2,000	21,000	—	—	—	6,000
		80,000	105,000	72,000	22,300	13,300	7,000	10,000	—	—	—	54,000
1889		—	—	—	—	—	—	—	—	343,063	—	—
		—	—	—	—	—	—	—	—	174,155	—	—
1890		—	—	—	—	—	—	—	—	—	—	—
1891		—	—	—	—	—	—	—	—	—	—	—
1892		—	—	—	—	—	—	—	—	—	—	—
1893		—	—	—	—	—	—	—	—	—	—	—
1894		—	—	—	—	—	—	—	—	—	—	—
1895		—	—	—	—	—	—	—	—	—	—	—
1896		—	—	—	—	—	—	—	—	—	—	—
1897		—	—	—	—	—	—	—	—	—	—	—
1898		—	—	—	—	—	—	—	—	—	—	—
1899		—	—	—	—	—	—	—	—	—	—	—
		130,000	48,000	67,000	37,200	50,000	—	20,800	11,000	—	—	20,800
1900		158,000	39,200	98,000	94,000	64,000	—	19,200	12,000	—	—	14,440
1901		144,600	45,000	45,000	8,060	—	—	4,600	—	13,960	29,620	3,640

Year/ /Country	*England*	*Ottoman Empire*	*France*	*Italy*	*Austria*	*Tunisia*	*Germany*	*Belgium*	*Egypt*	*U.S.A.*	*Other Countries*
	122,000	44,000	48,000	52,000	58,000	—	16,400	10,000	—	—	8,360
1902	128,550	44,000	40,000	9,960	—	—	6,000	—	13,840	31,200	3,760
	78,000	39,520	39,200	58,070	55,200	—	16,000	8,000	—	—	8,400
1903	—	—	—	—	—	—	—	—	—	—	—
1904	—	—	—	—	—	—	—	—	—	—	—
1905	—	—	—	123,520	—	—	—	—	—	—	—
	—	—	—	26,120	—	—	—	—	—	—	—
1906	—	—	—	158,440	—	—	—	—	—	—	—
	—	—	—	22,800	—	—	—	—	—	—	—
1907	—	—	—	123,040	—	—	—	—	—	—	—
	—	—	—	42,160	—	—	—	—	—	—	—
1908	—	—	—	128,840	—	—	—	—	—	—	—
	—	—	—	27,046	—	—	—	—	—	—	—
1909	—	—	—	117,360	—	—	—	—	—	—	—
	—	—	—	64,240	—	—	—	—	—	—	—
1910	135,000	57,760	64,400	379,300	—	12,800	—	—	—	—	—
	91,000	65,000	48,000	475,680	—	18,000	—	—	—	—	—

Sources: British consular reports in Tripoli and Benghazi, 1885–1910, Anthony Cachia, *Libya Under the Second Ottoman Occupation 1835–1911* (Tripoli: Government Press, 1945), 104, Muhammad Naji and Muhammad Nuri *Tarabulus al Gharb* (Tripoli Dar al-Fikir, 1973), 43, and E. Rossi *Storica di Tripoli e della Tripolitania Dallo Conquesta Araba al 1911* (Beirut: Dar al-Thaqafa, 1974), 416.

Appendix C
Volume of Libyan Exports and Imports in 1900
(In British pounds sterling)

Exports			*Imports*		
Commodity	Value		Commodity	Value	
	(Lira)	(Pound)		(Lira)	(Pound)
Esparto	99,000	3,960	Flour	128,000	5,120
Esponge	77,000	3,080	British cotton		
			—clothes	86,000	3,440
Goatskin	58,000	2,320	—textiles	21,000	840
Ostrich feather	54,000	2,160	Tobacco	2,000	80
			Sugar	24,000	960
Ivory	10,000	400			
			Tea	12,000	480

Sources: E. Rossi, *Storica di Tripoli e della Tripolitania Dallo Conquesta Araba al 1911* (Beirut: Dar al-Thaqafa, 1974), 416; and A. Medana, "Il vilayet di Tripoli di Barbaria dell' anno 1901," *Bollettino de gli Affair Esteri* (November 1909), 88, 97, 100.

Appendix D
Trading Partners 1899–1902; Imports
(In British pounds sterling)

Country	*Value (in Thousands of Pounds)*			
	1899	1900	1901	1902
England	130.00	158.00	112.00	98.00
France and Tunisia	67.20	98.00	48.00	39.20
Turkey	48.00	39.20	44.00	39.52
Germany	20.80	19.20	16.40	16.00
Italy	37.20	94.00	52.00	58.07
Austria	50.00	64.00	58.00	55.20
Belgium	11.00	12.00	10.00	8.80
Other	20.80	14.44	8.36	8.40
Total	385.00	498.80	354.84	323.20

Source: British consular reports in Tripoli and Benghazi, 1899–1902.

Appendix E
Major Trading Partners; Libyan Exports
(In British pounds sterling)

Country	*Value (in Thousands of Pounds)*	
	1901	1902
England	144.60	128.55
France	54.06	40.90
Turkey	45.00	44.00
U.S.A.	29.62	31.20
Greece	28.56	19.56
Egypt	13.96	13.84
Italy	8.06	9.96
Germany	4.60	6.00
Other	3.64	3.76
Total	332.10	297.46

Sources: British consular reports in Tripoli, 1901–1902; Muhammad Naji and Muhammad Nuri, *Tarabulus al-Gharb* (Tripoli: Dar Maktabal al-Fikir, 1973), 42; and Anthony Cachia, *Libya Under the Second Ottoman Occupation 1835–1911* (Tripoli: Government Press, 1945), 104.

Appendix F
Transit Trade—Export from Tripoli (1862–1904)
(In British pounds sterling)

Year	*Ivory*	*Ostrich Feathers*	*Tanned Goatskins*	*Total*
1862	10	3	—	—
1863	13	6	—	—
1864	17	10	1.5	28.5
1865	15	12	1.5	28.5
1866	12	7	1	20
1867	—	—	—	—
1868	—	—	—	—
1869	25	12	2.1	39
1870	25	16	1.5	42.5
1871	40	30	8	78
1872	35	45	8	88
1873	30	40	—	—
1874	50	115	—	—
1876	60	132	—	—
1877	—	—	—	—
1878	31	187	3.5	222
1879	21	235	11	227
1880	24	167.5	75	194
1881	16	152.5	12	181
1882	14	179	8	201
1883	15	236	11	262
1884	8	184	3	195
1885	12	85	4	101
1886	28	30	4	62
1887	20	15	5.5	40.5
1888	24.5	40	9	73.5
1889	18	55	15	88
1890	22	95	18	135
1891	30	80	17	117
1892	—	—	—	—
1893	28	56	38	122
1894	22	48	44	114
1895	8	45	51	104
1896	7	55	49	110.5
1897	7	66	88	121
1898	1.5	70	65	136.5
1899	4.5	58	59	121.5
1900	6	54	58.5	118.5
1901	2	28	49	79
1902	—	—	—	—
1903	3	21	43	64
1904	2	23	37	60

Source: British consular estimates in Tripoli in the parliamentary papers, 1862–1904.

NOTES

Introduction

1. On the connection between early anticolonial resistance and later mass nationalist movements in the 1960s, see T. O. Ranger, "Connections Between 'Primary Resistance' Movements and Modern Mass Nationalism in East and Central Africa," *Journal of African History,* ix:3 (1968), 437–63. On Libya, see John Davis, *Libyan Politics: Tribe and Revolution* (London: IB Tauris, 1987); and on Gadhdhafi, see Knut S. Vikor, "Al-Sanusi and Qadhafi—Continuity of Thought?," *The Maghreb Review* 12:1–2 (1987), 25–28.

2. The best critiques of Eurocentrism are Edward Said, *Orientalism* (New York: Vintage Books, 1979); Bryan Turner, *Marx and the End of Orientalism* (London: George Allen and Unwin, 1978); and Samir Amin, *Eurocentrism* (New York: Monthly Review Press, 1989).

3. See Edmund Burke III, "The Image of the Moroccan State in French Ethnological Literature: A New Look at the Origins of Lyauty's Berber Policy," in Ernest Gellner and Charles Micaud, eds. , *Arabs and Berbers: From Tribe to Nation in North Africa* (Lexington, Mass.: D. C. Heath, 1972), 195–99. Also see Archie Mafeje, "The Ideology of Tribalism," *Journal of Modern African Studies* 9:2 (1971), 253–61.

4. For the classical formulation of the segmentary model, see E. E. Evans-Pritchard, *The Sanusi of Cyrenaica* (Oxford: Clarendon Press, 1949), 59–60. Today the most prominent advocate of this model is Ernest Gellner in *Saints of the Atlas* (Chicago: University of Chicago Press, 1969), 35–70. For the application of this model in political science, see John Waterbury, *The Commander of the Faithful* (New York: Columbia University Press, 1970). For a summary of critiques of the segmentary model, see David Seddon, "Economic Anthropology or Political Economy: Approaches to the Analysis of Pre-Capitalist Formation in the Maghrib," in John Clamer, ed. , *The New Economic Anthropology* (London: MacMillan Press, 1978), 61–107; Talal Asad, *The Idea of an Anthropology of Islam* (Washington, D.C.: Georgetown University Center for Contemporary Arab Studies, 1986), 8–11; and Lila Abu-Lughod, "Zones of Theory in the Anthropology of the Arab World," *Annual Review of Anthropology* 18 (1989), 280–87. For a

general critique of the anthropological analysis of kinship, see David Schneider, *A Critique of the Study of Kinship* (Ann Arbor: University of Michigan Press, 1984).

5. Daniel Lerner, *The Passing of Traditional Society: Modernization in the Middle East* (New York: Free Press, 1958), 47. Lisa Anderson's *The State and Social Transformation in Tunisia and Libya 1830–1980* (Princeton: Princeton University Press, 1986) provides information on Libyan social history not previously available in the English language. Yet, because of the author's modernization methodology, particularly that of Samuel Huntington, she views social change as external. In the case of Libyan social history, she views change to come from the modernizing states that ruled Libya, either Ottoman or Italian. Consequently, she fails to address the complex social and economic structure and the various contingencies that existed in nineteenth-century Ottoman Libya. For more details, see my review of this book published in *The Arab Journal of International Studies* 1:2 (Summer 1988), 110–15. Samuel Huntington's major work is *Political Order in Changing Societies* (New Haven: Yale University Press, 1968). For a critique of Huntington's writings, see Colin Leys, "Samuel Huntington and the End of Classical Modernization Theory," in Hamza Alavi and Theodor Shanin, eds., *Introduction to the Sociology of Development* (New York: Monthly Review Press, 1982), 332–49. For a systematic critique of modernization literature, see Irene Gendzier, *Managing Political Change* (Boulder, Co.: Westview Press, 1985).

6. Yves Lacoste, "General Characteristics and Fundamental Structures of Medieval North Africa," *Economy and Society* 3:1 (1974), 10–11. On the destruction of the Asiatic mode, see Karl Marx, "The Future of the British Rule in India," in Karl Marx and Frederick Engels, *On Colonialism* (New York: International Publishers, 1972), 81. For a critique of the Asiatic mode of production, see Perry Anderson, *Lineages of the Absolutist State* (London: Verso, 1974), 462–95. Unfortunately, Anderson retreats to essentialist orientalist images when he analyzes "The House of Islam" in the same book, 361–94.

7. See Aballah Laroui, *History of the Maghreb* (Princeton: Princeton University Press, 1982), 262–87. New scholarship shows the existence of world systems and capitalist trading economies in the thirteenth and fourteenth centuries. See K. N. Chaudhuri, *Trade and Civilization in the Indian Ocean: An Economic History from the Rise of Islam to 1750* (Cambridge: Cambridge University Press, 1985), 222, and Janet L. Abu-lughod, *Before European Hegemony* (New York: Oxford University Press, 1989), 353–54, 372.

8. H. A. Benzabih, "The jabal al-Akhdar: A Half Century of Nomadic Livelihood," in E. G. H. Joffe and K. S. Malachlon, eds., *Social and Economic Development of Libya* (Kent, England: MENAS, 1982), 148; and

Abdelai Doumou, "the State and Popular Alliances: Theoretical Preliminaries in the Light of Moroccan Case," in Peter Anyang 'Nyong'o, ed., *Popular Struggles for Democracy in Africa* (London: Zed Press, 1987), 48–69.

9. Ali Abdullatif Ahmida, "The Structure of Patriarchical Authority: An Interpretive Essay of the Impact of Kinship and Religion on Politics in Libya (1951–1960)," M. A. paper of distinction (political science), University of Washington, 1983. The notable and tribal chiefs of the hinterland dominated the top state bureaucracy between 1951 and 1960. For example, the parliament's two houses were controlled by the chiefs. See Malik A. Abushhawa, "The Political System of Libya, 1951–1969," M. A. thesis (political science), Faculty of Economics and Political Science, Cairo University, 1977, 157, 179.

10. E. P. Thompson, *The Making of the English Working Class* (New York: Vintage Books, 1966), 11.

11. Peter Gran, *Islamic Roots of Capitalism, 1760–1840* (Austin: University of Texas Press, 1979); see especially the introduction and chapter 7. The subaltern school in Indian social history is contributing a fresh look at the multiple voices in colonial India. See Gyan Prakash, "Writing Post-Orientalist Histories of the Third World: Perspectives from Indian History," *Comparative Studies in Society and History* 32:2 (April 1990), 383–408.

12. A good example of this mode of analysis is 'Umar Ali Ibn Isma'il, *Inhiyar Hukim al-Usra al-qaramanliyya fi Libia (1790–1835)* (Tripoli: Maktabat al-Firjani, 1966). For a critique of anachronistic nationalist approaches to Middle Eastern History, see Rifaat A. Abou El-Haj, "Social Uses of the Past: Recent Arab Historiography of Ottoman Rule," *International Journal of Middle East Studies*, 14 (1982), 182–201 and his article on Libyan History, "An Agenda for Research in History: The History of Libya Between the Sixteenth and the Nineteenth Centuries," 15 (1983), 311–13.

13. Magali Morsy, "Maghrebi Unity in the Context of the Nation-State: A Historian's Point of View," *The Maghreb Review*, 8:3–4 (1983), 70–76.

14. Abou El-Haj, "An Agenda for Research," 311–13. See also a recent book by Youssef M. Choueiri, *Arab History and the Nation State: A Study of Modern Arab Historiography, 1820–1980* (London: Routledge, 1989), and Partha Chatterjee, *Nationalist Thought and the Colonial World: A Derivative Discourse?* (London: Zed Press, 1984).

15. Lisa Anderson in her book, *State and Social Transformation in Tunisia and Libya,* and Abdallah Ali Ibrahim in "Evolution of Government and Society in Tripolitania and Cyrenaica (Libya) 1835–1911," Ph.D. dissertation, University of Utah, 1982, ignore the existence of regional economies beyond the borders of the state.

16. Harriet Friedman, "Household Production and the National Economy: Concepts for the Analysis of Agrarian Formations," *The Journal of Peasant Studies* 7:2 (1980), 162.

17. Friedman, "Household Production and the National Economy," 162.

18. Karl Marx, *The Poverty of Philosophy* (New York: International Publishers, 1963), 125.

19. E. P. Thompson, *The Making of the English Working Class*, 11, 68; for a review of the literature, see William Roy, "Class Conflict and Social Change in Historical Perspective," *Annual Review of Sociology* 10 (1984), 483–506.

20. Talal Asad, "The Bedouin as a Military Force: Notes on Some Aspects of Power Relations Between Nomads and Sedentaries in Historical Perspective," in Cynthia Nelson, ed., *The Desert and the Swan: Nomads in the Wider Society* (Berkeley: Institute of International Studies, University of California, 1973), 71.

21. On class factionalism see Nicos Poulantzas, "On Social Classes," *New Left Review* 70 (March–April 1973), 35–37, and Barrington Moore, Jr., *Social Origins of Dictatorship and Democracy* (Boston: Beacon, 1966). Also see Salim Tamari, "Factionalism and Class Formation in Recent Palestinian History," in Roger Owen, ed., *Studies in the Economic and Social History of Palestine in the Nineteenth and Twentieth Centuries* (Oxford, St. Antony College: Carbondale and Edwardsville, 1982), 177–202.

22. On the concept of peasantization, see Kent Post, "Peasantization and Rural Political Movements in West Africa," *Archives Europénnes de Sociologie* VIII:2 (1972), 266; on proletarianization, see Shulamit Carmi and Henry Rosenfeld, "The Origins of the Process of Proletarianization and Urbanization of the Arab Peasants in Palestine," *Annals of the New York Academy of Sciences* 220:6 (1974), 475–76, and Mahfoud Bennoune, "Origins of the Algerian Proletariat," *Merip Reports* 94 (February 1981), 5–12.

23. On state formation, see Ronald Cohen and Elman Service, eds., *Origins of the State* (Philadelphia: Institute for the Study of Human Issues, 1978); on tributary state formation, see Henry Rosenfeld, "The Social Composition of the Military in the Process of State Formation in the Arabian Desert," *Journal of the Royal Anthropological Institute of Great Britain and Ireland* 95 (1956), 75–86, 174–95.

24. See Samir Amin, "Modes of Production and Social Formation," *Ufahamu* IV:3 (Winter) 1974, 57–87.

25. For a survey and critique of empiricism, see Leszek Kolakowski, *The Alienation of Reason: A History of Positivist Thought* (New York: Doubleday, 1968); Stuart Woolf, "Statistics and the Modern State," *Compara-*

tive Studies in Society and History 31:3 (July 1989), 590–96; and Gayatri Chakravorty Spivak, "The Rani of Sirmur: An Essay in the Reading of Archives," *History and Theory* 24:3 (1985) 247–72.

26. See Jan Vansina, *Oral Traditions: A Study in Historical Methodology* (Chicago: Aldine Publishing Company, 1956) and *Oral Traditions and History* (Madison: University of Wisconsin Press, 1985). See also James C. Scott, *Weapons of the Weak* (New Haven: Yale University Press, 1985), 27–37.

27. There is a new literature on subaltern resistance, especially in the colonial social history of India. See the works of the subaltern studies group led by Indian scholar Ranajit Guha. For an overview, see Rosalind O'Hanlon, "Recovering the Subject, Subaltern Studies and Histories of Resistance in Colonial South Asia," *Modern Asian Studies* 22:1 (1988), 187–224; also see the pioneering study by Theodore Swedenburg, "Memories of Revolt: The 1936–39 Rebellion and the Struggle for a Palestinian National Past," Ph.D. dissertation (anthropology), The University of Texas at Austin, 1988.

Chapter 1

1. Ibrahim Ahmad Rizqana, *al-Mammlaka al-Libiyya* (Cairo: Dar alnahda al-'Arabiyya, 1964), 32, 39, 73.

2. Adolf Vischer, "Tripoli," *The Geographical Journal* XXXVII (Nov. 5, 1911), 487–88. Also see Jean Despois, "Types of Native Life in Tripolitania," *Geographical Review* 35 (1945), 356–57.

3. Adolf Vischer, "Tripoli."

4. Jamal al-Din al-Daynasuri, *Jughrafiyat Fezzan* (Benghazi: Dar-Libya lil-nashir Wa al-Tawzi, 1967), 265–66; Jean Despois, "Geographic Humaine" in *Mission Scientifique Du Fezzan (1944–45)* (Alger: Institut de Recherches Sahariennes De L'université D'Alger: Paris, 1946) 29, 63.

5. Lawrence Krader, "Pastoralism," *International Encyclopedia of Social Studies II* (1968) 453–61; for a comprehensive review of the literature on pastoralism, see A. M. Khazakov, *Nomads and the Outside World*, trans. by Julia Crookenden (Cambridge: Cambridge University Press, 1983).

6. Pellissier de Reymand, "La Regance de Tripoli," *Revue des Deux Mondes* XII (1855), 14, 16; and Hadi Abu-Lugma, *Dirassat Libiyya* (Benghazi: Maktabat Qurina, 1975), 63–64.

7. Abu-Lugma, *Dirassat*, 147–50. Enrico De Agostini, *Le populazioni della Tripolitania, notizle ethniche e storiche* (Tripoli uffico politico-

mililare, 1917), 2, 8, 12; and De Agostini, *Le populazioni della Cirenaica* (Benghazi 1922–23), 415, 427. A summary of his survey is "Sulla populazioni Della Libia," *Libia*: Rivista Trimestrale Di Studi Libia (Gennio-Marzo, 1954), 4–13.

8. See Y. W. Gregory et al., *Report on the work of the Commission sent by the Jewish Territorial Organization, under the Auspices of the Governor General of Tripoli to examine the Territory proposed for the purpose of a Jewish settlement in Cyrenaica* (London: Jewish Organization, 1909), 11.

9. On the Roman period see the essay by British archeologist Robert Goodchild, "Farming in Roman Libya," *Geographical Journal* XXV (1952), 70–80; and Rhods Murphy, "The decline of North Africa since the Roman occupation: Climate or Human" *Association of American Geographers* 41 (June 1951), 116–32.

10. G. F. Gautier, *Les Siècles Obscurs Du Maghreb* (Paris: Payot, 1972), 385–89; André Gulien, *Historie de L'Afrique de Nord* (Paris: Payot, 1931), 373–402; Jean Despois, *Le Dejbal Nefausa Tripolitaine*, Etude geographique (Paris: Larose, 1935), 291; Muhammad Talbi, "Law and Economy in Afriqiya (Tunisia) in the Third Islamic Century," in A. L. Udovitch. ed., *The Islamic Middle East, 700–1900* (Princeton, NJ: Darwin Press, 1981) 222–23, and Ibn Khaldun, *The Muqaddimah*, trans. by Franz Rosental (New York: Pantheon, 1958), 304–5.

11. Yves Lacoste, *Ibn Khaldun* (London: Verso, 1984), 76.

12. J. Poncet, "Le mythe de catastrophe hilalienne" *Annales Economies, Societés, Civilisations* XXII (1967), 1099–1120, and C. Cahen, "Quelques mots sur les hilalians et le nomadisme," *Journal of the Economic and Social History of the Orient* XI (1963), 130–33.

13. Lacoste, *Ibn Khaldun*, 66–67.

14. Lacoste, *Ibn Khaldun*, 35–64.

15. Lacoste, *Ibn Khaldun*, 67.

16. Mahmud Abu-Swa, "Ru 'Ya jadida Lil-Fatah al-Islami Li Libya" [A new look at the Islamic conquest of Libya], *Majallat al-Buhath al-Tarikhiyya* 8:1 (January 1986), 48–49.

17. Radi Daghfus, "al-'Awamil al-Iqtisadiyya Li-Hijarat Bani Hilal" [The economic factors behind the migration of Bani Hilal], *Awraq* (Madrid, April 1981) 147–63.

18. See Shawqi 'Abd al-Hakim, *Sirat Bani Hilal* [The epic of Bani Hilal] (Beirut Dar al-Taniwir, 1983); for analysis of the social use of the Hilali epic in popular culture of North Africa, see 'Abd al-Rahman Ayyub, "The Hilali Epic: Material and Memory," *Revue D'Histoire Maghrebine* 11:35–36 (Décembre 1984) 184–217. Also for contemporary political signifi-

cance of the Hilali epic, see Susan Slyomovics "Arabic Folk Literature and Political Expression," *Arab Studies Quarterly* 8:2 (1986) 178–85.

19. J. W. Gregory, et al., *Report on the Work*, 5–6.

20. Regional market economies were a widespread phenomenon in Africa and the Middle East. See two studies that illustrate this point: Paul E. Lovejoy and Stephen Bair, "The Desert-Side Economy of Central Sudan," *International Journal of African Historical Studies* VIII:4 (1975), 550–65, and Hala M. Fatah, "The development of regional markets of Iraq and the Gulf, 1800–1900," Ph.D. dissertation (history), University of California, Los Angeles, 1986.

Chapter 2

1. On tributary social formation, see Amin, "Modes of Production and Social Forms," *Ufahamu* IV:3 (Winter 1974), 66, and *Class and Nation* (New York: Monthly Review, 1980), 1–19, 46–70; also see Kate Currie, "Problematic Modes and the Mughal Social Formation," *The Insurgent Sociologist* 9:2 (1980), 9–21.

2. Muhammad Khalil Ibn Ghalbun, *al-Tidkhar Fi Man Malaka Tarabulus Wa Ma Kan Biha Min al-Akhbar* (The story of Tripoli and its history), 2nd ed. (Tripoli: Maktabat, al-Nur, 1967), 281.

3. Ettori Rossi, *Storia di Tripoli e Della Tripolitania dallo Conquesta Araba al 1911*, translated into Arabic by Khalifa al-Tillisi (Beirut: Dar al-Thaqafa, 1974), 277; Nocola Ziadeh, *Libya Fi al 'Usur al Hadithah* (Libya in modern times) (Cairo: Ma'ahad al-buhuth wa al-Dirassat al-'Arabiyah, 1966), 53; Muhammad B. 'Uthman al-Hashaishi, *Jala al-Karab an Tarabulus al-Gharb*, edited by Ali Mustafa al-Misrati (Beirut: Dar Lubnan, 1965), 99; and GB, PRO, Consul Alvarez, "Benghazi," the FO, "A Report on Trade and Commerce of Benghazi and Derna for the Years 1902–03," received on Nov. 5, 1904, 22.

4. Jean Despois, *La Colonization Italienne en Libye*, translated into Arabic by Hashim Haydar (Benghazi: Dar Libya, 1968), 57.

5. Abu A. Boahen, "The Caravan Trade in the Nineteenth Century," *Journal of African History* III:2 (1972), 350.

6. Dennis D. Cordell, "Eastern Libya, Wadai and the Sanusiya: A Tariqa and a Trade Route," *Journal of African History* 18:2 (1972), 21–36.

7. See B. G. Martin, "Five Letters From the Archives of Tripoli," *Journal of the Historical Society of Nigeria* (1962), 350–80.

8. Until now there has been no major scholarly study of this Saharan

Libyan state. Most of what we know of its history derives from Ibn Ghalbun and some western travelers such as Hornemann in 1789, Barth in 1849, and Nachtigal in 1869. A recently discovered manuscript written by an unknown writer and copied by the Tripolitanian notable al-Khuja is called *Tarikh Fezzan,* edited by Habib Wadaa al-Hisnawi (Tripoli: Center for Libyan studies, 1979).

9. Ibn Ghalbun, *al-Tidhkar,* 111–13.

10. Ibn Ghalbun, *al-Tidhkar,* 125–26.

11. 'Umar Ali Ibn Isma'il, *Inhiyar Hukm al-Usra al-Qaramanaliyya fi Libya (1790–1835)* (The Collapse of the Qaramanli Dynasty in Libya) (Tripoli: Maktabat al-Firjani, 1966), 205.

12. *Tarikh Fezzan,* edited by Habib Wadaa al-Hisnawi (Tripoli: Center for Libyan Studies, 1979), 73. Al-Hisnawi recently published his Ph.D. dissertation on the state of Awlad Muhammad. It is the most comprehensive study on this topic. Unfortunately during my research I was not aware of this book, *Fazzan Under Awlad Muhammad* (Sabha: Center for African Studies, Sabha University Press, 1990).

13. Tarikh Fezzan, 76.

14. Ibn Ghalbun, *al-Tidhkar,* 210.

15. Ibn Isma'il, *Inhiyar,* 40, 203.

16. Ibn Isma'il, 230, and Kola Folayan, "Tripoli and the War with the U.S.A., 1801–5," *Journal of African History* XIII:2 (1972), 261–70.

17. Folayan, "Tripoli and the War with the U.S.A., 261–70.

18. Ahmad al-Na'ib al-Ansari, *al-Mahal al-Adhb fi-Tarikh Tarabulus al-Gharb* (1), 2nd ed. (The Sweet Source for the History of Tripoli) (Tripoli: Maktabat al-Firjani, 1967), 330. On the career of al-Kanimi, see Louis Brener, "Muhammad al-'Amin al-Kanimi and Religion and Politics in Bornu," in John Ralph Willis, ed., *Studies in West African Islamic History I* (London: Frank Cass, 1979), 161–76.

19. Francis Rodd, ed., "A Fezzani Military Expedition to Kanem and Bagirmi in 1821," *Journal of the Royal African Society* XXXV (April 1936), 153–68.

20. Ahmad al-Na'ib al-Ansari, *al-Mahal al-Adhb fi-Tarikh Tarabulus al-Gharb* (1), 2nd ed. (The Sweet Source for the History of Tripoli) (Tripoli: Maktabat al-Firjani, 1967), 333–34.

21. Ibn Isma'il, *Inhiyar,* 302.

22. Ibn Isma'il, 301.

23. 'Abdul-Karim Rafeq, "Changes in the Relationship between the Ottoman Control Administration and the Syrian provinces from the sixteenth to the eighteenth centuries," in Thomas Naff and Roger Owen, eds., *Studies in Eighteenth Century Islamic History* (Carbondale: Southern Illinois University Press, 1977), 53, 58–59, 68.

24. Andrew C. Hess, "The Forgotten Frontier: The Ottoman North African provinces during the Eighteenth Century," in Naff and Owen, eds., *Studies*, 76.

25. Rodolfo Micacchi, *Tarabulus al-Gharb taht hukm al-Usra al-Qaramanliyya* [Tripoli Under Rule of the Qaramanli Dynasty], translated by Taha Fawzi (Cairo: Arab League, Institute of Higher Arab Studies, 1961), 134–35.

26. Ibn Ghalbun, *al-Tidhkar*, 207; 'Abdull Salam Adham and Abdallah Ibrahim, eds., *Wath'iq 'an Tarikh Libya fi al-Qarn al-Tasi' 'Ashar* (Documents of Libyan history in the nineteenth century) I (Tripoli: Center for Libyan Studies, 1983); see Doc. 15, 28; and also GB, FO, 101/91, Consul Jago to O'Conor 21, 12, 1901.

27. Paolo Della Cella, *Narrative of an Expedition from Tripoli in Barbary to the Western Frontier of Egypt in 1817 by the Bay of Tripoli*, translated by Anthony Aufrere (London: J. A. Arch, 1823), 7, 9–10.

28. Ibn Isma'il, *Inhiyar*, 85–210.

29. See Abdalla Laroui, *The History of the Maghreb: An Interpretive Essay*, translated by Ralph Manheim (Princeton, N.J.: Princeton University Press, 1977), 234, 238; Ettori Rossi, *Storia di Tripoli e Della Tripolitania dallo Conquesta Araba al 1911*, translated by Khalifa al-Tilisi (Beirut: Dar al-Thaqafa, 1974), 43, 132; and Jerome B. Weiner, "New Approaches to the Study of Barbary Corsairs (1)," *Revue D'Histoire Maghrebine* 13–14 (Jan. 1979), 205–8.

30. Kola Folayan, *Tripoli During the Reign of Yusuf Pasha Qaramanli* (ILE–IFE, Nigeria: The University Press, 1975), 29; also see USNA Report of the American Consul in Tripoli, "Marine Forces in Tripoli," May 16, 1801; and Ibn Isma'il, *Inhiyar*, 120–24, 226.

31. Ibn Isma'il, *Inhiyar*, 148, 230.

32. Ibn Isma'il, *Inhiyar*, 28.

33. Ibn Ghalbun, *al-Tidhkar*, 158, and al-Ansari, *al-Mahal*, 318–19.

34. al-Ansari, *al-Mahal*, 319, and G. F. Lyon, *A Narrative of Travels and Discoveries in Northern and Central Africa in the Years 1818–1820* (London: Francis Class, 1966 [1821]), 127, 227.

35. F. Hornemann, "The Journal of F. Hornemann's Travels from

Cairo to Murzuk in the Years 1797–98" in *Missions to the Niger,* E. W. B. Bovill, ed. (Cambridge: Cambridge University Press, 1969), 102.

36. F. Hornemann, "Journal," 102.

37. F. Hornemann, "Journal," 160.

38. G. Nachtigal, *Sahara and the Sudan, Tripoli and Fezzan,* vol. I, translated by B. B. Fisher and Humphery G. Fisher (New York: Barnes & Noble, 1974), 87, 122.

39. Nachtigal, *Sahara and the Sudan," 160.*

40. Ibn Ghalbun, al-Tidhkar, 153; and *Tarikh Fezzan,* 67.

41. Tarikh Fezzan, 67; and Hornemann, *Journal,* 100.

42. Hornemann, *Journal,* 100.

43. Ibn Ghalbun, *al-Tidhkar,* 158.

44. Ibn Isma'il, *Inhiyar,* 230.

45. Ibn Isma'il, *Inhiyar,* 227.

46. See Ibn Isma'il, *Inhiyar,* for the text of French and British treaties with Tripoli, 448–52, 478–79.

47. al-Ansari, *al-Manhal,* 235.

48. Ibn Isma'il, *Inhiyar,* 19–20.

49. Rifaat A. Abou El-Haj, *Formation of the Modern State,* unpublished; on the impact of European capital, see Sevket Pamuk, *The Ottoman empire and European Capitalism 1820–1913* (Cambridge: Cambridge University Press, 1987); and Resat Kasaba, *The Ottoman empire and the World Economy* (Albany: State University of New York Press, 1988).

50. Abou-El-Haj, *Formation of the State,* 64–66.

51. Kasaba, *Ottoman empire,* 50.

52. Donald Quataert, *Social Disintegration and Popular Resistance in the Ottoman empire, 1881–1908. Reactions to European Economic Penetration.* (Albany: State University of New York Press, 1983).

53. Nachtigal, *Sahara,* 122.

54. MDJL, Doc. 99, "A Report from the Governor of Fezzan Muhammad Sami," 1911, 4.

55. On the role of the Ghadamis traders see the newly published documents, Bashir W. Yushi', ed., *Ghadamis: Wathaig Tijariyah Tarikhiyya, Ijtimaiyah* (Ghadamis, Commercial, Historical, and Social Documents) (Tripoli: Center for Libyan Studies, 1982), 28. Marion Johnson estimated

their number to be 129 (19 in Kano, 4 in Sokoto, 3 in Zaria, 3 in Nupe, 4 in Adomawa, 6 in Zinder, 37 in Tunis, in addition to others in Tripoli) in "Calico Caravans: The Tripoli Kano Trade after 1880," *Journal of African History* 17 (1976), 11; and Louis Brenner, "North African Trading Community in the 19th Century Central Sudan," in *Aspects of West African Islam*, edited by D. F. McCall and N. R. Benett (Boston: Boston University Press, 1971), 138.

56. Yushi', *Ghadamis*, 339–45.

57. GB, Co 2/13, Lieut. H. Clapperton to R. Wilmont, Harson, 6 June 1825, Hans Fisher, "A Journey From Tripoli Across the Sahara to Lake Chad," *Geographical Journal* (March 1909), 265; and E. Pellissier De Reynaud, "Le Regence De Tripoli," *Revue des Deux Mondes* 12 (1955), 43.

58. A. Adu Boahen, *Britain, The Sahara, and the Western Sudan* (Oxford: Clarendon Press, 1964), 160, 164; and Eric Williams, *Capitalism and Slavery* (New York: Perigee, 1980), 135, 6.

59. Marion Johnson, "Tijarat rish al-Na'am Fi al-Nisf al-Awal min al Qarn al-Tasia Ashar" (Ostrich Feather Trade in the First Half of the 19th Century), *Majallat al-Buhuth al-Tarikhiyya* 1 (January 1981), 134.

60. See C. W. Newbury, "North Africa and Western Sudan Trade in the nineteenth Century: A Re-Evaluation," *Journal of African History* 7 (1966), 233–46; Stephen Bair, "Trans-Sahara Trade and the Sahel: Damergu, 1870–1930" 18 (1977), 37–60; Johnson, "Calico Caravans," and "Tijarat rish," and the synthetic study of Ahmad Said Fituri, "Tripolitania, Cyrenaica."

61. DMT, Malif al-'Aradi, Lands file; for more details see Kemal H. Karabat, "The Land Regimes, Social Structure, and Modernization in the Ottoman empire," in *Beginning of Modernization in the Middle East* (Chicago: University of Chicago Press, 1968), 69–70; Peter Sluglett and Marion Farouk Sluglett, "The Application of the 1858 Land Code in Greater Syria, Some Preliminary Observations," in Tarif Khalidi, ed., *Land Tenure and Social Transformations in the Middle East* (Beirut: American University Press, 1984), 410; and Rifaat Ali Abou-El-Haj, "An Agenda for Research in History."

62. 'Abd al-Qadir Jami, the governor of Ghat during the 1900s, estimated the number of palm trees in Fezzan around 1,175,000, producing 1,600,000 *kaylah*. One *kaylah* equals 8 kg, with a value of 2,400,000 piasters. See Jami's *Min Tarabulus al-Gharb Ila al-Sahra al-Kubra* (From Tripoli to the Great Sahara), translated from Turkish into Arabic by M. al-Usta (Tripoli: Dar al-Misrati, 1973), 87. Also, Naji, *Tarikh Tarabulus al-Gharb*, 70–71; Nachtigal, *Sahara*, 113–15, and Jean Despois, "Fezzan," *The Encyclopedia of Islam* #2, new ed. (Leiden: E. J. Brill, 1965), 877.

63. MDJL, Soc. Doc. 99, "A Report from the Governor of Fezzan Muhammad Sami," who requested from the state council in Tripoli approval for the assignment of 1,500 palm trees of the state *miri* land in the region to serve the mosques as *waqf* to replace the trees lost during the rebellion of 'Abd al-Jalil. See also Abdullsalam Adham and A. S. al-Dajani, eds., *Wathaiq Tarikh Libya al-Hadith: al-Wathaiq al-'Uthmaniya 1881–1911* (Documents of the Modern History of Libya: Ottoman Documents) (Benghazi: The University Press, 1974), 163.

64. Fraj Stambouli and 'Abdel-Kader Zghal, "Urban Life in Pre-Colonial North Africa," *The British Journal of Sociology* 27 (March 1976), 10–11.

65. The Italian Consul A. Medana estimated the *waqf* revenues of the Regency to be around 51,640 piasters. "Il Vilayet di Tripoli di Barbaria dell'Anno 1901," *Bollettin Deqli Affari Esteri* (Rome, Nov. 1904), 48. In 1910 the *waqf* revenues in Tripolitania were 50,000 Turkish lira. Francesco Coro, *Stettantesei Anni di Dominazione Turca in Libia, 1835–1911,* translated by K. al-Tillisi (Tripoli: Dar al-Firjani, 1971), 54.

66. Evans-Pritchard, *The Sanusi of Cyrenaica,* 77. According to Italian colonial sources, the total revenues of the Sanusi lodges were around 200,000 Italian lire in 1928; see Graziani, *Cirenica Pacificata,* 25.

67. Jamil Hilal, *Dirassat Fi al-Waqi' al-Libi* (Studies in Libyan Reality) (Tripoli: Maktabat al-Fikir, 3), 2, 124; and Keith S. McLachlan, "The Role of Indigenous Farming in the Agrarian Structure of Tripolitania in the 19th and 20th Centuries," in M. M. Buru et al., *Planning and Development in Modern Libya* (London: Middle East and North Africa Studies Press, 1985), 34–35.

68. E. G. H. Joffe, "Trade and Migration between Malta and the Barbary States 1835–1911," in Buru, *Planning,* 3. Also by the same author, "British Malta and the Qaramanli Dynasty 1800–1835," *Revue D'Histoire Maghrebine* 12: Année: 37–38 (Jain 1985), 32.

69. De Reynaud, "Le Regence De Tripoli," 43.

70. Flour was imported in 1866 when drought hit the Regency. USNA, June 3 and Dec. 3, 1866. Also in 1881 flour was imported from Turkey for the same reason; see Cachia, *Libya,* 40.

71. Andre Caunelle, "Le Semi-Nomadisme dans l'Ouest Libyen: Fezzan, Tripolitaine," in *UNESCO: Recherches Du Zone Aride* 19, *Nomads et Nomadisme au Sahara* (Paris: UNESCO, 1963), 104; Jacques Thiry, "Le Fezzan: Notes Historique et Socio-Economique," *Correspondance d'Orient Etudes* 3 (1963), 47; and Jean Despois, "Géographie Humaine," in *Mission Scientifique Du Fezzan, 1944–1945* (Alger: Institute de Recherches Saharienne de l'Université D'Alger, Paris, 1946), 63.

72. C. R. Pennell, "Political Loyalty and the Central Government in Pre-Colonial Libya," in E. G. H. Joffe et al., *Social and Economic Development of Libya* (London: Menas Press Ltd., 1982), 14. Also, A. S. al-Dajani mentions that the workers of the esparto trade worked for 14 hours a day, *Libya Qubayla al-Ihtilal al-Itali 1882–1922* (Libya Before the Italian Occupation) (Cairo: al-Matbaa al-Fanniyya, 1971), 222, 234, 238. In addition, the workers were paid a low wage of five francs a day. Haj Muhammad al-Usta, personal interview, Tripoli, 22 Sept. 1985; and Robert Harrison, "Migrants in the City of Tripoli," *The Geographical Journal* 57 (July 1967), 415.

73. Mark Dyer, "Export Production in Western Libya, 1750–1793," *African Economic History*, 13 (1984), 118.

74. Tekeste Negash, *Italian Colonialism in Eritrea 1882–1941, Policies, Praxis and Impact* (Uppsala: Sweden, 1987), 2.

75. For a review of the literature, see Lisa Anderson, "'Ara Gharbiyya Fi Islah Uthmani Fi Libya Fi Awakhir al Qarn al-Tasi' 'Ashar" (Western views of an Ottoman reform in Libya during the end of the 19th century," *Majallat al-Buhuth al-Tarakhiyya* 7 (1985), 111–25.

76. Angelo Del Boca, *Gli Italiani in Libia: Tripoli Bel Soul D'Amore 1860–1922* (Rome: Literza Figli, 1986), 41–42. Also, R. Mori, "La Pentrationi Pacifica Italiana in Libia dal 1907 al 1911 e il Banco di Roma," *Revista di Studi Politici Internationali* 24 (1957), 110–11.

77. Rachel Simon, "The Relations of the Jewish Community of Libya with Europe in the Late Ottoman Period," in J. L. Miege, ed., *Le Relations Intercommunautaires Juives in Mediterranée O"identale XIIIe–XXe. Siécles* (Paris: CNRS, 1984), 71, 74.

78. R. A. Webster, *Industrial Imperialism in Italy 1908–1915* (Berkeley: University of California Press, 1975), 152.

79. R. Mori, "La Penetrationi," 112, Del Boca, *Gli, Italiani in Libia*, 33, al-Zawi, *Jihad al-Abtal*, 34; A. Barbar, "Musraf Roma Wa-Dawur al-Sultat al-'Uthmaniyya Fi al-Wuquf Dida al-Tasalul al Itali Ila-Libya 1907–1911" (The Bank of Rome and the role of Ottoman authorities in resisting its penetration into Libya), *Majallat al-Buhuth al–Tarikhiyya* 2 (July, 1982), 241, and R. Simon, "The Socio-Economic Role of the Tripolitanian Jews in the Late Ottoman Period," in *Communantes Juives des Marges Sahariennes du Maghreb*, ed. M. Abitbol (Jerusalem, 1982), 323–24.

80. DMT, Malaf al-'A'ilat (File of Notable Families); al-Zawi, *Jihad al Abtal*, 34; Francis McCullagh, *Italy's War for a Desert* (Chicago: F. G. Browne, 1913), 18.

81. See Francesco Crispi, *Memoirs*, vol. II, translated by M. Princhard-Agnetti (London, 1923), 474–75; Giovanni Giolitti, *Memoirs of My*

Life, translated by Edward Storer (New York: Howard Fertig, 1973), 260; Charles Lapworth, *Tripoli and the Young Italy* (London: Stephen Sweft, 1912), 59; and A. Barbar, "Masraf Roma," 241–43.

82. Barbar, "Masraf Roma," 240.

83. During the Young Turk liberal phase in 1908, a free press and some political associations were allowed. Many nationalist papers appeared. See Ali M. al-Misrati, *Sahafat Libya Fi Nisf Qarn* (Libyan Journalism in half a century) (Beirut: Dar al-Kashaf, 1960), and Shaban Fituri Gashut, "The Development of Libyan Newspapers 1860–1972: A History and Interpretation," Master's thesis, University of Kansas, 1972. The Italian Consulate and the Bank of Rome published their own papers through Jewish merchants such as Gustavo Arbib. Among these Italian papers were *Il Gournale di Tripoli, L'eco di Tripoli* and *Il Messagerio di Tripoli*. See Simon, "The Socio-Economic Role," 327.

84. Georges Remond, *Aux Camps Turca Arabes, Notes de Guerre en Cyrenaique que en Tripolitaine 1912*, 2nd ed., translated into Arabic by Muhammad A. El-Wafi (Tripoli: al-Mu'assa al 'Ama, 1983), 281.

85. Renzo De Felice, *Jews in an Arab Land: Libya, 1835–1970*, translated by Judith Romani (Austin: University of Texas Press, 1985), 18, and Barbar, "Masraf Roma," 242–47.

86. Barbar, "Masraf Roma," 241.

Chapter 3

1. Youssef Toni, "Tribal Distribution and Racial Relationships of the Ancient and Modern Peoples of Cyrenaica," Jamiat 'ayn Shams. Kulliyat al-Adab, *Hawliyat Kulliyat al-Adab* [Fine Arts College, Ayn Shams University, Annals of the College of Arts, Cairo] 8 (1963), p. 172.

2. Toni, "Tribal Distribution," 189.

3. De Agostini, "Sulle popolazioni Della Libia," 7, 12.

4. Dennis Cordell, "The Awlad Sulayman of Libya and Chad: Power and Adaptation in the Sahara and Sahel," *Canadian Journal of African Studies* 19:2 (1985), 325, 28.

5. Caunelle, "Le Semi-nomadisme Dans l'Oues Libyen," 101.

6. For an overview of the structure of Libyan tribes, see Emorys L. Peters, "Cultural and Social Diversity in Libya," in A. J. Allan, ed., *Libya Since Independence: Economic and Political Development* (New York: St. Martins Press, 1982), 103–7.

7. On tribal laws, especially the *Mi 'ad*, the senior Shayks council, see Massimo Colucci, "Il Diritto Consuetudinario della Cirenica," *Rivista Giuridica Del Medio Estremo Oriente E Guistizia Colonial* 1 (1932).

8. See Feraud, *Annales Tripolitaines*, 251; A. Caunelle, "Le Nomadisme de Zintan (Tripolitaine et Fezzan), *Travaux de l'institut de Recherches Sahariennes* 16:2 (1957), 97; and A. Caunelle, "Le nomadisme des Megarha (Fezzan), "*Travaux l'Institut de Recherches Sahariennes* 12 (1954), 63.

9. Jean Despois, *Le Djebel Nefousa (Tripolitaine): Etude Geographique* (Paris: Lurose-Editeurs, 1935), 135.

10. P. Lombardi, "Italian Agrarian Colonization During the Colonial Period," in Joffe, ed., *Social and Economic*, 95; and Segre, *The Fourth Shore*, 146.

11. G. H. Blake, *Misurata: A Market Town in Tripolitania* (Durham, England: University of Durham, 1968), 24, 30.

12. Jean Despois, "Development of Land Tenure in Northern Africa," in L. Dudley Stamp, ed., *A History of Land Use in Arid Regions* (Paris: UNESCO, 1961), 220–21.

13. On sharecropping in Tripolitania see Jamil Hilal, "Agriculture and Socioeconomic Change in the Region of Misallata, Tripolitania," *Dirassat: Libyan Economic and Business Review*, Benghazi University, 5:1 (Spring 1969), 97; on Cyrenaica, see al-Hashaishi "Jala," 100; and on Fezzan see Caunelle, "Le Seminomadisme," 108–109 and Despois, *Geographie Humaine*, 134, 236.

14. Hilal, "Agriculture and Socioeconomic Change," 97.

15. Hilal, "Agriculture and Socioeconomic Change," 78.

16. J. I. Clarke, "The Si'aan Pastoralists of the Jafara," in S. G. Willimott and J. I. Clarke, eds., *Field Studies in Libya* (Durham, England: University of Durham, 1960), 52.

17. Caunelle, "Le Semi-Nomadisme," 108–9.

18. Doc. 51, in Adham and Ibrahim, *Wathaiq*, 164; N. Slousch, "La Tripolitaine sous la Domination des Karamanli," *Revue de Monde Musulman* vi: 11 (Nov. 1908), 437; and Allen Streicker, "Government and Revolt in the Tripoli Regency, 1795–1855," Master's thesis, Northwestern University, 1970, 36, 79–80.

19. Peters, "Cultural and Social Diversity," 106.

20. Doc. 47, in Yushi', *Ghadamis*, 109; and Cordell, "The Awlad Sulayman of Libya and Chad," 330.

21. See P. Shinar, "Notes on the Socio-Economic and Cultural Role of

the Sufi Brotherhoods and Maraboutism in the Modern Maghreb," *Proceedings of the First International Congress of Africanists* (1962), 272–85.

22. GB, Naval Intelligence, *A Handbook of Libya* (London: H. M. Stationary Office, 1928), 46–51.

23. *Verso El Fezzan*, translated by Taha Fawzi (Tripoli: Maktabat al-Firjani, 1973), 85.

24. R. Graziani, *Cirenica Pazcificata*, translated into Arabic by Ibrihim B. Amir (Benghazi: Dar al-Andalus, 1974), 124; and Humphery J. Fisher and Virginia R. Fisher, "Firearms in Central Sudan," *Journal of African History* 12 (1974), 215–39.

25. Michel F. le Gall, "Pashas, Bedouins and Notables: Ottoman Administration in Tripoli and Benghazi 1881–1902," Ph.D. dissertation (history), Princeton University, 1986, 186.

26. GB, FO, Report of Consul J. R. Hay, 160/4, Dec. 1839.

27. GB, FO, Report of Consul A. Dickson, 12 Oct., 1911.

28. De Agostini, *Popolazioni Della Tripolitania*, xix; and Joffe, "Social and Political Structure," 23–24.

29. USNL 6/61, McCaurey to Webster, July 6, 1843.

30. GB, PRO, FO 195: 1375, Drumond Hay to Dufferin, June 5, 1881. Again in 1911 when Italy invaded Libya, many Tunisian tribesmen fought with their Libyan brothers against the Italian army. See for details Muhammad al-Marzuqi, *Dima' 'ala al-Hudud* (Blood on the borders) (Tunis-Tripoli: Al-Dar al-Arabiyah lil Kitab, 1975), 27, 49–80.

31. De Agostini, *Popolazioni Della Tripolitania*, xx; and Caunelle, "Le Seminomadisme," 106.

32. De Agostini, *Popolazioni Della Tripolitania*, xix; Caunelle, "Le Semi-nomadisme," 106.

33. 'Abd al-Jalil made a number of political alliances through marriage. He was married to the sister of the Sultan of Bornu, two of his sisters married two leading coast aristocrats of that sultanate, and a third sister was married to the Sultan of Morocco. See Adu Boahen, *Britain, the Sahara, and the Sudan*, 137. Also, 'Abd al-Jalil tried to negotiate a commercial treaty with France, offering to divert the Saharan trade toward French Algeria; see E. Subtil, "Histoire de Abd el Gelil, Sultan du Fezzan, Assassiné 1542," *Revue de L'orient* V (1844).

34. 'Abd al-Qadir Jami, *Min Tarabulus al Gharb*, 87.

35. J. Lethielleux, *Le Fezzan Ses Jardins Ses Palmiers* (Tunis: Imprimerie Bascone & Muscat, 1949), 45–46.

36. MDJL, Soc. Doc. 99, "A Report from the Governor of Fezzan," 2–5.

37. Subtil, "Histoire," 9–10; USNA, McCaulley to Secretary of State, May 5, 1942; and Boahen, *Britain, the Sahara*, 134, 136.

38. The Awlad Sulayman in Kanem raided other tribes more often than in Libya. Raiding was possible because no strong state existed in this frontier region. See Nachtigal, 338, 397.

39. Caunelle, "Le Nomadisme des Megarha," 63.

40. Marion Johnson, "Calico Caravans," 109.

41. The Yushi' merchant family sent its sons throughout their network of the Sahara trade in Ghat, Timbuktu, Sudan, Tripoli, and Tunis. See Doc. 30 in Yushi' *Ghadamis*, 82.

42. Doc. 47 in Yushi', *Ghadamis*, 109.

43. Doc. 66 in Adham and al-Dajani, *Wathaiq*, 182.

44. The people of Sukana told the traveler James Richardson that 'Abd al-Jalil cut down 20,000 trees. *Travels in the Great Desert of the Sahara in the Years of 1845 and 1846*, vol. II (London: Frank Cass and Co., 1970), 411; and Doc. 137 in Adham and al-Dajani, *Wathaiq*, 232.

45. Doc. 99, "Report of the Governor of Fezzan Muhammad Sumi: 1911," 4.

46. G. A. Krause, "Aufzeichnungen uber die Stadt Ghat in der Sahara," *Zeitschrift der Gesellschaft für Erdkunde* 17 (1882), translated into Arabic by 'imad Ghanim, *Thurath al-Sha'b*, Tripoli (April–June 1982), 137.

47. On the class structure of the Tuareg, see Johannes Nicolaison, *Ecology and Culture of the Pastoralist Tuareg* (Copenhagen: National Museum, 1963), 10–12.

48. 'Abd al-Qadir Jami (Jamey Bey) the Ottoman governor of Ghat in 1900, reported that "men were tyrannized by their wives, poor men have no liberty. This is by reason of the laws of inheritance by what all the real estate is the property of women." "Ghat and its Surroundings," *The Geographical Journal* xxxiv:2 (1909), 173; see also Nicolaison, *Ecology and Culture*, 115–22, 457; John Gulick, *The Middle East: An Anthropological Perspective* (Pacific Palisades, CA: Goodyear Publishing, 1972), 83; H. T. Norris, *The Tuaregs* (Wilts, England: Aris & Philips Ltd., 1974), 607; and Lars Eldblom, Interview, June 22, 1991, Potsdam, New York.

49. Abou El-Haj, "The Nature of the State."

50. Le Gall, "Pashas," 102–3, and GB, PRO, FO 101–91, Jago to O'Conor, Dec. 21, 1901.

51. Le Gall, "Pashas," 117.

52. Doc. 98 in Adham and al-Dajani,*Wathaiq*, 163.

53. Doc. 102, in Adham and al-Dajani,*Wathaiq*, 169

54. E. W. Bovill, *The Golden Trade of the Moors*, 2nd ed. (Oxford: Oxford University Press, 1978), 110–22.

55. GB, PRO, FO 160/12:23, Oct. 29, 1852.

56. USNA, 781, June 10, 1856.

57. GB, PRO, FO, 160:24, May 17, 1891.

58. Hornemann in Bovill, *Missions*, 103; and Nachtigal, *Sahara*, 169.

59. De Agostini, *Popolazioni Della Tripolitania*, 350, 364.

60. On the population of Ghadamis see Imad Ghanim, *al-Fusul al-Arba'ah* (April 1979), 97; on Murzaq and Ghat, see Coro, *Settantesci*, 134, 149, and De Agostini, *Popolazioni Della Tripolitania*, 202. The best study on the social history of these oases is Lars Eldblom, *Structure Fonciere Organisation Et Structure Social* (Unickol–Lund, 1968).

61. Nachtigal, *Sahara*, 122; Coro, *Settantesci*, 134; and Rossi, *Storia*, 416.

62. Despois, *Géographie Humaine*, 182–83.

63. Harrison, "Migrants," 415; and al-Dajani, "Libya Qubayla," 222, 224, 238.

64. Hilal, *Dirassat*, 124; Despois, *Géographie Humaine*, 182; and by the same author, *Le Djebal Nefousa*, 166–67.

65. Le Gall, "Pashas," 93.

66. See Post, "Peasantization," 229.

67. McLachlan, "The Role of Indigenous Farming," 34–35; Despois, "Types of Native Life," 356–57; and Le Gall, "Pashas," 92.

68. Le Gall, "Pashas," 93.

69. Goldberg, Harres, and R. Rosen, "The Itinerant Jewish Peddlers in Tripolitania at the End of the Ottoman Period and Under Italian Rule," 305–10.

70. al-Dajani, *Libya Qubayla*, 262.

71. On the role of Jewish merchants see Rachel Simon, "The Socio-economic Role of the Tripolitanian Jews," *Communities*, 321–28; if Maltese merchants, see Joffe, "Trade and Migration," and "British Malta and the Qaramanli. "

72. On the origins of this European patronage system see Edward Rae, *The Country of the Moors* (London: John Murray, 1877), 54, 78.

73. Anthony Cachia, *Libya Under the Second Ottoman Occupation: 1835–1911* (Tripoli: Government Press, 1945), 1021, Adham and al-Dajani, *Wathaiq*, 296–98.

74. Simon, "The Socio-Economic Role of the Tripolitanian Jews," 323–27.

75. al-Zawi, *Jihad*, 34.

76. Le Gall, "Pashas," 207; and *Baladiyat Tarabulus 1870–1970* (Municipality of Tripoli) (Tripoli: Idarat al-Athar, 1972).

77. al-Misrati, *Sahafat*, 18; see the classic essay by Albert Hourani on the role of the 'Ayan in the Ottoman empire: "Ottoman Reforms and the Politics of the Notables," in William Falk and Richard Chambers, eds., *The Beginnings of Modernization in the Middle East: The Nineteenth Century* (Chicago: University of Chicago Press, 1968), 41–68.

78. T. al-Zawi, *A'lam Libya* (Beirut: Dar Ihiya al Kutb al-Aribiyya, 1961), 14, 155.

79. MDJL, "Malaf al Amlak al-Musadara," (File of confiscated land by the colonial authorities), the district of Jffara, 22.

80. al-Marzuqi, *'Abd al-Nabi*, 623.

81. On the rivalry between the Suwayhli and the Muntasir clans, see Fushaykah, *Ramadan*, 11, 25, 46.

82. Some of the papers reflected Italian interests, such as *Il Giornel di Tripoli* 1909; *Eco di Tripoli* and *Il Messaggero di Tripoli*; others were pan-Islamist, such as *Tarabulus al Gharb* 1866, *al-Mirsad*, and *Abu-Qasha*, to mention a few. See al-Misrati, *Sahafat*, 13–118.

83. Hasan al-Faqih Hasan *al-Ywumiyat al-Libiyya 1551–1832* (Tripoli: Center for Libyan Studies, 1984), 20–21; and al-Zawi, *A'lam*, 14, 135, 200, 280, 291.

84. al-Zawi, *A'lam*, 342.

85. On the Muntasir family, see DMT, *Malaf al 'Aylat al Libiyyia*, 'Aialat al-Muntasir (The Muntasir Family) (The File of the Notable Families).

86. al-Faqih Hasan, Doc. 53–55, 17–131.

87. J. A. N. Brehony, "Seminomadism in the Jabal Tarhune," in Willimott, ed., *Field studies*, 63.

88. Ibn Isma'il, *Inhiyar*, 231; and M. A. al-Twair, "al-Zira'ah fi Waliyat Tarabulus al-Gharb 'athn'a al-Hukm al 'Authmani al-Mubashir

Laha, 1835–1911" (Agriculture in the Regency of Libya during the direct Ottoman rule), *Revue D'Histoire Maghrebiene*, 12éme Année:39–40 (Dec. 1985), 515–56. Many tribes settled. According to De Agostini's figures in 1913, 357,000 people were settled in Tripolitania and Fezzan, 128,000 were still seminomads and only 85,000 were nomads. De Agostini, *Popolazioni Della Tripolitania*, xviii. These figures can be accepted as accurate for the settled and urban populations, since these areas were under the rule of the colonial state. However, De Agostini's figures for the hinterland's population should be questioned, especially for the seminomadic and nomadic tribes. They are speculative, collected during wartime, and do not account for the many mobile tribesmen. But since no better data have been discovered, I will continue to quote his numbers with caution.

89. Lethielleux, *Le Fezzan*, 26–27.

90. Abdallah Ali Ibrahim, "Evolution of Government and Society in Tripolitania and Cyrenaica (Libya), 1835–1911," Ph.D. dissertation (history), University of Utah, 1982, 230.

91. Lethielleux, *Le Fezzan*, 45–46; Despois, *Géographie Humaine*, 236–37; and Lars Eldblom, *Land Tenure—Social Organization and Structure: A Comparative Sample Study of the Socio-Economic Life in Three Libyan Oases of Ghat, Mourzouk, and Ghadamis* (Uppsala: Scandinavian Institute of African Studies, 1969), 12, 15.

92. Caunelle, "Le nomadisme des Guedudfa," 350.

93. Louis Dupree, "The Non-Arabic Ethnic Groups of Libya," *Middle East Journal* xii (Winter 1958), 37–39.

94. Nachtigal, *Sahara*, 63–65, 86; Despois, *Géographie Humaine*, 134–35; and Lethielleux, *Le Fezzan*, 33.

95. De Agostini, *Popolazioni Della Tripolitania*, 364.

96. Lethielleux, *Le Fezzan*, 46.

97. Lethielleux, *Le Fezzan*, 46; and Eldblom, *Land Tenure*, 15.

98. William Dalton, "Patronage in Libyan Rural Development," *Nomadic Peoples* 18 (June 1985), 53–54.

99. Despois, *Géographie Humaine*, 237; and Caunelle, "Les Goueyda d'ouenzerik," 171.

100. Despois, *Géographie Humaine*, 233; and Lethielleux, *Le Fezzan*, 33.

101. De Agostini, *Popolazioni Della Tripolitania*, 364.

102. Despois, *Géographie Humaine*, 237; Lethielleux, *Le Fezzan*, 33, 46; and Caunelle, "Le seminomadisme," 108.

Chapter 4

1. A typical colonial approach to the Sanusiyya treated the order as a fanatical anti-Western movement. An example of this approach is the French writer Henri Duveyrier's *Le confrerie Musulmane de Sidi Mohammed Ben Ali es-Senousi et son domaine géographique de 1300–1883* (Paris: 1884, a reissue with an introduction by Carlo Nallino, Rome 1918). The work of Evans-Pritchard, *The Sanusi of Cyrenaica* (1948), though informative, is basically an apology for British colonialism. N. Ziadeh's *The Sanusyah* (1958) is dated and has many mistakes. The best scholarly study of the order is al-Dajani, *al-Haraka al Sanusiyya* (1967, 1988), especially the intellectual and political history. Yet there is no study of the political economy of the order to date.

2. Hasan Salaheddin Salem, "al-awda' al-Qabaliyya Fi Sharq Libya Fi al-'ahd al-'Uthmani al-Thani" (Tribal conditions in eastern Libya during the second Ottoman period), *Majallat al-Buhuth al-Tarikhiyya* 6:1 (1984), 20–21; and Le Gall, "Pashas," 197.

3. The Sanusi order sent two delegations to Istanbul for a tax exemption status for its *waqf* lodge lands. Sultan 'Abd al-Majid and, after him, his brother, Sultan 'Abd al-'Aziz, granted the order two imperial *Firmans* exempting the order's land from taxes under the status of *waqf*, or *Habus*. See recently published documents translated by the late 'Abdullsalam Adham (hereafter called Adham's collection) in Ahmad Sidqi al-Dajani, *al-Haraka al-Sanusiyya: nimuha wa Intsharuha Fi al-Qaran al-Tasi 'a 'Ashar* (The Sanusi order: Its origins and development during the nineteenth century), 2nd ed. (Cairo: 1988) 307–8, 311, 343; and Evans-Pritchard, *The Sanusi*, 91–92.

4. GB, PRO, FO 160/89, Memorandum on troop strength in Tripoli and Benghazi, June 9, 1889, FO, in which Consul Drumond Hay estimated the Turkish troops in Benghazi at around 2,000 (Dec. 14, 1889); and FO, Consul Alfred Dickson reported that the number of Turkish troops in the Regency declined to just 3,000 because of a rebellion in Yemen (Oct. 12, 1911).

5. GB, *Handbook of Libya*, 46–51.

6. Doc. 49 of Adham's Collection in al-Dajani, *al-Haraka*, 2nd ed, 353; and al-Hashaishi, *Jala*, 90.

7. Paolo Della Cella, *Narrative of an Expedition from Tripoli in Barbary to the Western Frontier of Egypt in 1817 by the Bay of Tripoli*, translated xfrom Italian by Anthony Aufrere (London: Jhou and Arthur Arch, 1822), 194.

8. James Hamilton, *Wanderings in North Africa* (London: John Murray, Albemarie St., 1856), 9.

9. Hamilton, *Wanderings,* 7.

10. al-Hashaishi, *Jala,* 52.

11. Della Cella, *Narrative,* 22, 221.

12. De Agostini, *Le Popolazioni Della Cirenaica, notizie etnice e storiche* (Benghazi: Governo Della Cirenaica, 1922–23) 415, 427.

13. Evans-Pritchard, *Sanusi,* 45.

14. De Agostini, *La Popolazioni Della Cirenaica,* 444.

15. Evans-Pritchard, *Sanusi,* 34.

16. Toni, "Tribal Distribution," 172.

17. Toni, "Tribal Distribution," 169, and Abbas, *Tarikh,* 151.

18. E. E. Evans-Pritchard, "Tribes and Their Divisions," in *Handbook of Cyrenaica,* part vii (Cairo: British Military Administration, 1947), 67; Ziadeh, *Libya Fi al-'usur,* 16; and Emorys L. Peters, "The Tied and the Free: An Account of Patron-Client Relationship among the Bedouin Pastoralists of Cyrenaica," in J. G. Peristiany, ed., *Contributions to Mediterranean Sociology: Mediterranean Rural Communities and Social Change* (Paris, the Hague: Mouton, 1968) 168–75.

19. De Agostini, *Le popolazioni Della Cirenaica,* 184–86.

20. De Agostini, *Le popolazioni Della Cirenaica,* 246–99.

21. De Agostini, *Le popolazioni Della Cirenaica,* 225, 227.

22. Saad Abu-oaf, "Legal Aspects of Tribal Lands and Settlement in Libya," in FAO *Report to the Government of Libya,* Development of tribal lands and settlements project, viv (April 1969), 3.

23. Ahmad Hasanain, *Fi Sahara, Libya* (Cairo, 1923), 188.

24. Peters, "Cultural and Social Diversity," 111.

25. James Hamilton, *Wanderings,* 56; and Abu-zeid, "The Sedentarization of Nomads in the Western Desert of Egypt," *International Social Science Journal* x:4 (1959), 550.

26. GB, PRO, FO Report of Consul Justin Alvarez from Benghazi, April 16, 1891.

27. FO, Alvarez, May 21, 1900.

28. FO, Alvarez, November 5, 1904; and Coro, *Settantiasei,* 114.

29. Evans-Pritchard, *Sanusi,* 37.

30. FO, Alvarez, years 1890, 1898, 1902. Also see more details on the

trade to Malta in E. G. H. Joffe, "British Malta and the Qaramanli Dynasty: 1800–1835," 32; and by the same author, "Trade and Migration between Malta and the Barbary States 1835–1911," 3.

31. al-Hashaishi, *Jala*, 98; and Cachia, *Libya*, 40, 104.

32. Della Cella, *Narrative*, 7, 51, 220, 224.

33. Toni, "Tribal Distribution," 177.

34. Peters, "Cultural and Social Diversity," 112.

35. Hasanain, *Fi Sahara*, 201; DMT, Report of the Ottoman Court Official Sadiq al-Muaid of a Visit to Sayyid al-Mahdi al-Sanusi in Kufra, 1890, 2.

36. GB, PRO, FO, A report of the British Consul Alvarez in Benghazi, April 16, 1891.

37. FO, Consul Alvarez in Benghazi, May 21, 1900.

38. FO, Consul Alvarez in Benghazi, November 5, 1904.

39. Johnson, "Calico Caravans," 50; and Dennis Cordell, "Eastern Libya, Wadai and the Sanusiyya: A Tariqa and a Trade Route," *Journal of African History* xxviii: 1 (1977), 34.

40. Boahen, *Britain, The Sahara*, 114.

41. J. L. Miege, "La Libye et La Commerce Transsaharien au xix. Siecle," *Revue de L'occident Musulman et de La Mediterranee* 19 (1975), 143.

42. See Hasanain, *Fi Sahara*, 48–49; the Sanusi Court Historian Muhammad Fu'ad Shukri, *al-Sanusiyya Din Wa-Duwla* [The Sanusiyya, a religion and a state] (Cairo: Dar al Fikir al-'Arabi, 1948), 27; and al-Dajani, *al-Haraka*, 1st ed., 266.

43. Evans-Pritchard, *Sanusi*, 49.

44. H. S. Salem, "al-Dar'ib al'Uthmaniyya fi Tarabulus al-Gharb Mutasarwifiayt Benghazi" [Ottoman taxes: Benghazi's country during the second half of the seventeenth century], *Majallat al-Buhath al-Tarikhiyya* 6:1 (1984), 20–21.

45. Salem, "al-Awda' al-Qabaliyya," 23.

46. Anderson, "Nineteenth Century Reform in Libya," *International Journal of Middle East Studies* 16 (1984), 336.

47. The center of the Sanusi influence was the lodge of Mizda, which was founded and administered by the Sunni family among the Jabal tribes of the Zintan, Awlad Busaif, Rijban, and Mashashiyya. See Adham's collection in al-Dajani, *al-Haraka*, Doc. 25, 324.

48. al-Zawi, *Jihad*, 253.

49. Hasanain, *Fi Sahara Libya*, 48-49.

50. See John Wright, "Outside Perceptions of the Sanusi," *Maghreb Review* 13: 1–2 (1988), 63–69.

51. See Edmond Burke III, "Understanding Arab Protest Movements," *Arab Studies Quarterly* 8:4 (1988), 336–38.

52. John Ralph Wills, "Jihad fi Sabil—Allah—Its Doctrinal Basis in Islam and Some Aspects of Its Evolution in Nineteenth-Century West Africa," *Journal of African History* viii:3 (1967), 395–415.

53. Ahmad Sudqqi al-Dajani, *Ahadith'an Libya Fi al-Qurn al-Thamin wa al-Tasi' 'Ushar* (Tripoli: Dar al-Misurati, 1968), 83. For details see also Ibrahim A. Abulqasim "Libyan Immigrants in the Agency of Tunis, 1881–1861." Ph.D. dissertation (history), University of Tunis, 1988.

54. A. S. El-Horeir, "Social and Economic Transformations," 218.

55. El-Horeir, "Social and Economic Transformations," 218.

56. On the life of Al-Fasi see R. S. O'Fahey, *Enigmatic Saint: Ahmad Ibn Idris and the Idrisi Tradition* (Evanston, Ill.: Northwestern University Press, 1990). Muhammad Ibn Ali al-Sanusi, "Iqaz al-Wisnan" [The awakening of the sleeping], 15–20, and "al-Masa'il al-'Ashr" [The ten matters], 11–13 in *al-Majmu 'a al-Mukhtara* [The Collected Works] (Beirut: Dar al-Kitab al-Lubnani, 1968).

57. al-Dajani, *al-Haraka*, 62–63.

58. al-Sanusi, "Iqaz al-Wisnan," 8.

59. al-Sanusi, "al-Durar al Saniyya fi Akhbar al-Sulala al-Idrisiyya" [The shining jewellers for the genealogy of the Idrisi family], in *Collected Works*, 6, 183.

60. Muhammad al-Taiyyb al-Ashhab, *al-Mahdi al-Sanusi* (Tripoli: Matba'at Maji Bilino, 1952), 69. Michel Le Gall argues that the Ottoman Porte did not grant tax exemption to the Sanusi. But even if he could not find a record of it in Istanbul the fact remains that the Sanusi Zawayya did not pay taxes. Le Gall needs to balance his evidence with local sources and archives. See his otherwise challenging article "The Ottoman Government and the Sanusiyya: A Reappraisal," *International Journal of the Middle East* 21C (1989), 96–97.

61. Doc. 21, Adham's collection in al-Dajani, *al-Haraka*, 318.

62. al-Sanusi, "Izaq al-Wisnan," 15–19.

63. al-Sanusi, "Izaq al-Wisnan," 15–19.

64. al-Sanusi, "al-Salsabil al Mu'in fi al-Turq al-'Rba'in" [The Reliable Source for the Forty Paths] in *Collected Works,* 6.

65. al-Dajani, *al-Haraka,* 161; al-Sanusi "'al-Mas'il" in *Collected Works,* 9; for comparison between the Sanusiyya and other Sufi-orders in the nineteenth century, see B. J. Martin, *Muslim Brotherhoods in Nineteenth Century Africa* (Cambridge: Cambridge University Press, 1976), 99–124.

66. Muhammad al-Taiyyb al-Ashhab, *al-Sanusi al-Kabir* [The Grand Sanusi] (Cairo: Maktabt al Qahira, n.d.), 24.

67. al-Dajani, *al-Haraka,* 270.

68. al-Ashhab, *al-Sanusi al-Kabir,* 150.

69. El-Horeir, "Social and Economic Transformations," 108–9.

70. Evans-Pritchard, *Sanusi,* 14.

71. al-Dajani, *al-Haraka,* 160.

72. Shukri, *al-Sanusiyya,* 49; Evans-Pritchard, *Sanusi,* 79; and al-Dajani, *al-Haraka,* 1st ed., 239.

73. al-Dajani, *al-Haraka,* 1st ed., 238; and Hasanain, *Fi Sahara Libya,* 46.

74. Rosita Forbes, "Across the Libyan Desert to Kufra," *The Geographical Journal* 58:2 (Aug. 1921), 88, 100; Hasanain, *Fi Sahara Libya,* 54, 193; and Cordell, "Eastern Libya," 31.

75. Humphrey J. Fisher and Virginia Rowland, "Firearms in the Central Sudan," *Journal of African History* xii:2 (1971), 223; Joseph P. Smaldone, "The Firearms Trade in the Central Sudan in the Nineteenth Century," in Daniel McCall and Norman Bennett, eds., *Aspects of West African Islam* (Boston: Boston University African Studies Center, 1971), 154, 59; and Shakri, *al-Sanusiyya,* 64.

76. Abner Cohen, "Cultural Strategies in the Organization of Trading Diasporas," in Claude Meillassoux, ed., *The Development of Indigenous Trade and Markets in West Africa* (London: Oxford University Press, 1971), 266. The descriptions of the Sanusiyya as an escapist movement by Ziadeh's *Sanusiya* or B. J. Martin's categories, in *Muslim Brotherhood,* of militant, moderate, and conservative movements where the Sanusiyya was described as moderate miss the complexity and the context of the nineteenth century. The Grand Sanusi provided moral example, education, and trade organization. These were revolutionary in the context of the time.

77. 37 in Libya, 6 in Hijaz, 8 in Egypt, and 1 in Tunis; during his son's leadership, 1859–1902, the lodges' number increased to 107: 30 in

Libya, 11 in Egypt, 6 in Central Sudan, 1 in Algeria, and 7 in Hijaz. See the Sanusi historian Muhammad A. al-Ashhab, *al-Sanusi al-Kabir*, 38, 42.

78. G. W. Murray, *Sons of Ishma'el: A Study of the Egyptian Bedouin* (London: George Routledge, 1935), 227.

79. There is confusion in the literature on the date of the final defeat of the Awlad Ali and their exile in Egypt: De Agostini mentions, in his study of the population of Cyrenaica, the year 1865 (p. 196), but Murray mentions the year 1789 (p. 30).

80. Murray, *Sons of Ishma'el*, 31, 289.

81. For more details, see Ali Barakat, *Tatwur al-Milkiyya al-Zira'iyya Fi Misr Wa 'Athuruha 'Ala al-Haraka al-Siyasiyya 1813–1914* [The Evolution of Landlordship in Egypt and its Impact on the Political Movement] (Cairo: Dar al-Thaqafa al-Jadida, 1977), 261–276.

82. Murray, *Sons of Ishmael*, 113.

83. Shukri, *al-Sanusiyya*, 52.

84. Adham's collection, Doc. 49, in al-Dajani, *al-Haraka*, 2nd ed., 352.

85. al-Ashhab, *al-Mahdi*, 35.

86. al-Ashhab, *al-Mahdi*, 35.

87. El-Horeir, "Social and Economic Transformations," 95.

88. El-Horeir, "Social and Economic Transformations," 93.

89. al-Ashhab, *Barqa*, 216.

90. al-Ashhab, *al-Mahdi*, 46.

91. Enrico Ensapato, *al-'Alagat al-Italiyya al Libiyya, 1902–1930* [Italian-Libyan Relations], translated into Arabic by 'Umar al-Baruni (Tripoli: Center for Libyan Studies, 1980), 120–21.

92. Cordell, "Eastern Libya, Wadai," 32.

93. Evans-Pritchard, *Sanusi*, 78–79.

94. Evans-Pritchard, *Sanusi*, 77.

95. Evans-Pritchard, *Sanusi*, 81–82; and C. C. Adams, "The Sanusis," *The Muslim World* xxxvi: 1 (Jan. 1946), 32.

96. Evans-Pritchard, *Sanusi*, 79.

97. Ahmad al-Sharif's decision was aimed at using Ottoman legal sovereignty to counter the expansion of the French in the Sahara. The Sanusi needed the protection of the Ottoman empire because they had not yet declared their own state. Thus the claim of the French would be refuted by

claiming central Sudan and southern Libya as Ottoman territories. Kilani Lataywish of the Magharba tribe was appointed governor of Kufra in 1910. See Shukri, *al-Sanusiyya*, 100, and Evans-Pritchard, *Sanusi*, 102.

98. Ahmad al-Sharif's declaration was published in the Egyptian journal *al-Manar* 15 (1921), 109–111; see also Muhammad 'Issa Salihiya, "The Libyan Papers Documented Secret, Letters of Ahmad al-Sharif, 1875–1933" (in Arabic), *Annals of the College of Arts*, Kuwait University, I (1980), 9; and Shukri, *al-Sanusiyya*, 140.

Chapter 5

1. Bipan Chandra, "Karl Marx, His Theories of Asian Societies and Colonial Rule," *Review* v:1 (Summer 1981), 84.

2. Thomas Hall, "Peripheries, Regions of Refuge, and Non-State Societies: Toward a Theory of Reactive Social Change," *Social Science Quarterly* 64 (1983), 582–97; Lionel Cliffe, "Class Formation as an 'Articulation' Process: East African Cases," in Alavi and Shanin, eds., *Introduction*, 262–87; and Salah Hamzowi, "Non-Capitalist Relations of Production in Capitalist Society: The Khammessat of Southern Tunisia," *Journal of Peasant Studies* 6:4 (July 1979), 444–70. On the non-European roots of capitalism outside of Europe, see Janet Abu-Lughod, *Before European Hegemony*, 353–54, 372; K. N. Chaudhuri, *Trade and Civilization in the Indian Ocean*, 222, and Peter Gran, *Islamic Roots of Capitalism*. On the role of collaboration, see Ronald Robinson, "Non-European Foundations of European Imperialism: Sketch for a theory of collaboration," In Roger Owen and Bob Sutcliffe, eds., *Studies in the Theory of Imperialism* (London: Longman, 1972), 117–40.

3. Perry Anderson, "Portugal and the End of Ultra-Colonialism," *New Left Review* (May–June 1962), 92–93, 98, 101–2; and Antonio Gramsci, *Selections from the Prison Notebooks*, 8th ed., translated and edited by Quintin Hoare and Geoffrey Newell Smith (New York: International Publishers, 1985), 68.

4. Luigi de Rosa, "Economics and Nationalism in Italy (1861–1914), *The Journal of European Economic History* 11:3 (Winter 1983), 537–38.

5. Luigi Villari, *Italian Foreign Policy Under Mussolini* (New York: Devin-Adair, 1950), 66–67; Maxwell H. Macartney and Paul Cremona, *Italy's Foreign and Colonial Policy 1914–1937* (London: Oxford University Press, 1938), 273, 284.

6. Paolo De Vecchi, *Italy's Civilizing Mission in Africa* (New York: Brentano's, 1912), 7, 40, 78–79. Also see Chevalier Tullio Irace, *With the Italians in Tripoli* (London: John Murry, 1912), viii–xvi.

7. Macksmith, *Mussolini's Roman Empire,* 41.

8. Macartney and Cremona, *Italy's Foreign and Colonial Policy,* 276–77.

9. Ernest N. Bennett, *With the Young Turks in Tripoli* (London: Methuen, 1912), 6–7; see a similar argument for French colonial images of West Africa, A. S. Kanya-Forstner, "French Expansion in Africa: The Mythical Theory," in Owen and Sutcliffe, eds., *Studies in the Theory of Imperialism,* 277–93.

10. Charles Lapworth, *Tripoli and the Young Italy,* chapter III.

11. See Gramsci, *Modern Prince,* 31–37, and also his *Selections from the Prison Notebooks,* 68. On the role of the northern industrial bourgeoisie, see Webster, *Industrial Imperialism,* 333–39.

12. Italy's population had jumped from 26 million in 1861 to 36 million in 1911; it reached 41 million in 1931. See Villari, *Italian Foreign Policy,* 66–67.

13. See Negash, "*Italian Colonialism,*" 2. For more details on the background of the war, see M. B. Akpan, "Liberia and Ethiopia, 1884–1914: The Survival of Two African States," in Adu Boahen, ed., *UNESCO General History of Africa* (Berkeley: University of California Press, 1985), 268–70.

14. Khakifa al-Tillisi, *Ma'arik al-Jihad al-Libi Min Khilal al-Khitat al-Italiyya* [The battles of resistance through Italian military plans] (Tripoli: al-Musu'a al-'Ama, 1982), 72, 76; and Graziani, *Verso El Fezzan,* 381–97.

15. al-Tillisi, *Ma'arik al-Jihad,* 78.

16. In postcolonial Libyan historiography, "collaboration" with the Italian colonial state as soldiers and administrators is poorly studied. There is a tendency to reduce the motives of the *Mutalinin,* the ones who had "gone Italian," to a lack of moral character, e. g., the work of Muhammad Said al-Gashshat. Such reductionist views ignore the social background and the complexity of motives of these Libyans who had to live through colonialism. Yet scholarship on anticolonial resistance in East and parts of North Africa is now quite sophisticated. On East Africa, see John Iliffe, "The Social Organization of the Maji Maji Rebellion," *Journal of African History* viii:3 (1967), 495–512; on North Africa see Edmund Burke, III *Prelude to Protectorate in Morocco: Precolonial Protest and Resistance 1860–1912* (Chicago: University of Chicago Press, 1976); Ross Dunn, *Resistance in the Desert: Moroccan Responses to French Imperialism 1881–1912* (Madison, Wisc.: University of Wisconsin Press, 1977); and also the articles by Peter Von Sivers, Julia Clancy-Smith, and Fanny Colonna in Edmund Burke, III and Ira Lapidus, eds., *Islam, Politics and Social Movements* (Berkeley: University of California Press, 1988).

17. See reports of two eyewitnesses: British journalists E. Bennett, *With the Turks*, p. 186; and Francis McCullagh, *Italy's War for a Desert* (Chicago: F. G. Browne, 1913), 18.

18. McCullagh, *Italy's War,* 3; and Lapworth, *Tripoli,* 85.

19. Giolitti, *Memoirs*, 260, 279.

20. Tullio Irace, *With the Italians*, 20.

21. See Ahmad Dia al-Din al-Muntasir's letter to S. al-Baruni in Za'ima al-Baruni, ed., *Safat Khalida Min al Jihad:* I [Glorious pages of resistance: Sulayman al-Baruni's papers] (Cairo: Mtba'at al-Istiqlal, 1964), 149–50.

22. Enrico De Leone, *La Colonizzione Dell' Africa Del Nord* (Padaua: Cedam-Casa Editrice dott. Antonio Milani, 1957), 390.

23. al-Zawi, *Jihad*, 34.

24. See DMT 188, "Malf al 'A'ilat al-Libiya" [files of Libyan notable families].

25. Fushayka, *Ramadan*, 29–33.

26. Ahmad became the *qaimmaqam* of Tarhuna and a member of the Ottoman state council in Tripoli. But in 1908, the young Turks regarded him as a pro-sultan Abd al-Hamid and blocked his election to the parliament. His father Umar was a *qaimmaqan* of Syrte. See Fushayka, *Ramadan*, 25, 33. Also, DMT 88, the Muntasir family's file.

27. Fushayka, *Ramadan*, 112.

28. The Muntasirs were rewarded for their collaboration with the Italians. 'Umar al-Muntasir became the *qaimmaqam* of Syrte, his son Salim was appointed the *qaimmaqam* of Misurata, and his son Ahmad became advisor to the Italian governor. See T. al-Zawi, *Jihad*, 118; and R. Graziani, *Versos El Fezzan*, 162.

29. ASAMI 150–53 (1919), cited in Lisa Anderson, "States, Peasants and Tribes," 173. Also see the letter of Ahmad al-Muntasir to S. al-Baruni in Za'ima al-Baruni, *Safahat Khalida*, 149–59; and DMT 88, "Malaf al-'A'ilat al Libiya: 'A'ilat al-Muntasir. "

30. 'Aghil Barbar, "The Tarabulus (Libyan) Resistance to the Italian Invasion: 1911–1920," Ph.D. dissertation (history) University of Wisconsin, Madison, 1980, 266; and De Leone, *La Coloniz-zione*, 390, 420.

31. al-Zawi, *Jihad*, 118.

32. In 1913 the Italians removed 'Abd al-Nabi by appointing him Mutasarrif of al-Jufra and arrested Saif al-Nasir's family. See al-Zawi, *Jihad*, 183; and Ishayka, *Ramadan*, 232.

33. Simon, "The Socio-Economic Role of the Tripolitanian Jews," 324.

34. De Felice, *Jews in the Arab Land*, 28, 40.

35. De Felice, *Jews in the Arab Land*, 351.

36. Goldberg, *Book of Mordechai*, 184, 187.

37. See al-Haj 'Umar S. al-Firjani (interview, June 7, 1978), in Mabruk al-Sa'di, ed., *Mawusu'at Riwayat al-Jihad* [A collection of oral histories of the Libyan *Jihad*] (Tripoli: Libyan Studies Center, 1983), 101. Also see Caunelle, "Le nomadisme des Zintan," 97; al-Zawi, *Jihad*, 183; and Graziani, *Verso El Fezzan*, 42, 188–89.

38. al-Haj Imnayna S. al-Gharbi (interview, May 31, 1978), *Mawusu'at*, 91; al-Zawi, *Jihad*, 480, 502; and Graziani, *Cirenaica*, 43.

39. Graziani, *Verso El Fezzan*, 110; and al-Gashshat, *Ma'arik*, 345.

40. Muhammad M. Ali al-Hamil (interview, July 3, 1978), *Mawusu'at*, 190; and al-Zawi, *Jihad*, 502.

41. For a brief history of this Libyan warlord, see al-Zawi, *Jihad*, 502–15. Also see Caunelle, "Le Fezzan Soul Bey Khalifa," *Bulletin de Liaison Saharienne* 9:32 (1959), 298–302.

42. Muhammad A. Khalifa Muftah (interview, April 24, 1978), *Mawusu'at* 30–31; and al-Gashshat, *Ma'arik*, 12.

43. al-Zawi, *Jihad*, 233.

44. Despois, *Le Djebal*, 308, 319; and 'Abd al Jalil al-Tahir, *al-Mujtama' al-Libi* [Libyan Society] (Beirut: al-Maktaba al-'Asriyya, 1968), 33.

45. De Agostini, *La Popolazioni della Tripolitania*, xx; and Hadi Abu Lugma, "Ethnic Elements in the Western Coastal Zone of Tripolitania," in Willimott and Clarke, eds., *Field Studies in Libys*, 113–15.

46. Streicker, "Government and Revolt," 36, 79–80.

47. al-Marzuqi, *'Abd al-Nabi*, 62–63.

48. Khalifa al-Tillisi, *Ba'ada al-Gardabiyya* [After al-Gardabiyya] (Beirut: Dar al-Thaqafah, 1973), 213; and al-Zawi, *Jihad*, 186.

49. For a biography of Ramadan, see Fushayka, *Ramadan al-Suwayhli*.

50. PRO, FO 371/4888, September 2, 1920.

51. al-Marzuqi, *Abd al-Nabi*, 201.

52. Muhammad Said al-Ghashshat, *Ma'arik al Difa' 'An al-Jabal al-Gharbi* (Tripoli: al-Munsha al-'Ama, 1983), 99; al-Tillisi, *Ba'd al-Gardabiyya*, 257.

53. al-Zawi, *'Umar al-Mukhtar,* 128; and Evans-Pritchard, *Sanusi,* 159–60.

54. See *Mudhakarat Anwar Pasha* [Memoirs of Anwar Pasha], edited by Orkhan Quluglo and translated into Arabic by A. El-Horeir (Tripoli: Libyan Studies Center, 1979); and *Mudhakarat al-Zubat al-Atrak* [Memoirs of Turkish officers], translated into Arabic by Wajdi Kadak, and edited by 'Imad Hatim (Tripoli: Libyan Studies Center, 1979).

55. Shaykh Shakib Arslan, the ideologue of the Muslim movement in Europe, played a major role in publicizing the invasion of Libya. See William Cleveland, *Islam Against the West: Shakib Arslan and the Campaign for Islamic Nationalism* (Austin: University of Texas Press, 1985), 100–102.

56. For a detailed study of the Italian-Ottoman agreement, see Muhammad 'Abd al-Karim al-Wafi, *al-Tariq Ila Lauzzane* [*The road to Lausanne*] (Tripoli: Dar al Firjani).

57. al-Zawi, *Jihad,* 160–61; al-Baruni, *Safaht* (I), 423; and De Leone, *La Colonizzione,* 387.

58. al-Baruni, *Safahat* (I), 464–67.

59. Rosabla Davico, "La Guerrilla Libyenne 1911–1932," in *Abd el-Karim et la Republique du Rif* (Paris: Maspero, 1976), 434–35; and Simon, *Libya,* 188.

60. al-Baruni, *Safahat* (I), 467.

61. al-Baruni, Suf B. 'Askar, and 3,000 fighters surrendered their arms to the French as they retreated to Tunisia. See Barbar, "Tarabulus (Libyan) Resistance," 262.

62. al-Zawi, *Jihad,* 184; and al-Tillisi, *Ba'd al-Gurdabiyya.*

63. al-Zawi, *Jihad,* 186.

64. al-Zawi, *Jihad,* 193–96.

65. al-Zawi, *Jihad,* 196; also see the story of the revolt narrated by one of the guerrillas, 'Abd al-Qadir Muhammad Ahmad (interview, June 7, 1978), in al-Sa'adi, *Mawusu'at,* 167; De Leone, *La Colonizzione,* 429; and al-Tillisi, *Ma'jam,* 275.

66. al-Tillisi, *Ma'arik,* 45–46.

67. Simon, *Libya,* 221; and al-Tillisi, *Ma'arik,* 45–46.

68. See Khalifa al-Tillisi, *Ma'jam Ma'arik al-Jihad fi Libya 1911–1931* (Tripoli-Tunis: al-Dar al-'Arabiyya, 1980), 405–8; De Leone, *La Colonizzione,* 448; and Evans-Pritchard, *Sanusi,* 122.

69. al-Tillisi, *Ma'jam*, 408.

70. al-Tillisi, *Ma'riq*, 51–52.

71. See El-Horeir, "Social and Economic Transformations."; and Salihiyya, *Safahat Majhula*, 13–17.

72. Evans-Pritchard, *Sanusi*, 126; and Lisa Anderson, "States, Peasants and Tribes," 284.

73. See the letter from Idris to Ahmad al-Sharif in Shakri, *al-Sanusiyya*, 191; and Salihiyya, *Safahat*, 18.

74. Salihiyya, *Safahat*, 17.

75. See Wright, "Outside Perceptions of the Sanusi," 62–69. By 1920 British travelers began to report about the Sanusi in positive terms. See Rosita Forbes, "Across the Libyan Desert to Kufra," 82, 85; and by the same author, "The Sanusi as a factor . . . ," 176.

76. See the letter of Idris to Ahmad al-Sharif in Shakri, *al-Sanusiyya*, 191; al-Zawi, *Jihad*, 282, 287.

77. al-Zawi, *Jihad*, 266, 301.

78. Salihiya, *Safahat*, 17.

79. Salihiya, *Safahat*, 17.

80. See al-Zawi, *Jihad*, 266–67; and Graziani, *Cirenaica*, 89.

81. See Fushayka, *Ramadan*.

82. al-Zawai, *Jihad*, 232–33.

83. al-Zawai, *Jihad*, 313, 317, 322, 324, 329; for 'Azzam's view, see Jamil 'Arif, ed., *Safahat Min al-Mudhakarat al-Siriyya Li 'Awal 'Amin Lil-jami'a al-'Arabiyya* [Pages from the memoirs of the first secretary of the Arab League] (Cairo: al-Maktab al-Masri al-Hadithy, n.d.), 199, 202, 209.

84. al-Zawi, *Jihad*, 322, 324; and 'Arif, *Safahat*, 210–14.

85. al-Zawi, *Jihad*, 259–60; for the Italian view, see De Leone, *La Colonizzione*, 506–7.

86. The dispute over the authority of the parliament led to the resignation of the Republic's representatives; see al-Zawi, *Jihad*, 370, 386.

87. See al-Baruni, *Safahat* (I), 166; Farhat al-Zawi in Remond, *Aux Camps*, 147; al-Zawi, *Jihad*, 90; Ahmad al-Sharif in Salihiyya, *Safahat*, 34; Umar al-Mukhtar, in al-Zawi, *'Umar al-Mukhtar*, 11. The oral histories of ordinary guerrillas echoed the same motives; see al-Sa'di, *Mawusu'at*, 189.

88. Bennett, *With the Young Turks*, 187; McCullagh, *Italy's War*, 292; and Abbott, *Holy War*, 120.

89. See Muhammad Said al-Gashshat, *Sada al-Jihad fi al 'Adab al Sha'bi* [Echo of Libyan jihad in popular literature] (Beirut: Dar-Lubnan, 1970).

90. Remond, *Aux Camps*, 144.

91. Remond, *Aux Camps*, 144.

92. al-Zawi, *Jihad*, 512.

93. al-Baruni, *Safahat* (I), 431–32.

94. Remond, *Aux Camps*, 102; De Leone, *La Colonizzione*, 387.

95. al-Zawi, *Jihad*, 257, 301; Fushayka, *Ramadan*, 117, 123; and al-Baruni, *Safahat* (I), 89.

96. Muhammad Ibrahim Lutfi al-Masri, *Tarikh Harb Tarabulus* [History of Tripoli's war] (Banha: Matba'at al'Amir Faruq 1942), 52, 64–65.

97. al-Zawi, *Jihad*, 244–49.

98. al-Zawi, *Jihad*, 398; al-Marzuqi, *Abd al-Nabi*, 121.

99. PRO, FO: 371/380b. May 4, 1920.

100. See the report of one of Ramadan's officers, Muhammad S. Hwaydi, in al-Marzuqi, *Abd al-Nabi*, 140–43; Fushayka, *Ramadan*, 244–45; and al-Zawi, *Jihad*, 399.

101. Most Libyan historians of the Tripolitanian resistance avoided mentioning the Jabal civil war, e. g., Shaykh T. al-Zawi, *Jihad*, 309; K. al-Tillisi, *Ba'd al-Gardabiyya*; while al-Gashshat, who wrote on this subject in his books *Khalifa* and *Ma'arik*, was partial to his tribe, the al-Zintan.

102. See the letters of the Jabal notables and chiefs in al-Gashshat, *Khalifa*, 351–98; and by the same author, *Ma'ariq*, 407–521; see also the oral histories of guerrillas, the al-Sa'adi interviews in *Mawusu'at*.

103. Abu-Lugma, "Ethnic Elements," 113–15, and De Agostini, *La Popolozione* xx.

104. al-Zawi, *Jihad*, 183.

105. al-Zawi, *Jihad*, 232–33.

106. al-Zawi, *Jihad*, 333–34.

107. al-Zawi, *Jihad*, 405; Graziani, *Verso El Fezzan*, 37.

108. al-Zawi, *Jihad*, 405; al-Gashshbat, *Khalifa*, 170, and by the same author, *Ma'ariq*.

109. al-Zawi, *Jihad*, 409; Graziani, *Verso El Fezzan*, 45.

110. al-Zawi, *Jihad,* 422–23.

111. al-Zawi, *Jihad,* 423.

112. al-Zawi, *Jihad,* 325–27.

113. Adrian Pelt, *Libyan Independence and the United Nations* (New Haven: Yale University Press, 1970), 19.

114. De Leone, *La Colonizzione,* 514.

115. al-Zawi, *Jihad,* 40.

116. al-Zawi, *Jihad,* 340.

117. al-Tillisi, *Ma'arik,* 56.

118. Graziani, *Verso El Fezzan,* 39, 49, 108, 153.

119. al-Zawi, *Jihad,* 514.

120. al-Zawi, *Jihad,* 514 and Graziani, *Verso,* 290–91.

121. al-Tillisi, *Ma'arik,* 78.

122. al-Marzuqi, *Abd al-Nabi.*

123. Graziani, *Cirenaica,* 32; and al-Tillisi, *Ma'arik,* 56.

124. D. Mack Smith, *Mussolini's Roman Empire,* 41.

125. See *al-Manar* (Cairo), January 23, 1912.

126. Graziani, *Cirenaica,* 279.

127. See A. J. Nicholls, "German," in *European Fascism,* edited by J. J. Woolf (London: Weidenfeld and Nicolson, 1970), 65.

128. On 'Umar al-Mukhtar, see al-Zawi, *'Umar al-Mukhtar* (Tripoli: Dar al-Firjani, 1970); and A. Barbar, ed., *'Umar al-Mukhtar, Nashatuhu Wajihaduh 1862–1931* ['Umar al-Mukhtar, his upbringing and jihad] (Tripoli: Libyan Studies Center, 1983).

129. al-Zawi, *'Umar al-Mukhtar,* 11, 84; M. Salihiyya, "al Adwar Fi Harakat al Jihad al-Libi," [Tribal camps in Libyan jihad], *Majallat Kuliyat al 'Adab,* Kuwait University, 13 (1978), 152; and see the letter from 'Umar al-Mukhtar to Ahmad al-Sharif in Idris El-Horeir, "Mawaqif Khalida Li 'Umar al-Mukhtar" [Memorable attitudes of 'Umar al-Mukhtar], *Majallat al-Buhuth al-Tarikhiyya* 2 (July 1988), 74.

130. Knud Holmboe, *Desert Encounter: An Adventurous Journey Through Italian Africa,* translated by Helga Holbek (New York: G. P. Putnam's Sons, 1937), 150.

131. Idris El-Horeir, "Mawaqif Khalida," 74.

132. Salihiyya, *Safahat*, 38; on Gaja Abdallah, see Said A. al-Hindiri, *al-'Alagat al-Libiya al-Chadiyya 1882–1975* [Libyan-Chadian relations] (Tripoli: Libyan Studies Center, 1983), 93; and A. El-Horeir, "Social and Economic Transformations" 93–94.

133. al-Zawi, *'Umar al-Mukhtar*, 188–89; and Graziani, *Cirenaica*, 48.

134. al-Zawi, *'Umar al-Mukhtar*, 100.

135. See Salihiyya, "al-Adwar," 153–54; and A. Barbar, "Al 'Asul al-Iqtisadiyyawa al-Ijtima'iyya Li-Harakat 'Umar al-Mukhtar" [The Economic and Social Bases of 'Umar al-Mukhtar's Movement, 1923–31] in A. Barbar, ed., *'Umar al-Mukhtar*, 80–89; and Grazian, *Cirenaica*, 92–94.

136. Salihiyya, "al-'Adwar," 154; Barbar, "Al-Asul," 82.

137. Salihiyya, "al-'Adwar," 156–59.

138. Salihiyya, "al-'Adwar," 159; and Graziani, *Cirenaica*, 102, 113.

139. According to Graziani, there were 20,000 guns in Cyrenaica between 1922 and 1928 (*Cyrenaica*, 124), and around 6,000 active guerrillas, declining to 500 by 1930 (*Cirenaica*, 33–34).

140. Graziani, *Cirenaica*, 196.

141. The Italian government offered al-Mukhtar a salary of 50,000 Italian francs a month if Sayyid al-Rida made peace with them, but al-Mukhtar refused. Al-Mukhtar's response was published later in the nrespaper *al-Watan* (Benghazi), 143 (1949).

142. Graziani, *Cirenaica*, 102, 150, 231.

143. Graziani, *Cirenaica*, 231; al-Tillisi, *Ma'jam*, 441–44; and al-Zawi, *'Umar*, 169.

144. See al-Zawi, *'Umar*, 165; and Yusuf al-Barghathi, "al-Mu'taqalat" [Concentration camps] in Salahaldin H. Salem and Habib W. al-Hisnawi, eds., *Dirassat Fi al-Tarikh al-Libi* (II) [Studies in Libyan history] (Tripoli: Libyan Studies Center, 1984), 315.

145. Muhammad al-Tayyib al-Ashhab, *Barqa al-'Arabiyya* [Arab Cyrenaica] (Cairo: Maktabat al-Hawari, 1947), 482; Evans-Pritchard, *Sanusi*, 189; and G. Rochat, "Il genocidie Cirenico e La Storigrafia Coloniale," *Belfagor* xxxv (1980), 449–56.

146. See University of Benghazi *Diwan al Shi'r al Sha'bi (I)* [Collection of popular poetry] (Benghazi: University of Benghazi Press, 1977), 228–37.

147. Holmboe, *Desert Encounter*, 137.

148. Holmboe, *Desert Encounter*, 137.

149. Holmboe, *Desert Encounter*, 304; and al-Zawi, *'Umar*, 213.

150. Salihiyya, *Safahat*, 6.

151. Salihiyya, *Safahat*, 39.

Conclusion

1. John Shotter, "Rhetoric and the Recovery of Civil Society," *Economy and Society* 18:2 (May 1989), 150.

2. See Bryan Turner, "Orientalism and the Problem of Civil Society in Islam," in Asaf Hussain et al., eds., *Orientalism Islam, and Islamists* (Brattleboro: Amana Books, 1984), 14–24; Asad, *The Idea of an Anthropology*, 8–9; and Abou El-Haj, "An Agenda for Research," 316.

3. On the study of the subaltern resistance see Ranajit Guha's essay, "On Some Aspects of the Historiography of Colonial India," in *Subaltern Studies I: Writings on South Asian History and Society*, edited by Ranajit Guha (New Delhi: Oxford University Press, 1982), 1–8, and Scott, *Weapons of the Weak*, 305–50.

4. See C. A. Hamilton, "Ideology and Oral Tradition: Listening to the Voices From Below," *History in Africa* 14 (1987), 67–86.

GLOSSARY

'abd (pl. 'abid). slave

'agha. lord, master; commander of the janissary military troops. In Cyrenaica, an *'agha* is an aide to the head of a religious lodge

'alim (pl. *'ulama*).scholar or specialist on Islamic law

'atwa (pl. *'atawat*). tribute

'ayan. notables

'a'ilat 'a'ilah. family, household

baraka (pl. *barakat*). God's blessing; a person who is blessed with *baraka* is called *murabit* and *sharif*

bait. house, household

bay'a. oath of fealty; homage, consent

Bilad al-Sudan. lit., the land of the blacks; the name given by Arabs to the region south of the Sahara and between the Nile and the Atlantic Ocean prior to European colonialism

Cologhli or **Kolughli.** from Turkish Kolughlu, descendants of intermarriage between Turkish troops and local North African women

dalu or **dalaw.** goatskin water container drawn up by a donkey and guided by a peasant called *jabbad* in Southern Libya

dariba (pl. *dara'ib*). tax

dhikr (pl. *'adhkar*). Sufi term for chanting and repetition of certain words, or poems in praise of God

din. religion

duwr (pl. *'adwar*). division, turn; a division of anticolonial tribal resistance in Libya during the colonial period

ferman or faraman. Ottoman imperial decree, edict, letter of commission or appointment

fallah or **fellah** (pl. *fallahin*). peasant

fatha or **fatiha**. start, the opening of each chapter of the Quran; prayer to gain the help or the blessing of God

fatwa (pl. *fatawa* and *fatawi*). formal legal opinion given by an *'alim* or jurist of standing to a question given to him by a judge or individual

habs or **habus** (pl. *hubus*). North African term for *waqf* or religious endowment

hadith. reported words and deeds of the prophet Muhammad by reliable chain of transmitters and scholars of Islamic law. The Quran and the hadith constitute the major authoritative sources of Islamic law

hamada. stony desert plateau; among the largest in Libya is hamada al-Hamra, located between southern Tripolitania and northern Fezzan

ikhwan. brothers, brethren, members of a religious order

ijtihad. scholarly free interpretation of Islamic law by qualified scholar of standing. The conventional view is that *ijtihad* was closed by the twentieth century and *taqlid* or conformity was accepted in Islamic law. This static view has been challenged as many scholars pointed out that even if conservative *'ulama* closed the gates of *ijtihad*, people still reinterpret the law in new ways

ijaza. graduation certificate for outstanding students of Islamic law

iltizam. tax concession on agriculture

imam. leader of prayers attached to a mosque; leader of the community or the state in Shii and Kharaiji Islam

jabbad. peasant hired to irrigate a farm of a landlord in exchange for a share of the crop according to initial agreement. The sharecropper *jabbad* draws water from a well using a donkey

jabal. mountain

janissary. Ottoman military corps till the beginning of the nineteenth century

jihad. religious struggle against inner-base impulses and desires, and also against the infidels who threaten the land of Islam

jaziya. tax levied on non-Muslims living under Muslim rule

khalifa (pl. *khulafa*). caliph, successor of the prophet, title of the ruler of the Muslim state

khammas (pl. *khammasa*). sharecropper in North Africa, often receives a fifth of the harvest in exchange for his labor

lahma. in western Libya refers to clan or subtribe

magharssa. contract between a sharecropper and landowner in North Africa. The sharecropper agrees to plant and irrigate palm and olive trees in exchange for a share of these trees by the time of the first harvest

mahalla. state military expedition or camp to subdue a rebellion and collect tributes in nineteenth-century North Africa

miriland. state land

mithiqal. weight, currency unit of gold

mtalian or **talian** (pl. *mutalinin*). "gone Italian," *harqi* in Algeria, a term used in Libya to describe Libyans who collaborated with the Italian colonial state as soldiers and bureaucrats

mu'alim (pl. *mu'alimin*). teacher

mudir. administrator of a subdistrict or *nahiya*

mufti. scholar of outstanding knowledge in religious matters who gives formal legal opinion or fa-wa to questions given to him by a judge

mujahid (pl. *mujahidin*). fighter against infidels, see *jihad*

mulk. property, private property

muqadm. foreman, military officer, head of a religious lodge

murabit (pl. *murabtin*). saint, individual who has *baraka*, client tribesmen in Cyrenaica

mutasarrif. provincial governor of a district or mutasarrifiyya in Ottoman Libya in the second half of the nineteenth century

pasha. governor-general of a province or *wilayat*; big landlord, high military or ministerial person in the Ottoman empire. The governor of Ottoman Libya in Tripoli was called *pasha*. The rules of the independent Qaramanli state retained the title of *pasha* from 1711 to 1835

Porte. the office of grand vizier in Istanbul, the highest political office in the Ottoman empire

qabila (pl. *qaba'il*). tribe

qadi or **kadi**. judge

Quran or **Koran**. the written words of Allah as revealed to the prophet Muhammad; Muslim holy book

qaimmaqam. administrator of a district or *qaimmaqamiyya* in Ottoman Libya in the second half of the nineteenth century

Quraish. prophet Muhammad's tribe; one of the most powerful tribes in seventh-century Arabia, which controlled the city of Mecca. Muslims have always accorded respect to the descendants of Quraish. Some Muslim jurists even required Quraishi kinship as a qualification for leadership of the Muslim community

Sa'adi. from Sa'da, the ancestress of the ten Sa'adi tribes of Cyrenaica. These tribes were members of the Arab Hilali conquering tribes of North Africa in the eleventh century. Hence they have owned most of the fertile land and water resources at the expense of early Arab and Berber Murabtin tribes in Cyrenaica. These ten tribes are 'Abid, 'Urufa, 'Awagir', Magharba, 'Abadydat, Hasa, 'Aylat-Faid, Drasa, and Bra'sa

sagai. water carrier, sharecropper peasant who is hired to irrigate a landowner's farm in exchange for a percentage of the harvest or a salary in North Africa

sadaqa (pl. *sadaqat*). alms, voluntary contribution of alms for the sake of God's rewards

sharif (pl. *asfraf* or *shurufa*). noble; a person who is believed to descend from the prophet's family through his daughter Fatima

shari'a. law, Islamic law; includes the Quran, the deeds and the statements of prophet Muhammad, the consensus of the Muslim community and the reasoning of the *ulama*

shaykh. elder, dignitary, leader of prayers at a mosque, *'alim*, tribal chief

saniya (pl. *swani*). well, farm in North Africa

sidi or **sayyid** (pl. *sadah* or *assyad*). colloquial from *Sayyidi*, Sir; respected person of status from *sharifi* or *murabitic* background in North Africa

shwashna. descendants of freed black slaves in North Africa

Sufi. mystic; a major trend in Islam that stresses the inner spiritual experience. In North Africa Sufi Islam dominated popular culture from the fourteenth century

sultan. title of ruler, the ruler of the Ottoman empire

sunna. the deeds and statements of the prophet Muhammad as accepted by a reliable chain of transmitters. Muslims who believe in the Sunna are called *Sunni*

suff (pl. *sufuf*). line, tribal confederation and alliance in southern Tunisia, Tripolitania, and Fezzan in Libya during the nineteenth century

takhris. process of estimating the harvest of olive or palm trees by state tax collectors in nineteenth-century Ottoman Libya

tanzimat. lit., in Turkish, "beneficent legislation"; Ottoman reforms from 1839 to 1876

tariqa (pl. *turaq*). path, religious Sufi order

'umma. Islamic community

'ushr (pl. *'ashar*). tithe, 10 percent tax on agricultural produce known also as *zakat*, one of the five pillars of Islam

wabbar. person who fertilizes palm trees in Fezzan

wadi (pl. *'awdiya* or *widiyan*). valley

wald (pl. *'awlad*). child, boy, descendant, e.g., Awlad Sulayman

wali (pl. *wulat*). provincial governor of *wilayat* in the Ottoman empire

walii (pl. *'awliya'*). saint, *murabit* who is believed to have *baraka* in North Africa. After the death of a *walii* his tomb or lodge becomes a shrine and a place of sanctity

waqf. religious endowment, see **habs**

watan. homeland

wilayat. in Turkish *iyala* and *vilayet*; province of the Ottoman empire. A wilayat is made of a district, *mutasarrifiyya*, a subdistrict, *qaim-maqamiyya*, and a sub-subdistrict, a *mudiriyya* or *nahiya*. This was the administrative system of the Ottoman empire during the second half of the nineteenth century

zakat. alms, see **'ushr**

zawiya (pl. *zawaya*). lodge, mosque, hospice, and school complex of a religious Sufi order, e.g., the Sanusiyya.

REFERENCES

Archives

Tripoli: 1. Dar al-Mahfuzat al-Tarikhiyya (DMT). 2. Markaz Dirassat Jihad al-Libiyyin (MDJL).

Rome: Archivo Storico de Ministero Africa Idaliana (ASMAI), Ministero degli Affari Esteri.

London: Public Record Office (PRO).

Washington, D.C.: United States National Archives (USNA).

Unpublished Papers and Dissertations

Abou El-Haj, Rifaat A. *The Nature of the State* (unpublished manuscript).

Abushhawa, Malik. "The political system in Libya (1951–1969)," M.A. thesis (political science), Cairo University, 1977.

Abu-Swa, Mahmud. "The Arabization and the Islamization of the Maghreb: Social and economic reconstruction of the history of the Maghreb during the first two centuries of Islam," Ph.D. diss. (history), UCLA, 1984.

Ahmida, Ali A. "The structure of patriarchal authority: An interpretive essay on the impact of kinship and religion on politics in Libya between 1951–1960," M.A. paper of distinction, University of Washington, Seattle, 1983.

Anderson, Lisa S. "States, peasants and tribes: Colonialism and rural politics in Tunisia and Libya," Ph.D. diss. (political science), Columbia University, 1980.

Barbar, 'Aghil M. "The Tarabulus (Libyan) resistance to the Italian invasion: 1911–1920," Ph.D. diss. (history), University of Wisconsin, Madison, 1980.

Cordell, Dennis. "The Awlad Sulayman of Libya and Chad: A study of raiding and power in Chad basin in the nineteenth century," M.A. thesis, University of Wisconsin, Madison, 1972.

Fatah, Hala. "The development of regional markets of Iraq and the Gulf, 1800–1900," Ph.D. diss. (history), UCLA, 1986.

Fituri, Ahmad S. "Tripolitania, Cyrenaica, and Bilad al-Sudani trade relations during the second half of the nineteenth century," Ph.D. diss. (history), University of Michigan, 1982.

Gashut, Shaban F. "The development of Libyan newspapers 1860–1972: A history and interpretation," M.A. thesis, University of Kansas, 1972.

El-Horeir, 'Abdul Mola S. "Social and economic transformations in the Libyan hinterland during the second half of the nineteenth century: The role of Sayyid Ahmad al-Sharif," Ph.D. diss. (history), UCLA, 1981.

Ibrahim, Abdallah A. "Evolution of government and society in Tripolitania and Cyrenaica (Libya) 1835–1911," Ph.D. Diss., University of Utah, 1982.

Le Gall, Michel F. "Pashas, bedouins and notables in the Ottoman administration in Tripolitania, Benghazi 1881–1902," Ph.D. diss. (history), Princeton University, 1986.

Pamuk, Sevket. "Foreign trade, foreign capital and the peripheralization of the Ottoman empire, 1830–1913," Ph.D. diss. (economics), University of California, Berkeley, 1978.

Salem, Salaheddin H. "The genesis of political leadership in Libya, 1952–1969," Ph.D. diss. (history), George Washington University, 1973.

Streiker, Allen. "Government and revolt in the Tripoli Regency 1795–1969," M.A. thesis, Northwestern University, 1970.

Swedenburg, Theodore. "Memories of revolt: The 1936–39 rebellion and the struggle for a Palestinian national past," Ph.D. diss. (anthropology), University of Texas, Austin, 1988.

Interviews

Shalgam, 'Abdal-Rahman, August 8, 1985, Rome.

al-Usta, Haj Muhammad, September 22, 1985.

al-Hisnawi, Habib Wadaa, September 25, 1985, Tripoli.

Eldblom, Lars, June 22, 1991, Potsdam, New York.

Newspapers

Abu Qasha, al-Mirsad, al-'Adl (Tripoli).

Published Material: Books and Articles

'Abd al-Haqim, Shawqi. *Sirat Bani Hilal.* Beirut: Dar al-Tanwir, 1983.

Abou El-Haj, Rifaat A. "An agenda for research in history: The history of Libya between the sixteenth and the nineteenth centuries." *International Journal of Middle East Studies* 15 (1983).

———. *Formation of the Modern State.* Albany: State University of New York Press, 1991.

———. "Social user of the past: Recent Arab historiography of Ottoman rule." *International Journal of Middle East Studies* 14 (1982).

Abu-Lugma, Hadi. *Dirassat Libiyya.* Benghazi: Maktabat Qurina, 1975.

Abu-Lughod, Janet. *Before European Hegemony.* New York: Oxford University Press, 1989.

Abu-Lughod, Lila. "Zones of theory in the anthropology of the Arab world." *Annual Review of Anthropology* 18 (1989).

Abu-Oaf, Saad. "Legal aspects of tribal lands and settlement in Libya." In FAO *Report to the Government of Libya,* April 1969.

Abu-Swa, Mahmud. "Ru'ya jadida lil-fatah al-Islami li-Libya" *Majallat al-Buhuth al-Tarikhiyya* 8:1 (Tripoli, January 1986).

Abu-Zeid, Ahmad. "The sedentarization of nomads in the western desert of Egypt." *International Social Science Journal* X:4 (1959).

Adams, C. C. "The Sanusis." *Muslim World* XXXVI:1 (January 1946).

Adham, A. and A. Ibrahim, eds. *Watha'iq 'An Tarikh Libya fi al-Qarn al Tasic Ushr (I) Thawrath Ghuma al-Mahmudi.* Tripoli: Center for Libyan Studies, 1983.

Ahmida, Ali A. "Colonialism and the formation of the Arab states: The Tunisian and Libyan experiences." *The Arab Journal of International Studies* 1:2 (Summer 1988).

Akpan, M. B. "Liberia and Ethiopia, 1884–1914: The survival of two African states." In A. Boahen, ed., *UNESCO General History of Africa.* Berkeley: University of California Press, 1985.

Alavi, Hamiza, and Theodor Shanin, eds. *Introduction to the Sociology of Developing Societies.* New York: Monthly Review Press, 1982.

Amin, Samir. "Modes of production and social formation." *Ufahamu* IV:3 (Winter 1974).

———. *Class and Nation Historically and in the Current Crisis.* New York: Monthly Review Press, 1980.

Anderson, Lisa S. "Nineteenth-century reform in Ottoman Libya." *International Journal of Middle East Studies* 16 (1984).

———. *The State and Social Transformation in Tunisia and Libya 1830–1980.* Princeton: Princeton University Press, 1986.

Anderson, Perry. *Passages from Antiquity to Feudalism*, London: New Left Review Press, 1974.

———. "Portugal and the end of ultra-colonialism." *New Left Review* (May–June 1962).

al-Ansari, Ahmad N. *al-Manhal al-'Adhb fi Tarikh Tarabulus al-Garb.* Vol. I. Tripoli: Makiabat al-Firjani, n.d.

Anwar Pasha. *Mudhakarat Anwar Pasha* [Memoir of Anwar Pasha]. Tripoli: Center for Libyan Studies, 1979.

Anyan'nyong'o, Peter, ed. *Popular Struggle for Democracy in Africa.* London: Zed Press, 1987.

Asad, Talal. "Anthropology and the analysis of ideology." *Man* 14:4 (December 1979).

———. *The Idea of an Islamic Anthropology.* Washington, D.C.: Georgetown University Press, 1986.

———. "Two European images of non-European rule." In Asad, ed., *Anthropology and the Colonial Encounter.* Atlantic Highlands, New York: Humanities Press, 1988.

al-Ashhab, Muhammad T. *Barga al-'Arabiyya.* Cairo: Maktabat al-Hawari, 1947.

———. *Al-Mahdi al-Sanusi.* Tripoli: Matbaat Maji, 1952.

———. *Al-Sanusi al-Kabir.* Cairo: Matbaat al-Qahira, n.d.

Ayyub, 'Abd al-Rahman. "The Hilali epic: Material and memory." *Revue D'Histoire Maghrebine* II (December 1984).

Bair, Stephen. "Trans-Sahara trade and the Sahel: Damegu, 1930–1970." *Journal of African History* 18 (1977).

Baladiyat Tarabulus in 1870–1970. Tripoli: Idarat al-Athar, 1972.

Barakat, Ali. *Tatwur al-Milkiyya al-Zira'iyya fi Misr wa Atharaha 'Ala al-Haraka al-Siyasiyya 1813–1914.* Cairo: Dar al-Thaqafa al-Jidida, 1977.

Barbar, 'Aghil, ed. *'Umar al-Mukhtar.* Tripoli: Center for Libyan Studies, 1983.

———. "Masraf Roma Wa-Dawur al Sultat al-'Uthmaniyya Fi al-Wuquf Dida al-Tasalul al Ifali Ila-Libya" Majallat al-Buhut al-Tarikhiyya 2 (July 1982).

Barth, Henry. *Travels and Discoveries in North and Central Africa in the Years 1849–1855.* Philadelphia: Key Stone Publishing Co., 1890.

al-Baruni, Za'ima S., ed. *Safahat Khalida Min al-Jihad.* Cairo: Miba'at al-Istiqlal, 1964.

Bennett, Ernest. *With the Young Turks in Tripoli.* London: Methuen and Co., 1912.

Bennoune, Mahfaud. "Origins of the Algerian proletariat." *MERIP Reports* (February 1981).

Berman, J. "The concept of articulation and the political economy of colonialism." *Canadian Journal of African Studies* 18:21 (1984).

Blake, G. H. *Misurata: A Market Town in Tripolitania.* Durham, England: University of Durham, 1968.

Boahen, Adu. "The caravan trade in the nineteenth century." *Journal of African History* 111:2 (1972).

———. *African Perspectives on Colonialism.* Baltimore: Johns Hopkins University Press, 1987.

Bovill, E. W. *The Golden Trade of the Moors.* 2nd ed. Oxford: Oxford University Press, 1928.

Brener, Robert. "Agrarian class structure and economic development in pre-industrial Europe." *Past and Present* 70 (February 1976).

Brener, Robert. "The origins of capitalist development: A critique of neo-Smithian Marxism." *New Left Review* 104 (July–August 1977).

Brenner, Louis. "Muhammad al-Amin al-Kanimi and religion and politics in Bornu." In John Ralph, ed., *Studies in West African Islamic History* I. London: Frank Cass, 1979.

———. "North African trading community in the nineteenth century central Sudan." In D. F. McCall and N. R. Benett, eds., *Aspects of West African Islam.* Boston: The University Press, 1971.

Brewer, Anthony. *Marxist Theories of Imperialism.* London: Routledge & Kegan Paul, 1980.

Burke III, Edmund. "The image of the Moroccan state in French ethnological literature." In E. Gellner and Charles Micaud, eds., *Arabs and*

Berbers: From Tribe to Nation in North Africa. Lexington, Mass.: D. C. Heath, 1972.

———. Prelude to *Protectorate in Morocco. Pre-Colonial Protest and Resistance 1860–1912*. Chicago: University of Chicago Press, 1976.

———. "Understanding Arab protest movements," *Arab Studies Quarterly* 8:4 (1988).

Burke III, Edmund, and Ira Lapidus, eds. *Islam, Politics, and Social Movements*. Berkeley: University of California Press, 1988.

Cachia, Anthony. *Libya Under the Second Ottoman Occupation 1835–1911*. Tripoli: Government Press, 1945.

Cahen, Claud. "Quelques mots sur les hilaliens et le nomadisme." *Journal of Economic and Social History of the Orient* XI (1963).

Carmi, Shulamit, and Henry Rosenfeld. "The origins of the process of proletarianization and urbanization of the Arab peasants in Palestine." *Annals of the New York Academy of Sciences* 220:6 (1974).

Caunelle, Andre. "Le Fezzan sous bey Khalifa." *Bulletin de Liaison Saharienne* 9:32 (1958).

———. "Le Nomadisme de Zintan (Tripolitaine et Fezzan)." *Travaux de l'Institut de Recherches Sahariennes* 9:32 (1958).

———. "Le nomadisme de Megarha (Fezzan)." *Travaux de l'Institute de Recherches Sahariennes* 12:2 (1954).

———. "Le semi-nomadisme dans l'ouest Libyen: Fezzan, Tripolitaine." In UNESCO Recherches Du Zone Aride 19, *Nomades et Nomadisme au Sahara*. Paris: UNESCO, 1963.

Chakrabarty, Dipesh. "Post-coloniality and the artifice of history: Who speaks for 'Indian' Pasts?" *Representations* 37 (Winter 1992).

Chakravarty-Spivak, Gayatri. "The Rani of Sirmur: An Essay in Reading the Archives." *History and Theory* 24:3 (1985).

Chandara, Bipan. "Karl Marx, his theories of Asian societies and colonial rule." *Review* V:1 (Summer 1981).

Chatterjee, Partha. *Nationalist Thought and the Colonial World: A Derivative Discourse?* London: Zed Press, 1986.

Chaudhuri, K. N. *Trade and Civilization in the Indian Ocean: An Economic History from the Rise of Islam to 1750*. Cambridge: Cambridge University Press, 1985.

Chirot, Daniel. "Changing fashion in the study of social causes of economic and political change." In James Short, ed., *The State of Sociology:*

Problems and Perspectives. Beverly Hills, CA: Sage Publications, 1981.

Clamer, John, ed. *The New Economic Anthropology*. London: MacMillan, 1978.

Clancy-Smith, Julia. "Saints, Mahdis, and Arms: Religion and resistance in nineteenth century North Africa," in Edmund Burke III and Ira Lapidus, eds., *Islam, Politics, and Social Movements*. Berkeley: University of California Press.

Clarke, J. I. "The Si'aan pastoralists of the Jafara." In S. G. Willimott and J. I. Clarke, eds. *Field Studies in Libya*. Durham, England: Durham University Press, 1960.

Cleveland, William. *Islam Against the West: Shakib Arslan and the Campaign for Islamic Nationalism*. Austin: University of Texas Press, 1985.

Cliff, Lionel. "Class formation as an 'articulation' process: East African cases." In Alavi and Shanin, eds. *Introduction*.

Cohen, Abner. "Cultural strategies in the organization of trading diasporas." In C. Meillassoux, ed., *The Development of Indigenous Trade and Markets in West Africa*. London: Oxford University Press, 1971.

Cohen, Ronald, and Elman Service, eds. *Origins of the State*. Philadelphia: Institute for the Study of Human Issues, 1978.

Collins, Robert, ed. *The Partition of Africa*. New York: John Wiley & Sons, 1969.

Colonna, Fanny. "The transformation of a saintly lineage in North West Aures Mountains (Algeria): Nineteenth and twentieth centuries," in Edmund Burke III and Ira Lapidus, eds., *Islam, Politics, and Social Movements*. Berkeley: University of California Press.

Colucci, Massimo. "Il diritro consuetudinario della Cirenaica." *Rivesita Giuridica Del Medio Estremo Oriente E Giustizia Colonial* 1 (1932).

Cordell, Dennis. "The Awlad Sulayman of Libya and Chad: Power and adaptation in the Sahara and Sahel." *Canadian Journal of African Studies* 19:2 (1985).

———. "Eastern Libya Wadai and the Sanusiyya: A Tariqa and trade route." *Journal of African History* 18:2 (1972).

Coro, Francesco. *Stettantessei Anni di Dominizione Turca in Libia, 1835–1911*. Tripoli: Dar al-Firjani, 1971.

Currie, Kate. "Problematic modes and the Mughal social formation." *The Insurgent Sociologist* 9:2 (1980).

Daghfus, Radi. "al-'Awamil al-Iqtisadiyya Li-Hijarat bani Hilal." *Awraq*. (April 1981).

Dajani, Ahmad S. *Ahadith 'An Tarikh Libya*. Tripoli: Dar al-Misurati, 1968.

———. *al-Haraka al-Sanusiyya*, 2nd ed., Cairo: al-Matba'a al Faniyya, 1988.

———. *Libya Qubayla al-Ihtilal al-Itali: 1882–1911*. Cairo: al-Matba'a al Faniyya, 1971.

Dajani, Ahmad S., and Abd al-Salam Adham, eds. *Watha'iq Tarikh Libya al-Hadith: al Watha'iq al 'Uthmaniyya, 1881–1911*. Benghazi: The University Press, 1974.

Dalton, William. "Patronage in Libyan rural development." *Nomadic Peoples* 18 (June 1985).

Davico, Rosabla. "La Guerrilla Libyenne 1911–1932." In *Abd el-Karim et la Republique du Rif: Actes du colloque international d'etudes historiques et sociologiques, 18–20 Janvier 1973*. Paris: Maspero, 1976.

Davis, Horace. "Nations, colonies and social classes: The position of Marx and Engels." *Science and Society* 29 (1965).

Davis, John. *Libyan Politics: Tribe and Revolution: An Account of the Zuwayya and their Government*. London: I. B. Tauris, 1987.

Daynasuri, J. *Jughrafiyat Fezzan*. Benghazi: Dar Libya, 1967.

De Felice, Renzo. *Jews in an Arab Land, 1836–1970*. Austin: University of Texas Press, 1985.

Del Boca, Angelo. *Gli Italiani in Libia: Tripoli Bel Soul D'Amore 1860–1922*. Rome: Literza Figli, 1986.

De Leone, Enrico. *La Colonizzione Dell Africa Del Nord*. Padaua: CE-Dam, 1957.

Della Cella, Paolo. *Narrative of an Expedition from Tripoli in Barbary to the Western Frontier of Egypt in 1817 by the Bay of Tripoli*. London, 1822.

De Reynaud, P. "La régence de Tripoli." *Revue des Deux Mondes* XII (1855).

De Rose, Luigi. "Economics and nationalism in Italy (1861–1914)." *The Journal of European Economic History* 11:3 (Winter 1983).

Despois, Jean. *La Colonization Italienne en Libye*. Benghazi: Dar Libya, 1968.

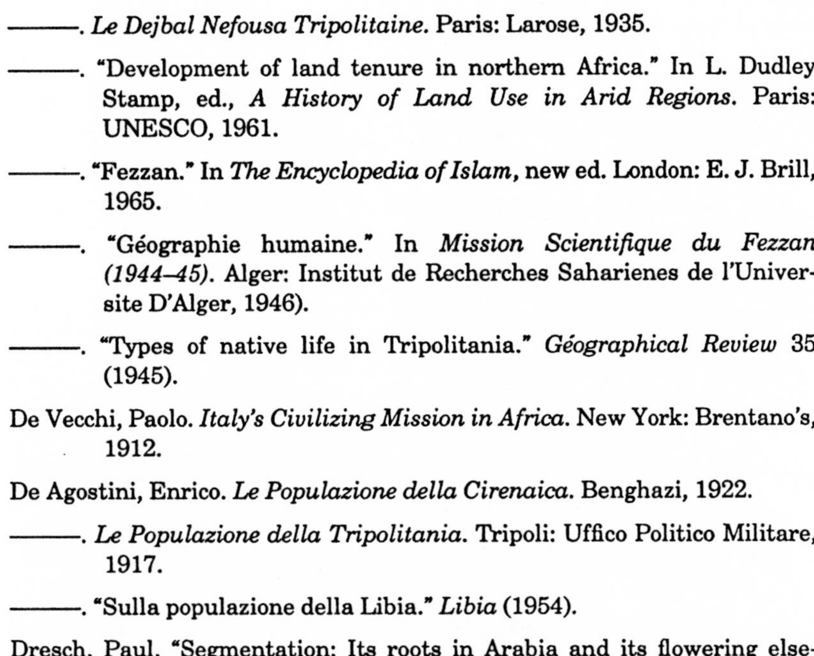

———. *Le Dejbal Nefousa Tripolitaine.* Paris: Larose, 1935.

———. "Development of land tenure in northern Africa." In L. Dudley Stamp, ed., *A History of Land Use in Arid Regions.* Paris: UNESCO, 1961.

———. "Fezzan." In *The Encyclopedia of Islam,* new ed. London: E. J. Brill, 1965.

———. "Géographie humaine." In *Mission Scientifique du Fezzan (1944–45).* Alger: Institut de Recherches Saharienes de l'Universite D'Alger, 1946).

———. "Types of native life in Tripolitania." *Géographical Review* 35 (1945).

De Vecchi, Paolo. *Italy's Civilizing Mission in Africa.* New York: Brentano's, 1912.

De Agostini, Enrico. *Le Populazione della Cirenaica.* Benghazi, 1922.

———. *Le Populazione della Tripolitania.* Tripoli: Uffico Politico Militare, 1917.

———. "Sulla populazione della Libia." *Libia* (1954).

Dresch, Paul. "Segmentation: Its roots in Arabia and its flowering elsewhere." *Cultural Anthropology* 3 (1988).

Dunn, Ross E. *Resistance in the Desert: Moroccan Responses to French Imperialism, 1881–1912.* Madison: University of Wisconsin Press, 1977.

Dupree, Louis. "The non-Arabic groups of Libya." *Middle East Journal* XII (Winter 1958).

Duvayrier, Henri. *Le Confrèrie Musulmane de Sidi Mohammed Ben Ali el-Senousi et Son Domaine Géographique en 1800–1883.* Paris, 1884; Rome, 1918.

Dyer, Mark. "Export production in western Libya, 1750–1793." *African Economic History* 13 (1984).

Eldblom, Lars. *Land Tenure—Social Organization and Structure.* Uppsala: Scandinavian Institute of African Studies, 1969.

Elster, Jon. *Making Sense of Marx.* London: Cambridge: Cambridge University Press, 1985.

Ensapato, Enrico. *al-'Alaqat al-Italiyya al-Libiyya 1902–1930.* Tripoli: Center for Libyan Studies, 1980.

Evans-Pritchard, E. E. *The Sanusi of Cyrenaica.* Oxford: Oxford University Press, 1949.

———. "Tribes and their divisions." In *Handbook of Cyrenaica*. Cairo: British Military Administration, 1947.

al-Faqih Hasan, H. *al-Ywumayat al-Libiya (I) 1551–1832*. Tripoli: Center for Libyan Studies, 1984.

Feraud, Charles. *Annales Tripolitaine*. Paris, 1927. (Arabic translation by Muhamad A. al-Wafi, Tripoli, 1973. Reprinted in 1983.)

Fisher, Hans. "A journey from Tripoli across the Sahara to Lake Chad." *Géographical Journal* (March 1909).

Fisher, Humphrey, and Virginia Fisher. "Fire arms in central Sudan." *Journal of African History* 12 (1974).

Folayan, Kola. "Tripoli and the war with the U.S.A., 1801–5." *Journal of African History* XIII:2 (1972).

———. *Tripoli During the Reign of Yusuf Pasha Qaramanli*. IFE, Nigeria: University of IFE Press, 1975.

Forbes, R. "Across the Libyan desert to Kufra." *Geographical Journal* 58:2 (1921).

———. "The Sanusi as a Factor in North African Development," *Journal of the Central Asian Society*, VIII (1921).

Frank, Andre Gounder. *Capitalism and Underdevelopment in Latin America*. New York: Monthly Review Press, 1969.

Friedman, Harriet. "Household production and the national economy: Concepts for the analysis of agrarian formations." *The Journal of Peasant Studies* 7:2 (1980).

Fushayka, Muhammad M. *Ramadan al-Suwayhli*. Tripoli: Dar al-Farjani, 1974.

Gautier, G. F. *Les Siciles Obscurs du Maghreb*. Paris: Payot, 1972.

Geertz, Clifford. "The integrative revolution: Primordial sentiments and civil politics in the new states." In Geertz, ed., *Old Societies and New States: The Quest for Modernity in Asia and Africa*. New York: Free Press, 1963.

Gendzier, Irene. *Managing Political Change*. Boulder, Colo.: Westview Press, 1985.

Gerth, H. H. and C. W. Mills, eds. *From Max Weber*. New York: Oxford University Press, 1946.

al-Gashshat, Muhammad S. *Khalifa Bin 'Askar*. Beirut: Dar al-Masira, 1978.

———. *Ma'arik al-Difa' 'An al-Jabal al-Gharbi.* Tripoli: al-Munsh' al-'Ama, 1983.

———. *Sada al-Jihad fi al 'Adab al-Sha'bi.* Beirut: Lubnan, 1970.

Giddens, Anthony. *Capitalism and Modern Social Theory.* Cambridge: Cambridge University Press, 1971.

Giolitti, Giovanni. *Memoirs of My Life.* New York: Howard Fertig, 1973.

Glavanis, Kathy, and Pandeli Glavanis, eds. *The Rural Middle East, Peasant Lives and Modes of Production.* London: Zed Press, 1989.

Goldberg, Harvey E., ed. *The Book of Mordechai.* Philadelphia: Institute for the Study of Human Issues, 1980.

Goldfrank, Walter. "Silk and steel: Italy and Japan between the two world wars." In Edmund Burke III, ed., *Global Crises and Social Movements.* Boulder, Colo.: Westview Press, 1988.

Goodchild, Robert. "Farming in Roman Libya." *Géographical Journal* XXV (1952).

Gorin, Zeev. "Socialist societies and the world system theory: A critical survey." *Science and Society* XLIX:3 (Fall, 1985).

Gramsci, Antonio. *Selections from the Prison Notebooks.* 8th ed. New York: International Publishers, 1985.

———. *The Modern Prince and Other Writings.* 9th ed. New York: International Publishers, 1983.

Gran, Peter. *Islamic Roots of Capitalism.* Austin: University of Texas Press, 1977.

Graziani, Rodolfo. *Cirenaica Pacificata.* Benghazi: Dar al-Andulus, 1974.

———. *Verso El-Fezzan.* Tripoli: Maktabat al-Firjani, 1973.

Great Britain Naval Intelligence. *A Handbook of Libya.* London: H. M. Stationery Office, 1928.

Gregory, Y. W. *Report on the Work of a Commission Sent by the Jewish Organization.* London: Jewish Organization, 1909.

Guha, Ranajit, ed. *Subaltern Studies I: Writings on South Asian History and Society.* New Delhi: Oxford University Press, 1982.

Gulick, John. *The Middle East: An Anthropological Perspective.* Pacific Palisades, Calif.: Goodyear Publishing, 1972.

Gulien, Andre. *Histoire de L'Afrique de Nord.* Paris: Payot, 1931.

Hall, Thomas. "Incorporation in the world system, toward a critique." *American Sociological Review* 51 (June 1986).

———. "Peripheries, regions of refuge, and non-state societies: Toward a theory of reactive social change." *Social Science Quarterly* 64 (1983).

Hallaq, Wael. "Was the gate of ijtihad closed?" *International Journal of Middle East Studies* 16 (1984).

Hamilton, C. A. "Ideology and oral tradition: Listening to the voices from below." *History in Africa* 14 (1987).

Hamilton, James. *Wanderings in North Africa.* London: John Murry, 1956.

Hamzowi, Salah. "Non-capitalist relations of production in capitalist society: The Khammesat of southern Tunisia." *Journal of Peasant Studies* 6:4 (July 1979).

Harrison, Robert. "Migrants in the city of Tripoli." *Geographical Journal* 57 (July 1967).

al-Hashaishi, Muhammad B. *Jala al-Karab 'an Tarabulus al Gharb.* Beirut: Dar Lubnan, 1965.

Hassanin, Ahmad. *Fi Sahara' Libya.* Cairo, 1923.

Helfgott, Leonard. "Tribalism as socioeconomic formation in Iranian history." *Iranian Studies* 10 (1977).

Hermassi, Elbaki. *al-Mujtama' Wa al-Dawla fi al-Maghreb al-'Arabi.* Beirut: Center of Arab Unity Studies, 1987.

———. *Leadership and National Development in North Africa.* Berkeley: University of California Press, 1972.

Hess, Andrew. "Fire-arms and the decline of Ibn Khaldun's military elite." *Archivum Ottomanicum* IV (1972).

———. "The forgotten frontier: The Ottoman North African provinces during the eighteenth century." In Thomas Naff and Roger Owen, eds., *Studies in Eighteenth Century Islamic History.* Carbondale, Ill.: Southern Illinois University Press, 1977.

Hilal, Jamil. "Agriculture and socioeconomic change in the region of Misillata, Tripolitania." *Dirassat: Libyan Economic and Business Review* (Benghazi University) 5:1 (Spring 1969).

Hindiri, Said. *al-'Alaqat al-Libiyya al-Chadiyya 1882–1975.* Tripoli: Center for Libyan Studies, 1983.

al-Hisnawi, Habib W. *Fazzan Under Awlad Muhammad* Sabha: Center for African Studies, Sabha University Press, 1990.

———, ed. *Tarikh Fezzan.* Tripoli: Center for Libyan Studies, 1979.

Holumboe, Knud. *Desert Encounter: Adventurous Journey Through Italian Africa.* New York: G. P. Putnam's Sons, 1937.

El-Horeir, Idris. "Mawaqif Khalida li 'Umar al-Muktar." *Majallat al-Buhath al-Tarikhiyya* 2 (July 1988).

Hornemann, F. "The journal of F. Hornemann's travels from Cairo to Marzuk in the years 1797–98." In E. W. B. Bovill, ed., *Missions to the Niger.* Cambridge: Cambridge University Press, 1969.

Hourani, Albert. "Ottoman reform and the politics of notables." In W. Polk and R. Chambers, eds., *Beginnings of Modernization in the Middle East: The Nineteenth Century.* Chicago: University of Chicago Press, 1968.

Huntington, Samuel. *Political Order in Changing Societies.* New Haven, Conn.: Yale University Press, 1968.

Ibn Ghalbun, Muhammad K. *al-Tidhkar fi man Malaka Tarabulus Wa Makan Piha Min al'Akbar.* 2nd ed., Tripoli: Maktabat al-Nur, 1967.

Ibn Isma'il, 'Umar A. *Inhiyar Hukim al-Usra al-Qaramanliyya fi Libya (1790–1835).* Tripoli: Maktabat al-Firjani, 1966.

Ibn Khaldun, 'Abd al-Rahman. *The Muqaddimah: An Introduction to History.* Princeton, N.J.: Princeton University Press, 1967.

Iliffe, John. "The social organization of the Maji Maji rebellion." *Journal of African History* viii:3 (1967).

Inalik, Halil. "The socio-political effects of the diffusion of fire-arms in the Middle East." In V. J. Parry and M. G. Yapp, eds., *War, Technology and Society in the Middle East.* Oxford: Oxford University Press, 1975.

Jami, 'Abd al-Qadir (Jamey Bey). "Ghat and its surroundings." *Geographical Journal* XXXIV:2 (1909).

———. *Min Tarabulus al-Garb Ila al-Sahra al-Kubra.* Tripoli: Dar al-Misurati, 1973.

Joffe, E. G. H. "British Malta and the Qaramanli Dynasty (1800–1835)." *Revue D'Histoire Maghrebine* (1985).

———, ed. *Social and Economic Development of Libya.* Kent, England: MENAS, 1982.

Johnson, Marion. "Calico caravans: The Tripoli Kano trade after 1880." *Journal of African History* 17 (1976).

———. "Tijarat rish al Na'am fi al-nisf al Awal min al-Qarn al-Tasi' Ashar." *Majallat al-Buhuth al-Tarikhiyya* 1 (Jan. 1982).

Kanya-Forster, A. S. "French expansion in Africa: The mythical theory." In Roger Owen and Bob Sutcliffe, eds. *Studies in the Theory of Imperialism*. London: Longman, 1972.

Karbat, Kemal. "The land regime, social structure, and modernization in the Ottoman empire." In *Beginnings of the Modernization in the Middle East*. Edited by William R. Polk and Richard L. Chambers. Chicago: University of Chicago Press, 1968.

Kasaba, Resat. *The Ottoman empire and the World Economy*. Albany, N.Y.: State University of New York Press, 1988.

Kay, Geoffrey. *Development and Under-development: A Marxist Analysis*. London: St. Martin's Press, 1973.

al-Khatibi, Abd al-Kabir. *al-Naqad al-Muzdawaj*. Beirut: Dar al-Awda, n.d..

Khazanov, A. M. *Nomads and the Outside World*. Cambridge: The Unversity Press, 1983.

Kolakowski, Leszek. *The Alienation of Reason: A History of Positivist Thought*. New York: Doubleday, 1968.

Krader, Lawrance. "Pastoralism." In *Encyclopedia of Social Sciences* II (1968).

Krause, G. A. "Aufzeichnungen über die Stadt Ghat in der Sahara." *Thurath al-Sha'b* (Tripoli), April–June 1982.

Lacoste, Yves. *Ibn Khaldun*. London: Verso, 1984.

Lapworth, Charles. *Tripoli and the Young Italy*. London: Stephen Swift, 1912.

Laroui, Abdalla. *The History of the Maghreb*. Princeton, N.J.: Princeton University Press, 1977.

Le Gall, Michel. "The Ottoman government and the Sanusiyya: A reappraisal." *International Journal of Middle East Studies* 21 (1989), 91–106.

Lerner, Daniel. *The Passing of Traditional Society in the Middle East*. New York: Free Press, 1958.

Lethielleux, J. *Le Fezzan: ses Jardins et ses Palmiers*. Tunis: Imprimerie Bascone & Muscat, 1949.

Leys, Colin. "Samuel Huntington and the end of the classical modernization theory." In Hamiza Alavi and Theodor Shanin, eds., *Introduction to the Sociology of Developing Societies*. New York: Monthly Review Press, 1982.

Lovejoy, Paul, and Samuel Bair. "The desert side economy of central Sudan." *International Journal of African Historical Studies* VIII:4 (1975).

Lustick, Ian. *State-Building Failure in British Ireland and French Algeria.* Berkeley, Calif.: Institute of International Studies, 1985.

Lyon, G. F. *A Narrative of Travels and Discoveries in Northern and Central Africa in the Years 1818–1820.* London: Francis Class, 1966 [1821].

Macarthey, Maxwell, and Paul Cremona. *Italy's Foreign and Colonial Policy 1914–1937.* Oxford: Oxford University Press, 1938.

Mack Smith, Denis. *Mussolini's Roman Empire.* New York: Penguin Books, 1977.

Magdoff, Harry. *Imperialism.* New York: Monthly Review Press, 1978.

Martin, B. G. "Five letters from the archives of Tripoli." *Journal of the Historical Society of Nigeria* (1962).

———. *Muslim Brotherhoods in Nineteenth Century Africa.* Cambridge: Cambridge University Press, 1976.

Marx, Karl. *The Poverty of Philosophy.* New York: International Publishers, 1963.

Marx, K., and F. Engels. *On Colonialism.* New York: International Publishers, 1972.

al-Marzuqi, Muhammad. *'Abd al-Nabi Bil-Khayre.* Tunis-Tripoli: al-Dar al-'Arabiyya Lil Kitab, 1978.

———. *Dima 'Ala al Hudud.* Tunis-Tripoli: al-Dar al-Arabiyya lil Kitab, 1975.

al-Masri, Muhammad I. *Tarikh Harb Tarabulus.* Banha: Matbaat al Amir Faruq, 1942.

McCullagh, Francis. *Italy's War for a Desert.* Chicago: F. G. Browne, 1913.

McLachlan, Keith S. "The role of indigenous farming in the agrarian structure of Tripolitania in the nineteenth and twentieth centuries." In M. M. Buru, et al., eds., *Planning and Development in Modern Libya.* London: Middle East and North Africa Studies Press, 1985.

Medana, A. "Il vilayet di Tripoli di Barbaria dell' anno 1901," *Bollettino de gli Affair Esteri* (November 1909).

Meillassoux, Claude. "From reproduction to production." *Economy and Society* 1 (1972).

———. *Maidens, Meal, and Money*. Cambridge: Cambridge University Press, 1981.

Micacchi, Rodolfo. *Tarabulus al-Garb Tahf Hukm al-Usra al-Qaramanliyya*. Cairo: Arab League Institute for Higher Arab Studies, 1961.

Miege, J. L., ed. *Le Relations Intercommunautaires juives Mediterranée occidentale XIIIe–XXe Siecles*. Paris: CNKS, 1984.

———. "La Libye et la commerce trans Saharien aux XIX. Siecle." *Revue l'Occident Musulman an et de la Mediterranée* 19 (1975).

al-Misurati, Ali M. *Sahafat Libya Fi Nisf Qurn*. Beirut: Dar al-Kashaf, 1960.

Mommsen, Wolfgang. *Theories of Imperialism*. Chicago: University of Chicago Press, 1980.

Moore, Jr., Barrington. *Social Origins of Dictatorship and Democracy*. Boston: Beacon Press, 1966.

Mori, R. "La pentratiloni Pacifica Italiana in Libia del 1907 al 1911 e il Banco di Roma." *Revista di Studi Politici International* 24 (1957).

Morsy, Maghali. *North Africa 1800–1900*. London: Longman, 1987.

———. "Maghrebi unity in the context of the nation–state: A historian's viewpoint." *Maghreb Review* 8:3–4 (1983).

Mouzelis, Nicos. "Modernization, underdevelopment, uneven development: Prospects for a theory of third world formation." *Journal of Peasant Studies* 7:3 (April 1980), 370.

Murphy, Rhods. "The decline of North Africa since the Roman occupation: Climate or human." *Association of American Geographers* 41 (June 1951).

Murray, G. W. *Sons of Ismael: A Study of the Egyptian Bedouin*. London: George Routledge, 1935.

Nachtigal, G. *Sahara and the Sudan, Tripoli and Fezzan*. Vol. I. New York: Barnes & Noble, 1974.

Naff, T., and R. Owen, eds. *Studies in Eighteenth Century Islamic History*. Carbondale, Ill.: Southern Illinois University Press, 1977.

Naji, Muhammad, and Muhammad Nuri. *Tarabulus al-Garb*. Tripoli: Dar Maktabal al-Fikir, 1973.

Negash, Tekeste. *Italian Colonialism in Eritrea 1882–1941: Policies, Praxis and Impact*. Uppsala, Sweden: 1987.

Newbury, C. W. "North Africa and the western Sudan in the nineteenth century: A re-evaluation." *Journal of African History* 7 (1966).

Nicolaison, Johannes. *Ecology and Culture of the Pastoralist Tuareg.* Copenhagen: The National Museum, 1963.

Norris, H. T. *The Tuaregs, Their Islamic Legacy and its Diffusion in the Sahel.* Wilts, England: Aris and Phillips, 1975.

Nyang, Sulayman S. *Islam, Christianity, and African Identity.* Brattleboro, Vt.: Amana Books, 1984.

O'Brien, Jay. "Toward a reconstruction of ethnicity: Capitalist expansion and cultural dynamics in Sudan." *American Anthropologist* 55:4 (Dec. 1986), 898–907.

O'Fahey, R. S. *Enigmatic Saint: Ahmad Ibn Idris and the Idrisi Tradition.* Evanston, Ill.: Northwestern University Press, 1990.

O'Hanlon, Rosalind. "Recovering the subject: Subaltern studies and histories of resistance in colonial south Asia." *Modern Asian Studies* 22:1 (1988).

O'Hanlon, Rosalind and David Washbrook. "After orientalism: Culture, criticism, and politics in the third world," *Comparative Studies in Society and History* 34:1 (January 1992).

Owen, Roger, ed. *Studies in the Economic and Social History of Palerstine in the Nineteenth and Twentieth Centuries.* Oxford: Carbondale & Edwardsville, 1982.

Owen, Roger, and Bob Sutcliffe, eds. *Studies in the Theory of Imperialism.* London: Longman, 1972.

Pamuk, Sevket. *The Ottoman empire and European Capitalism, 1820–1913.* Cambridge: Cambridge University Press, 1987.

Parakash, Gyan. "Postcolonial criticism and Indian historiography." *Social Text* 31–32 (1992).

———. "Writing post-orientalist histories of the third world: Perspectives from Indian historiography." *Comparative Studies in Society and History* 32:2 (1990).

Pelt, Adrian. *Libyan Independence and the United States.* New Haven, Conn.: Yale University Press, 1970.

Peters, Emorys L. "Cultural and social diversity in Libya" In A. J. Allan, ed., *Libya Since Independence.* New York: St. Martin's Press, 1982.

———. "The tied and the free: An account of patron-client relationship among the Bedouin pastoralists of Cyrenaica." In J. G. Peristially, ed., *Contributions to Mediterranean Sociology.* Paris: Mouton, 1968.

Polk, W., and L. Chambers, eds. *Beginnings of Modernization in the Middle East. The Nineteenth Century*. Chicago: University of Chicago Press, 1968.

Poncet, J. "Le mythe de catastrophe hilalienne." *Annales Economies, Sociétés, Civilisations* XXII (1967).

Post, Kent. "Peasantization and rural political movements in West Africa." *Archives Européennes de Sociologie* VIII:2 (1972).

Poulantzas, Nicos. "On social classes." *New Left Review* 70 (March–April 1973), 3.

Quataert, Donald. *Social Disintegration and Popular Resistance in the Ottoman Empire 1881–1908*, New York: New York University Press, 1983.

Rae, Edward. *The Country of the Moors*. London: John Murray, 1877.

Rafeq, 'Abdul-Karim. "Changes in the relationship between the Ottoman administration and the Syrian provinces from the sixteenth to the eighteenth centuries." In Thomas Naff and Roger Owen, eds., *Studies in the Eighteenth Century Islamic History*. Carbondale, Ill.: Southern Illinois University Press, 1977.

Ranger, T. O. "Connections between primary resistance movements and modern mass nationalism in East and Central Africa." *Journal of African History* ix:3 (1968).

Remond, George. *Aux Camps Turca Arabes*. 2nd ed., Tripoli: al-Mu'assa al'Ama, 1983.

Rey, Pierre-Philippe. "Class alliances." *International Journal of Sociology* XII:2 (1982).

Richardson, James. *Travels in the Great Desert of the Sahara in the Years of 1845 and 1846*. Vol. II. London: Frank Cass, 1970.

Rizqana, Ibrihim A. *al-Mammlaka al-Libiyya*. Cairo: Dar al-Nahda al-'Arabiyya, 1964.

Robinson, Ronald. "Non-European foundations of European imperialism: Sketch for a theory of collaboration." In R. Owen and B. Sutcliffe, eds., *Studies in the Theory of Imperialism*. London: Longman, 1972.

Rochat, G. "Il genocidie Cirenico e la storigrafia coloniale." *Belfagor* XXXV (1980).

Rodd, Francis, ed. "A Fezzani military expedition to Kanem and Bagirmi in 1821." *Journal of the Royal African Society* XXXV (April 1936).

Rodney, Walter. "The imperialist partition of Africa." *Monthly Review* 21:11 (April 1970).

Rosenfeld, Henry. "The social composition of the military in the process of state formation in the Arabian desert." *Journal of the Royal Anthropological Institute of Great Britain and Ireland* 95 (1956).

Rossi, E. *Storica di Tripoli e della Tripolitania Dallo Conquesta Araba al 1911*. Beirut: Dar al-Thaqafa, 1974.

Roth, Guenther. *Scholarship and Partisanship: Essays on Max Weber*. Berkeley: University of California Press, 1971.

Roy, William. "Class conflict and social change in historical perspective." *Annual Review of Sociology* 10 (1984).

al-Sa'di, Mabruk, ed. *Mawusu'at Riwayat al-Jihad*. Tripoli: Center for Libyan Studies, 1983.

Said, Edward. *Orientalism*. New York: Vintage Books, 1979.

Salem, S. H. "al-Awda' al Qabaliyya in Sharq Libya fi al 'ahd al-Uthmani al-thani." *Majallat al-Buhuth al-Tarikhiyya* 6:1 (1984).

———. "al-Dar'ib al 'uthmaniyya fi Tarabulus al-gharb mutasarifiyt Benghazi." *Majallat al-Buhuth al-Tarikyiyya* 6:1 (1984).

Salem, S. H., and H. W. al-Hisnawi, eds. *Dirassat Fial-Tarikh al-libi* (11). Tripoli: Center for Libyan Studies, 1984.

Salihiyya, Muhammad I. "al-Adwar fi harakat al-jihad al-Libi." *Majallat Kuliyat al-Adab* (Kuwait University) 13 (1978).

———. "The Libyan papers documented secret, letters of Ahmad al-Sharif, 1875–1933" (in Arabic). *Annals of the College of Arts* (Kuwait University) I (1980).

al-Sanusi, Muhammad B. *al-Majmu'a al-Mukhtara*. Beirut: Dar al-Kitab al-Lubnani, 1968.

Schneider, David. *A Critique of the Study of Kinship.*. Ann Arbor: University of Michigan Press, 1984.

Scott, James. *Weapons of the Weak*. New Haven, Conn.: Yale University Press, 1985.

Segre, Claudio. *Fourth Shore: The Italian Colonization of Libya*. Chicago: University of Chicago Press, 1974.

Shinar, P. "Notes on the socioeconomic and cultural role of the Sufi brotherhoods and maraboutism in the modern Maghreb." *Proceedings of the First International Congress of Africanists* (1962).

Shotter, John. "Rhetoric and the recovery of civil society." *Economy and Society* 18:2 (May 1989).

Shukri, Muhammad F. *al-Sanusiyya*. Cairo: Dar al-Fikir al-Arabi, 1948.

Simon, Rachel. *Libya Between Ottomanism and Nationalism*. Berlin: Klaus Schwarz Verlag, 1987.

———. "The relations of the Jewish community of Libya with Europe in the late Ottoman period." In J. L. Miege, ed., *Les Relations Intercommunutaires Juives en Mediterranée Occidentale*. Paris: CNRS, 1984.

———. "The socioeconomic role of the Tripolitanian Jews in the late Ottoman period." In M. Abitbol, ed., *Communautes Juives des marges Sahariennes du Maghreb*. Jerusalem, 1982.

Skocpol, Theda. *States and Social Revolutions*. Cambridge: Cambridge University Press, 1979.

Slousch, N. "La Tripolitaine sous la domination de Karamanli." *Revue de Monde Musulman* VI:11 (1908).

Sluglett, Peter, and Marion Farouk Sluglett. "The application of the 1858 land code in greater Syria, some preliminary observations." In Tarif Khalidi, ed., *Land Tenure and Social Transformations in the Middle East*. Beirut: American University Press, 1984.

Slyomovics, Susan. "Arab folk literature and political expression," *Arab Studies Quarterly* 8 (1986).

Stambouli, Fraj, and 'Abd el-Kader Zghal. "Urban life in pre-colonial North Africa." *The British Journal of Sociology* 27 (March 1976).

Subtil, E. "Histoire de 'Abd el-Gelil, sultan du Fezzan assassiné 1842." *Revue de l'Orient* V (1844).

Tahir, 'Abd al-Jalil. *al-Mujtama' al-Libi*. Beirut: al-Maklaba al-'Asriyya, 1968.

Talbi, Muhammad. "Law and economy in Afriqiyya (Tunisia) in the third Islamic century." In A. L. Udovitch, ed., *The Islamic Middle East, 700–1900*.

Tamari, Salim. "Factionalism and class formation in recent Palestinian history." In Roger Owen, ed., *Studies in the Economic and Social History of Palestine in the Nineteenth and Twentieth Centuries*. Oxford: Carbondale & Edwardsville, 1982.

Taylor, John. *From Modernization to Modes of Production*. London: MacMillan, 1981.

Thiry, Jacques. "Le Fezzan notes historique et sociologique." *Correspondance d'Orient Etudes* 3 (1963).

Thompson, E. P. *The Making of the English Working Class*. New York: Vintage Books, 1966.

al-Tillisi, Khalifa. *Ba'da al-Ghardabiyya*. Beirut: Dar al-Thaqafa, 1973.

———. *Ma'jam Ma'arik al-Jihad Fi Libya, 1911–1931*. Tripoli-Tunis: al-Dar al-'Arabiyya Lil Kitab, 1980.

———. *Ma'arik al-Jihad al-Libi Min Khilal al-Khitat al-Harbiyya*. Tripoli: al-Munsha al-'Ama, 1982.

Toni, Youssef. "Tribal distribution and racial relationships of the ancient and modern people of Cyrenaica." Jami'at 'Ayan Shams. Kulliyat al-Adab *Hawliyat Kulliyat al-Adab* [Fine Arts College, Ain Shars University Annals of the College of Arts, Cairo]. 8 (1963).

Tullio Irace, Chevalier. *With the Italians in Tripoli*. London: John Murry, 1912.

Miss Tully. *Letters written during ten years' residence at the court of Tripoli*, edited by Seaton Dearden. London: A. Barker, 1957.

Turner, Bryan. *Marx and the End of Orientalism*. London: George Allen and Unwin, 1978.

———. "Orientalism and the problem of civil society in Islam." In Asaf Hussain, et al., eds., *Orientalism, Islam and Islamists*. Brattleboro, Vt: Amana Books, 1984.

al-Twair, M. A. "Agriculture in the Regency of Tripoli during the direct Ottoman rule." *Revue d'Histoire Maghrebine*, 12:39–40 (Dec. 1985).

Udovitch, A. L., ed. *The Islamic Middle East 700–1900*. Princeton, N.J.: Darwin Press, 1981.

University of Benghazi. *Diwan al-Shi'r al-Sha'bi* I. Benghazi: University of Benghazi Press, 1977.

Uzoigwi, G. N. "European partition and conquest of Africa: An overview." In Adu Boahen, ed. *UNESCO General History of Africa* 7 (1985).

Vansina, Jan. *Oral Traditions: A Study in Historical Methodology*. Chicago: Aldine Publishing Company, 1956.

———. *Oral Traditions and History*. Madison: University of Wisconsin Press, 1985.

Vikor, K. S. "Al-Sanusi and Qadhafi—Continuity of Thought?" *Maghreb Review* 12:1–2 (1987).

Villari, Luigi. *Italian Foreign Policy Under Mussolini.* New York: Devin-Adair, 1950.

Vischer, Adolf. "Tripoli." *Geographical Journal* XXXVII (Nov. 5, 1911).

Von Sivers, Peter. "Back to nature: The agrarian foundation of society according to Ibn Khaldun." *Arabica* XXVII:1 (1980).

———. "Rural Uprisings as Political Movements in Colonial Algeria," in Burke III and Lapidus *Islam, Politics and Social Movements.*

al-Wafi, Muhammad A. *al-Tariq Ila Lausanne.* Tripoli: Dar al-Firjani, 1980.

Wallerstein, Immanuel. "Comments on Stern's critical tests." *American Historical Review* 93:4 (Oct 1988).

———. *The Capitalist World Economy.* Cambridge: Cambridge University Press, 1980.

Warren, Bill. *Imperialism: Pioneer of Capitalism.* London: New Left Review Press, 1980.

Waterbury, John. *The Commander of the Faithful.* New York: Columbia University Press, 1970.

Webster, R. A. *Industrial Imperialism in Italy 1908–1915.* Berkeley: University of California Press, 1975.

Weiner, Jerome B. "New approaches to the study of Barbary corsairs (1)." *Revue d'Histoire Maghrebine* 13–14 (Jan. 1979).

Willimott, S. G., and J. I. Clarke, eds. *Field Studies in Libya.* Durham, England: Durham University Press, 1960.

Wills, John R. "*Jihad fi sabil Allah*: Its doctrinal basis in Islam and some aspects of its evolution in nineteenth century West Africa." *Journal of African History* VIII:3 (1967).

Wolf, Eric. *Peasant Wars of the Twentieth Century.* New York: Harper & Row, 1969.

———. *Europe and the People Without History.* Berkeley: University of California Press, 1982.

Wolpe, Harold. "The theory of internal colonialism: The South African case." In Ivar Oxaal, Tony Barnett, and David Booth, eds., *Beyond the Sociology of Development.* London: Routledge & Kegan Paul, 1975.

Woolf, J. J., ed. *European Fascism.* London: Weidenfeld and Nicolson, 1970.

Woolf, Stuart. "Statistics and the modern state." *Comparative Studies in Society and History* 31:3 (July 1989).

Wright, John. "Outside perceptions of the Sanusi." *Maghreb Review* 13:1–2 (1988).

Yushi', Bashir. *Ghadamis Watha'iq Tijariyya, Tarikhiyya, Ijtima'iyya.* Tripoli: Center for Libyan Studies, 1982.

al-Zawi, Tahir. *A'lam Libya.* Beirut: Dar Ihya al-Kutub al-Arabiyya, 1961.

———. *Jihad al-Abtal.* Beirut: Dar al-Fatah lil-Nashir, 1970.

———. *'Umar al-Mukhtar.* Tripoli: Maktabat al-Firjani, 1970.

El-Zein, Abdul Hamid. "Beyond ideology and theology: The search for the anthropology of Islam." *Annual Review of Anthropology* 6 (1977).

Ziadeh, Nicola. *Sanusiyah.* Leiden: E. J. Brill, 1958.

———. *Libya Fi al-'Usur al-Hadithah.* Cairo: Ma'had al-Buhuth wa al Dirassat al-'Arabiyya, 1966.

INDEX

Printed in the United States
29801LVS00004B/334-369